First Workshop on Abusive Language Online 2017

Held at ACL 2017

Vancouver, Canada
4 August 2017

ISBN: 978-1-5108-4580-0

ACL 2017

The First Workshop on Abusive Language Online

Proceedings of the Workshop

August 4, 2017
Vancouver, Canada

Sponsors

Primary Sponsor

Malcolm S. Forbes Center for Culture and Media Studies

Platinum Sponsors

Gold Sponsors

Silver Sponsors

The New York Times   Bloomberg

Introduction

We are very pleased to welcome you to the first Workshop on Abusive Language Online (ALW), held at ACL 2017 in Vancouver, Canada. The last few years have seen a surge in abusive behavior online, with governments, social media platforms, and individuals struggling to cope with the consequences and to produce effective methods to combat it. In many cases, online forums, comment sections, and social media interactions have become sites for bullying, scapegoating, and hate speech. These forms of online aggression not only poison the social climate of the online communities that experience it, but can also provoke physical violence and harm.

Addressing abusive language necessitates a multidisciplinary approach that requires knowledge from several fields, including, but not limited to: media studies, natural language processing (NLP), psychology, sociology, law, gender studies, communications, and critical race theory. NLP, as a field that directly works with computationally analyzing language, is in a unique position to develop automated methods to analyse, detect, and filter abusive language. By working across disciplinary divides, researchers in all these fields can produce a comprehensive approach to abusive language that blends together computational, social and legal methods.

We are therefore very happy to bring researchers of various disciplines together in this one-day workshop to discuss approaches to abusive language. The workshop consists of two invited speaker talks, two panels, and oral and poster presentations.

- Carol Todd

  Carol Todd founded the Amanda Todd Legacy in memory of her daughter Amanda after her death by suicide on October 10, 2012. Amanda's Legacy was created to bring increased awareness and conversations within families and communities about online exploitation, cyberabuse and internet safety. The goal has been to encourage a shift in thinking about bullying type behaviours (both on and offline) to those of REFLECTION and RESPECT as well as to destigmatizing the perceptions related mental health as it can relate to how we treat others.

- Brianna Wu

  Brianna Wu is a 2018 Democratic candidate for U.S. Congress in Massachusetts-District 8. Brianna is also head of development at GSX, a Boston independent videogame studio. Brianna came to national prominence when she and other women working in the tech industry were personally targeted by alt-right hate groups, including one spearheaded by Steve Bannon, now Chief Strategist to Donald Trump. Despite threats on her life and her family, Brianna has never wavered as a voice for the marginalized, including women, people of color and LGBT individuals.

We will be hosting the following researchers as our panelists:

- Lucas Dixon

  Lucas Dixon is Chief Scientist at Jigsaw, an incubator within Alphabet that builds technology to tackle some of the toughest global security challenges facing the world today. His work focuses on security, machine intelligence and data visualization..

- Pascale Fung

  Pascale Fung is a Professor at the Department of Electronic & Computer Engineering at The Hong Kong University of Science & Technology. She is the founding chair of the Women Faculty Association at HKUST and her research interests lies in building intelligent systems that can understand and empathise with humans.

- Sora Han

  Sora Han is an Associate Professor of Criminology, Law and Society at the School of Law at UC Irvine. She recently published her first book, Letters of the Law (Stanford University Press 2015), which recasts and extends the insights of critical race theory to produce new readings of American law's landmark decisions on race and civil rights.

- Elizabeth Losh

  Elizabeth Losh is an Associate Professor of English and American Studies at William and Mary with a specialization in New Media Ecologies. In addition to recent work on selfies and hashtag activism, she has also written a number of frequently cited essays about communities that produce, consume, and circulate online video, videogames, digital photographs, text postings, and programming code.

- Margaret Mitchell

  Margaret Mitchell is the Senior Research Scientist in Google's Research & Machine Intelligence group, working on advancing artificial intelligence towards positive goals. Her work combines computer vision, natural language processing, social media, many statistical methods, and insights from cognitive science.

- Vinodkumar Prabhakaran

  Vinodkumar Prabhakaran is a postdoctoral fellow in the computer science department at Stanford University. His research falls in the interdisciplinary field of computational sociolinguistics, in which he builds and uses computational tools to analyze linguistic patterns that reveal the underlying social contexts in which language is used.

- Jacqueline Wernimont

  Jacqueline is a founding co-Director of the HS Collab and an assistant professor of English at Arizona State University, where she specializes in literary history, feminist digital media, histories of quantification, and technologies of commemoration. Her current book project, tentatively titled Numbered Lives, traces a 500+-year history of technologies that attempt to quantify human life.

In addition, the workshop includes research papers from the community. We received 21 submissions, and accepted 14 (67% acceptance rate): 4 as oral presentations and 10 as poster presentations. For each paper, we assigned three reviewers from within NLP and at least one reviewer from outside of NLP to provide a different perspective on the research. The papers at the workshop cover a wide range of topics: for example, abusive language detection in different languages, analysis of abusive language across different domains, development of corpora and annotation guidelines for this field of NLP, to name a few.

We would like to thank all authors of the submitted papers, reviewers, presenters, invited speakers, and panelists. In addition, we thank our generous sponsors which helped us fund the travel costs for speakers and panelists: Brown University as our principal sponsor, StrainTek as a platinum sponsor, Google and Amazon as gold sponsors, and the New York Times and Bloomberg as silver sponsors.

It is our hope that this workshop can function as a starting point for more interdisciplinary work, approaches, and cooperation in analyzing and detecting abusive language online.

We wish you all a productive and inspiring workshop!

Zeerak, Wendy, Dirk & Joel

Organizers:

Zeerak Waseem, University of Sheffield
Wendy Hui Kyong Chun, Brown University
Dirk Hovy, University of Copenhagen
Joel Tetreault, Grammerly

Program Committee:

Swati Agarwal, IIIT Delhi, India
Fiona Barnett, Duke University, USA
Darina Benikova, University of Duisburg-Essen, LTL, Germany
Simone Browne, UT Austin, USA
Anneke Buffone, University of Pennsylvania, USA
Pete Burnap, Cardiff University, United Kingdom
Christina Capodilupo, Teachers College, Columbia University, USA
Guillermo Carbonell, University Duisburg-Essen, Germany
Pedro Cardoso, Synthesio, France
Gabriella Coleman, McGill, Canada
Bart Desmet, LT3, Ghent University, Belgium
Lucas Dixon, Jigsaw, USA
Nemanja Djuric, Uber ATC, USA
Jacob Eisenstein, Georgia Institute of Technology, USA
Hugo Jair Escalante, INAOE, Mexico
Lucie Flekova, UKP Lab, TU Darmstadt, Germany
Camille François, Jigsaw, USA
Matthew Fuller, Goldsmith, United Kingdom
Tanton Gibbs, Facebook, USA
Lee Gillam, University of Surrey, United Kingdom
Jen Golbeck, University of Maryland, USA
Erica Greene, New York Times, USA
Kevin Hamilton, University of Illinois, USA
Sora Han, University of California, Irvine, USA
Christopher Homan, Rochester Institute of Technology, USA
Veronique Hoste, Ghent University, Belgium
Ruihong Huang, Texas A&M, USA
Els Lefever, LT3, Ghent University, Belgium
Shuhua Liu, Arcada University of Applied Sciences, Finland
Elizabeth Losh, College of William and Mary, USA
Shervin Malmasi, Harvard Medical School, USA
Fumito Masui, Kitami Institute of Technology, Japan
Yashar Mehdad, Airbnb, USA
Rada Mihalcea, University of Michigan, USA
Mainack Mondal, Max Planck Institute for Software Systems, Germany
Manuel Montes-y-Gómez, INAOE, Mexico
Kevin Munger, NYU, USA
Srmuthi Mukund, A9.com Inc, USA
Preslav Nakov, Qatar Computing Research Institute, HBKU, Qatar

Courtney Napoles, Johns Hopkins University, USA
Chikashi Nobata, Apple, USA
Guy De Pauw, CLiPS - University of Antwerp, Belgium
Whitney Phillips, Mercer University, USA
Karolien Poels, University of Antwerp, Belgium
Daniel Preotiuc-Pietro, University of Pennsylvania, USA
Michal Ptaszynski, Kitami Institute of Technology, Japan
Awais Rashid, Lancaster University, United Kingdom
Björn Ross, University Duisburg-Essen, Germany
Paolo Rosso, Universitat Politecnica de Valencia, Spain
Masoud Rouhizadeh, Stony Brook University & University of Pennsylvania, USA
Christina Sauper, Facebook, USA
Molly Sauter, McGill University, Canada
Nishant Shah, Leuphana, ArtEZ University of the Arts, CIS (Bangalore), India
Thamar Solorio, University of Houston, USA
Jeffrey Sorensen, Jigsaw, USA
Dennis Tenen, Columbia University, USA
Jennifer Terry, University of California, Irvine, USA
Achint Thomas, Embibe Indiavidual Inc, India
Nanna Bonde Thylstrup, University of Copenhagen, Denmark
Lyle Ungar, University of Pennsylvania, USA
Anna Vartapetiance, University of Surrey, United Kingdom
Kristin Veel, University of Copenhagen, Denmark
Erik Velldal, University of Oslo, Norway
Ingmar Weber, Qatar Computing Research Institute, Qatar
Jacque Wernimont, Arizona State University, USA
Michael Wojatzki, University of Duisburg-Essen, Germany
Lilia Øvrelid, University of Oslo, Norway

Invited Speakers:

Brianna Wu, Giant Spacekat, USA
Carol Todd, Amanda Todd Legacy Society, Canada

Panelists:

Lucas Dixon, Jigsaw, USA
Pascale Fung, Hong Kong University of Science and Technology, Hong Kong
Sora Han, University of California, Irvine, USA
Elizabeth Losh, William and Mary, USA
Margaret Mitchell, Google, USA
Vinodkumar Prabhakaran, Stanford University, USA
Jacqueline Wernimont, Arizona State University, USA

Table of Contents

Conference Program

Friday, August 4, 2017

08:45–09:05 *Opening Remarks*

09:05–09:50 *Invited Talk A: Carol Todd*

09:50–10:35 *Panel A: Sora Han, Liz Losh, Lucas Dixon*

10:35–11:00 *Break*

11:00–12:30 *Paper Presentations*

11:00–11:20 *Dimensions of Abusive Language on Twitter*
Isobelle Clarke and Dr. Jack Grieve

11:20–11:40 *Constructive Language in News Comments*
Varada Kolhatkar and Maite Taboada

11:40–12:00 *Rephrasing Profanity in Chinese Text*
Hui-Po Su, Zhen-Jie Huang, Hao-Tsung Chang and Chuan-Jie Lin

12:00–12:20 *Deep Learning for User Comment Moderation*
John Pavlopoulos, Prodromos Malakasiotis and Ion Androutsopoulos

12:20–14:00 *Lunch*

14:00–15:30 *Poster Session*

Class-based Prediction Errors to Detect Hate Speech with Out-of-vocabulary Words
Joan Serrà, Ilias Leontiadis, Dimitris Spathis, Gianluca Stringhini, Jeremy Blackburn and Athena Vakali

One-step and Two-step Classification for Abusive Language Detection on Twitter
Ji Ho Park and Pascale Fung

Legal Framework, Dataset and Annotation Schema for Socially Unacceptable On-line Discourse Practices in Slovene
Darja Fišer, Tomaž Erjavec and Nikola Ljubešić

Abusive Language Detection on Arabic Social Media
Hamdy Mubarak, Kareem Darwish and Walid Magdy

Vectors for Counterspeech on Twitter
Lucas Wright, Derek Ruths, Kelly P Dillon, Haji Mohammad Saleem and Susan Benesch

Detecting Nastiness in Social Media
Niloofar Safi Samghabadi, Suraj Maharjan, Alan Sprague, Raquel Diaz-Sprague and Thamar Solorio

Technology Solutions to Combat Online Harassment
George Kennedy, Andrew McCollough, Edward Dixon, Alexei Bastidas, John Ryan, Chris Loo and Saurav Sahay

Understanding Abuse: A Typology of Abusive Language Detection Subtasks
Zeerak Waseem, Thomas Davidson, Dana Warmsley and Ingmar Weber

Using Convolutional Neural Networks to Classify Hate-Speech
Björn Gambäck and Utpal Kumar Sikdar

Illegal is not a Noun: Linguistic Form for Detection of Pejorative Nominalizations
Alexis Palmer, Melissa Robinson and Kristy K. Phillips

15:30–16:00   *Break*

16:00–16:45   *Invited Talk B: Brianna Wu*

16:45–17:30   *Panel B: Pascale Fung, Vinodkumar Prabhakaran, Jacqueline Wernimont, Margeret Mitchell*

17:30–17:40   *Wrapup*

Dimensions of Abusive Language on Twitter

Isobelle Clarke
Aston University
Birmingham, UK
clarkei@aston.ac.uk

Jack Grieve
University of Birmingham
Birmingham, UK
grievejw@gmail.com

Abstract

In this paper, we use a new categorical form of multidimensional register analysis to identify the main dimensions of functional linguistic variation in a corpus of abusive language, consisting of racist and sexist Tweets. By analysing the use of a wide variety of parts-of-speech and grammatical constructions, as well as various features related to Twitter and computer-mediated communication, we discover three dimensions of linguistic variation in this corpus, which we interpret as being related to the degree of interactive, antagonistic and attitudinal language exhibited by individual Tweets. We then demonstrate that there is a significant functional difference between racist and sexist Tweets, with sexists Tweets tending to be more interactive and attitudinal than racist Tweets.

1 Introduction

With the rise of trolling and other forms of abusive language online, many computational methods for detecting abusive language have been introduced. These classifiers have been trained on a wide range of linguistic features, including specific keywords (Xiang et al., 2012), Bag-of-Words (Warner and Hirschberg, 2012), character n-grams (Mehdad and Tetreault, 2016), word n-grams (Chen et al., 2012; Yin et al., 2009), part-of-speech n-grams (Davidson et al., 2017), and various syntactic features (Burnap and Williams, 2014). A variety of extra-linguistic features have also been considered, including gender (Waseem and Hovy, 2016), location (Waseem and Hovy, 2016), user behaviour and performance (Balci and Salah, 2015; Dadvar et al., 2013), and surrounding posts (Yin et al., 2009). Many of these methods assume that abusive language includes profanity and negative sentiment, but such features are not always present in abusive posts. Including offensive terms in the feature set can even hinder the accuracy of classifiers (Davidson et al., 2017), because profanity can be used for amplification and other non-abusive functions, leading to many false positives (Chen et al., 2012). Trolls have also developed more covert ways of abusing others, such as using creative spelling or avoiding offensive words (Hine et al., 2017). These strategies have been accounted for in part by examining the use of offensive words in context, applying spell-correction algorithms (Chen et al., 2012), consulting WordNet (Chen et al., 2012), and using character n-grams to deal with the noisiness of online communication (Mehdad and Tetreault, 2016).

Despite this growing body of research, functional variation in abusive language has yet to be investigated directly. At the most basic level, we do not know what is the general repertoire of styles for abusive language that exists online. One way to understand how the structure of language varies depending on its communicative purpose is multi-dimensional analysis (MDA) (Biber, 1988, 1989). MDA is generally based on the relative frequencies of many lexical and grammatical features measured across a corpus of texts representing a particular variety of language. The most important dimensions of linguistic variation are extracted from this dataset through a factor analysis, and then interpreted functionally based on the linguistic features and the individual texts that are most strongly associated with each dimension. In addition to providing a more complete understanding of the structure of abusive language, incorporating this type of information into abusive language classification systems should lead to more robust and principled methods.

Proceedings of the First Workshop on Abusive Language Online, pages 1–10,
Vancouver, Canada, July 30 - August 4, 2017. ©2017 Association for Computational Linguistics

The goal of this study is therefore to use MDA to identify the main dimensions of functional linguistic variation in a corpus of racist and sexist abusive Tweets (Waseem and Hovy, 2016). However, because MDA relies on the multivariate analysis of the relative frequencies of linguistic features, it is not suitable for analysing a corpus of Tweets, which typically include fewer than 30 words, and are therefore too short to allow for the relative frequencies of most features to be measured accurately. Rather than concatenate Tweets to form longer texts (e.g. Passonneau et al., 2014), for example by author, which would obscure text-level patterns, we therefore apply a new form of categorical MDA based on a multiple correspondence analysis of the simple occurrence of a variety of lexical and grammatical forms in individual Tweets to identify common patterns of functional variation in abusive Tweets. Finally, we investigate the degree to which the racist and sexist Tweets in our corpus vary in terms of these dimensions.

2   Method

Our dataset is based on the Twitter corpus used in Waseem and Hovy (2016), which contained 136,052 English Tweets, identified by searching for common racial, religious and sexist slurs and terms, as well as hashtags known to trigger hate speech over a 2 month period. With the help of an outside annotator, they coded 16,914 Tweets as either racist (1,972 Tweets by 9 users), sexist (3,383 Tweets by 613 users) or neither racist nor sexist (11,559). Using 'twitteR' package (Gentry, 2016), we downloaded the Tweets based on the Twitter IDs; however, at the time of download only 2,818 Tweets were still available, presumably because the relevant posts had been deleted. Of these Tweets, 628 had been coded as sexist and 858 as racist. Our analysis focuses on these 1,486 Tweets.

In general, research using MDA has been based on a feature set which has grown over time and which has changed depending on the variety and the language under analysis. There are, however, a core set of features related to basic parts-of-speech and grammatical constructions (Biber, 1988), which we have included in our analysis. These features include tense and aspect markers, place and time adverbials, personal pronouns, questions, nominal forms, passives, subordination,

complementation, adjectives and adverbs, modals, specialised verb classes, coordination, negation and other lexical classes, such as amplifiers, downtoners and conjunctions. In addition, as is generally the case in MDA studies (e.g. Grieve et al., 2010), we included additional features to refine our analysis for this particular variety of language, including hashtags, URLs, capitalisation, imperatives, comparatives, and superlatives. We then tagged our corpus for each of the 86 linguistic features. This was achieved by first tagging the Tweets for basic part-of-speech information using the Gimpel et al. (2011) Twitter Tagger. Based on the tagged corpus, we then automatically identified occurrences of our 86 features in the corpus by looking for specific tags, words, and sequences of tags and words, taking into account various exceptional forms found in this corpus.

Rather than measure the relative frequency of these forms across the texts in the corpus, we simply considered whether or not each of these features occurred in each of the texts, retaining the 81 features that occurred in at least 1% of the Tweets in our corpus. We then subjected this 81 feature by 1,486 text binary data matrix to a multiple correspondence analysis (MCA) in R using FactoMineR (Husson et al., 2017). MCA is essentially a dimension reduction method, which aims to represent high dimensional categorical data in low dimensional space, similar to factor analysis as used in traditional MDA for continuous data. MCA is predominantly used to analyse data from questionnaires and surveys (Husson et al., 2010), but it has also been used in linguistics, most notably in lexical semantics (e.g. Tummers et al., 2012; Glynn, 2009, 2014).

The MCA returns a positive or negative coordinate for each linguistic feature on each dimension as well as a value indicating the variables contribution to that dimension (Le Roux and Rouanet, 2010). If the variables' coordinates are of similar value, then this indicates that these variables often co-occur in Tweets. The MCA also assigns a positive or negative coordinate to each Tweet on each dimension, which can then be plotted to visualize the relationship between the Tweets on each dimension. Tweets with similar coordinates on a dimension will share linguistic features. Each dimension was interpreted by considering the functional properties shared by the linguistic features with the strongest contributions. Following Le

Table 1: The positive and negative features strongly contributing to the Dimensions

Dim	Coord	Features
2	+	Question mark (4), Question do (3.9), Accusative case (3.8), absence of Prepositions (3.5), absence of Nouns (3.3), 2nd person pronoun (3.1), absence of Proper nouns (2.9), Emoticons (2.4), absence of Articles (2.4), Nominative case (2.3), Other pronouns (2.2), WH-words (2.1), absence of Attributive adjectives (2.1), Initial DO (2), absence of Be as main verb (1.8), absence of Coordinating conjunctions (1.2), 1st person pronouns (1.2), Subject pronouns (1.1), Initial verbs (.9), WH-clause (.9), Exclamation marks (.8), Quotation marks (.7), absence of Mentioning (.7), Hashtags (.7), Interjections (.6)
	-	Existentials (5.5), Place adverbials (5.4), BE as main verb (3.3), Coordinating conjunctions (2.3), Proper nouns (2.3), absence of Nominative case (2), Articles (1.9), Quantifiers (1.9), Attributive adjectives (1.6), Synthetic negation (1.5), Predicative adjectives (1.2), Contrastive conjunctions (1.2), absence of Other pronouns (1.1), Nominalisations (1.1), Prepositions (1), Numerals (.9), absence of 2nd person pronouns (.9), absence of Accusative case (0.9), Perfect aspect (.7), Determiners (.7), absence of Question marks (.7)
3	+	Question DO (9), Question marks (6.8), 2nd person pronouns (6.8), absence of Subject pronouns (4.4), Initial DO (3.7), Initial verbs (3.2), Determiners (3), Nominalisation (2), Synthetic negation (2), Possessive pronouns (1.9), absence of 1st person pronouns (1.8), Other pronouns (1.7), absence of Nominative case (1.1), absence of Third person pronoun (1), Pro-verb DO (.9), Emoticons (.8), Existentials (.8), BE as main verb (.7)
	-	Subject pronouns (8.7), 1st person pronouns (6.2), Auxiliary BE (3.2), 3rd person pronouns (2.8), Object pronouns (2.5), absence of 2nd person pronouns (1.9), Progressive aspect (1.8), absence of Determiners (1.7), Verbs of perception (1.6), Nominative case (1.3), absence of Mentioning (1.2), absence of Question marks (1.2), absence of Other pronouns (.9), Passives (.8)
4	+	Predicative adjectives (4.5), Existentials (4.4), absence of Prepositions (3.7), absence of Proper nouns (3.5), BE as main verb (3.4), Place adverbials (3), Emoticons (2.5), absence of Nouns (2.3), Synthetic negation (2.3), absence of Capitalisation (2), Subject pronouns (1.9), 1st person pronouns (1.9), absence of Past tense (1.4), Interjections (1.3), absence of Auxiliary BE (1.2), Comparatives (1.1), absence of Articles (1), Requests (.9), absence of URLs (.8), Nominative case (.7)
	-	Auxiliary BE (7.3), Progressive aspect (4.6), Hashtags (3.9), Capitalisations (3.2), By-passives (3.3), URLs (3.1), Proper nouns (2.8), Public verbs (2.1), absence of BE as main verb (1.8), Past tense (1.5), Numerals (1.5), Question DO (1.3), Passives (1), Prepositions (1), Perfect aspect (1), absence of Subject pronouns (1), Articles (0.8), absence of Nominative case (0.7), absence of Predicative adjectives (0.7), Infinitives (0.7)

Roux and Rouanet (2010), we interpreted each dimension by considering all features with a contribution that exceeds 0.62, the average contribution of a feature on a dimension (100/162). In addition, the Tweets with the highest positive and negative coordinates on each dimension were subjected to a micro-analysis to confirm and refine these functional interpretations. Finally, the racist and sexist Tweets were compared on each dimension using Wilcoxon signed-ranked tests to see if there were any functional differences in these two forms of abusive language.

3 Results

We chose to use MCA to extract 4 dimensions based primarily on the functional interpretability of these dimensions. However, because longer Tweets are more likely to contain more features, it is also important to consider whether text length may have confounded our analysis. In standard MDA text length is controlled for by analysing the relative frequencies of features (i.e. by dividing the frequency of a feature in a text by the total number of words in the text), allowing texts of different lengths to be compared. In this case, relative frequencies are not reliable because Tweets are so short, which is why we measured the simple occurrence of forms rather than their relative frequencies and why we used MCA rather than Factor Analysis. To measure the degree to which our analysis was affected by variation in text length, we correlated the dimension coordinates returned by the MCA for each Tweet against Tweet length. Overall, we found that Dimension 1 is strongly positively correlated to Tweet length ($r = .72$), Dimension 2 is moderately negatively correlated ($r = -.33$), and Dimensions 3 and 4 are only weakly correlated ($r = .02$ and $r = -.23$). The strong correlation between Dimension 1 and Tweet length is reflected by the fact that the positive features that contribute most strongly to this dimension involve the occurrence of a wide range of forms, whereas the negative features that contribute most strongly involve the absence of a wide range of forms. By excluding Dimension 1 from our primary interpretative analysis, because it primarily reflects Tweet length, we were thus able to largely control for text length in our analysis, despite not analysing relative frequencies. The features that contribute the most to the remaining 3 dimensions, which we interpret below, are presented in Table 1.

3.1 Dimension 2: Interactive

Features with strong contributions and positive coordinates on Dimension 2 have an interactive function. For example, question marks, question DO, WH-words and initial DO are indicative of questions being asked. First and second person pronouns are used to involve the writer and the reader in the discourse. Verb-initial sentences are common in computer-mediated communication when the subject, often the author, is omitted because such information is retrievable from the context (Bieswanger, 2016). Hashtags are used to contribute to and interact with a discussion feed. Quotation marks are used to refer to someone elses speech/words. Interjections are immediate responses to stimuli and emoticons can be used to represent responsive facial expressions.

This interpretation is supported by Examples 1-4, which are Tweets that are strongly associated with positive Dimension 2. All four examples exhibit an interactive style. For example, each Tweet contains at least one second person pronoun. Example 2, 3 and 4 all contain a hashtag and are thus interacting with the feed, whereas Example 1 mentions another user and is therefore interacting directly with another account.

1. *@username Do you think implying someone cant get laid is sexist or abusive?*

2. *#QuestionsForMen Did you know that when you look at a girl - you rape her? http://...*

3. *#QuestionsForMen Did you know that scientists agree that women slut shame to make vaginas more valuable to you? http://t...*

4. *#DontDateSJWs unless you want them to date you, bang you, call you, stalk you THEN cry rape and do performance art. http://t*

Alternatively, features with strong contributions and negative coordinates on Dimension 2 are associated with a more informational style, maximising the amount of information being expressed in 140 characters. For example, existential *there* introduces things or statements. *Be* as main verb and predicative adjectives serve to identify a characteristic, role or attribute of a subject noun phrase. The use of numbers, attributive adjectives, quantifiers, place adverbials, prepositions and proper nouns allow for the expression of detailed descriptions and specific information. Nominalisations are similarly indicative of a high informational load. Contrastive conjunctions emphasise a contrast between two ideas and coordinating conjunctions link two sentences together. Synthetic negation can be used to increase the emphatic force of a statement (Tottie, 1983). This interpretation is also supported by the moderate negative correlation with text length, which reflects the fact that longer Tweets tend to be more informationally dense.

This interpretation is supported by Examples 5-8, which are Tweets that are strongly associated with negative Dimension 2. All four examples exhibit an informational as opposed to an interactive style. For example, each Tweet is made up of 1 or more declarative sentences, headed by the main verb 'to be', which is used to provide identifying information. Synthetic negation can also be seen in Examples 5, 7 and 8, where it is used to present information in an absolutist way.

5. *@username @username @username There is no comparing the vileness of Mohammed to Jesus or Buddha, or Lao Tse. He was simply a criminal*

6. *@username @username Muslims have been raping white girls with Labors approval for 16 years. Any ukip just got there.*

7. *@username @username @username There are no Jews in Saudi or many of the Gulf estates because the Muslims exterminated them.*

8. *@username @username @username There was no golden age. Jews were regularly slaughter by Muslims in pogroms.*

Overall, Dimension 2 is therefore interpreted as representing the degree of interactiveness exhibited by a Tweet. Notably, previous MDA studies (e.g. Biber, 1988, 1989; Grieve et al., 2010) have found a similar primary dimension, which opposes two of the most basic functions of language, namely interacting and informing.

3.2 Dimension 3: Antagonistic

Features with strong contributions and positive coordinates on Dimension 3 have an antagonistic function. For example, several of these features are associated with forming questions, including question DO and initial DO, verb initial, and question marks, which can be used to make demands of other users. Second person pronouns are also associated with antagonistic language especially when accompanied by the absence of first and third person pronouns as well as subject pronouns in general, which indicates that these Tweets are targeted at specific users. The co-occurrence of nominalisations with these features is associated with a high degree of specificity, whilst features such as possessive pronouns function to indicate possession, implying that someone is being targeted and challenged on specific information or possessions. A high degree of specificity in questions are common in adversarial discourse, for example in cross-examination questions, which are typically loaded and structured to confuse the witness and discredit their statement (Gibbons, 2008). Furthermore, emoticons and exclamation marks can be associated with more aggressive forms of online communication.

This interpretation is supported by Examples 9-12, which are Tweets that are strongly associated with positive Dimension 3. They all contain questions antagonistically directed to other users. Specifically, in all four cases, something has been noticed by the Tweeter and is now being opposed through questioning.

9. *@username Can you be legally forced into parental obligations? Can your genitals be cut at birth? Does your right to vote have an *?*

10. *If being pro-due process makes you pro-rape, does being anti-death penalty make you pro-murder? http://t...*

11. *#AskAWhiteFeminist Seriously, what rights dont you have, and why can none of you answer that question?*

12. *@username1 Do you approve of your pedophile prophet raping a 9 year old girl, like it says in 7 hadith?*

Alternatively, features with strong contributions and negative coordinates on Dimension 3 are associated with a more conciliatory style. Obviously, abusive language is inherently antagonistic; however, the absence of second person pronouns and the presence of subject and object pronouns, particularly third person pronouns and first person pronouns, indicates that Tweets scoring negatively on this Dimension are not targeting particular individuals. The co-occurrence of the progressive tense indicates that continuing action is being described. Object pronouns suggest that this action is affecting or influencing particular people. The co-occurrence of first person pronouns and verbs of perception suggest that the writer is giving their account of what they are perceiving, rather than opposing people directly.

This interpretation is supported by Examples 13-16, which are Tweets that are strongly associated with negative Dimension 3, all of which reflect an 'us versus them dichotomy', whereby descriptions of the actions of 'them' are either perceived by the person speaking or the actions of 'them' are influencing 'us'. Several of the Tweets are directed to more than one user suggesting that they are part of a conversation between friends/acquaintances. While the people being spoken about may find the messages abusive, they are not targeted to them, hence the language appears to be more collaborative than antagonistic, with people involved in the conversation sharing the same views, even though those views would be considered offensive by others.

13. *@username1 I saw him, but I rarely engage male fems zero point to it. They are just following orders*

14. *@username1 @username2 I actually wish they would just start using egalitarian so we can just let feminist mean the misandrist hypocrites.*

15. *@username1 @username2 Reminds me of Simpsons where grandpa was screaming Death at everything. Now its rape. http://...*

16. *@username1 @username2 @username3 They are breeding us out of existence in the westernised world. Islam will rule the world in time.*

Overall, Dimension 3 is therefore interpreted as representing the degree of antagonism exhibited by a Tweet. Previous definitions of trolling have suggested that such posts tend to be hostile and aggressive (Hardaker, 2010). Moreover, it has been shown that adversarial behaviour, such as anger and accusation are common online, especially when discussing ideological issues because the purpose is to dominate the discourse and such adversarial behaviour can perform this function (Herring et al., 1995).

3.3 Dimension 4: Attitudinal

Features with strong contributions and positive coordinates on Dimension 4 have an attitudinal function. For example, comparatives are used to describe people or things in relation to others. Predicative adjectives and BE as a main verb function to describe and identify particular attributes or characteristics of the subject. First person pronouns involve the Tweeter in the discourse, marking the post as a personal opinion. The co-occurrence of existential *there* with these features and the absence of nouns suggests that descriptions are being introduced rather than things, or that information is being introduced and then an opinion is given. Synthetic negation indicates that something is being contested.

This interpretation is supported by Examples 16-20, which are Tweets that are strongly associated with positive Dimension 4. All of these examples are expressions of opinions and personal stance through features such as first person pronouns, *be* as a main verb and adjectives.

17. *@username1 @username2 @username3 and we still get payed equally. That stupid myth bothers me to no end because theres really things -*

18. *@username1 No. You have proven your ignorance here to anyone who isnt as dumb as you. Its there for all to see but you dont know it.*

19. *@username1 I have no religion, but I can accommodate Jews, Hindus, Buddhists, Taoist, Atheists. But Islam is too cancerous*

20. *@username1 @username2 Except that there was no such sexual torture and she is a lying bitch*

Alternatively, features with strong contributions and negative coordinates on Dimension 4 do not share this attitudinal function. Instead, several features have a reporting function. For example, public verbs mark indirect or reported speech, the perfect tense is used to report on past events, and the progressive tense refers to continuing action. Passive constructions serve to emphasise the object acted upon, rather than the agent. Agentless passive constructions are common in ideological discourse as they can be used to reduce the agents prominence and therefore the blame or cause, whereas *by*-Passives take the information that would be typically new information and present it at the beginning of the sentence as given information and the agent is then moved to the end of the clause and presented as new information (Fairclough, 1992). URLs function to direct the reader to more information, including a website or an image. Numbers serve to add additional, specific information. The co-occurrence of URLs and numbers with ideological features suggests that they are functioning to support a point or provide proof, either in the form of additional textual or quantitative information. Capitalisation suggests that the writer is either emphasising a point or raising their voice.

This interpretation is supported by Examples 21-24, which are Tweets that are strongly associated with negative Dimension 4. The examples support this interpretation as the speakers point of view is not explicitly marked, but rather the action of others is being reported and supported with numbers and URLs.

21. *@username1 @username2 The Jews are trying to defend themselves against Muslims trying to exterminate them. http://...*

22. *In Islam women must be locked in their houses, and Muslims claim this is treating them well. http://...*

23. *@username1 @username2 The world is doing nothing. Islam is producing the terrorist activities and has been for 1400 years*

24. *Following the example of the pedophile prophet Mohammed in every detail, one ISIS militant is marrying a 7 year old child in Mosul. #Islam*

Overall, Dimension 4 is therefore interpreted as representing the degree of attitudinal judgment exhibited by a Tweet. Abusive language is by nature attitudinal and ideological. However, it has been shown that such beliefs can be realised in various ways, such as through explicit opinions or by telling stories, which present the other in a negative light (e.g. van Dijk, 1993). Thus, the degree of attitudinal judgement reflects the way in which the attitude is encoded.

Figure 1: Boxplots of Racist and Sexist Tweets for Dimension 2, 3, and 4

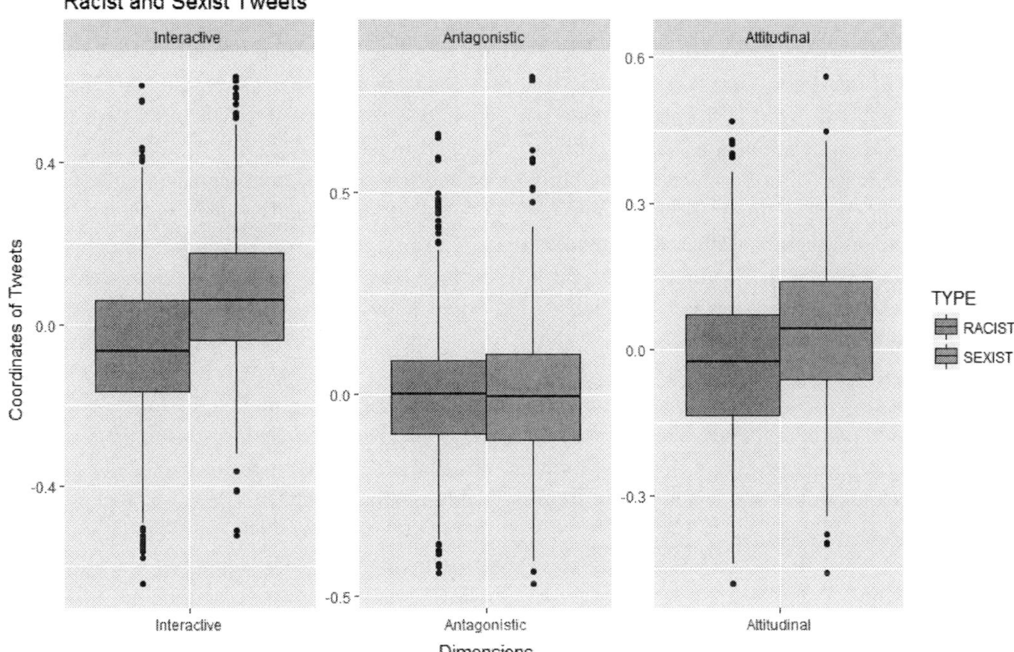

3.4 Racist versus Sexist Tweets

Following the interpretation of our three primary functional dimensions, we tested the extent to which racist and sexist Tweets differ along each of these dimensions. In particular, we used a Wilcoxon signed-ranked tests to test if there were any functional differences between the coordinates of racist and sexist Tweets on each dimension. In addition, we produced boxplots to help visualise each comparison (see Figure 1). Overall, we found significant differences ($p < .01$) between racist and sexist Tweets on Dimensions 2 and 4, with sexist Tweets tending to be more interactive and attitudinal than racist Tweets. We did not, however, find a significant difference in the degree of Antagonism between racist and sexist Tweets.

To interpret these findings, we considered previous studies on sexist and racist language and strategies. For example, in a study examining sexist strategies on two email lists, Herring et al. (1995) found that one silencing strategy employed in sexist language is to dismiss the points raised by others by referring to their 'triviality'. It is possible to see in Examples 17 and 18 that the significance of a point is being disputed. In Example 17, "stupid myth" not only represents something

as nonfactual through the word "myth", but also represents it as trivial and benign through "stupid". In Example 18, the intelligence of the speaker is being called into question, thereby discrediting the original posters statement and presenting it as trivial. Thus, it may be that expressions of attitudinal judgement, specifically by encoding that the previous post is trivial, are serving the over-arching aim to silence the individual. Another silencing strategy employed in sexist discourse is to regain control over the conversation by introducing new topics (Herring et al., 1995). This strategy may provide a reason for why sexist tweets are more interactive as the over-arching aim may be to regain control and therefore they may ask new questions and interact by introducing new topics.

In regards to racist language, van Dijk (1993) describes that racist ideologies have been shown to be reproduced through story-telling and argumentation. Specifically, stories are told by people from majority groups about minority groups in the form of complaints or negative events (van Dijk, 1993). Although stories are often associated with personal expression and opinion, stories are used to inform people, and can take the form of news reports. These stories are functionally less entertaining, but serve more to argue a point or persuade (van Dijk, 1993). It is possible to draw similarities with what van Dijk (1993) says here with the informational and reporting function of the racist Tweets. The argumentative and persuasive function of racist discourse is apparent in the racist Tweets with the use of URLs and numbers in Examples 21-24, which function here to provide supporting evidence. Furthermore, story-telling involves introducing a complication and providing contextual information, rather than interacting. This can be seen in Examples 5, 7 and 8 through the existential *there*, which functions to introduce new information. Thus, it may be suggested that racist Tweets are less interactive and attitudinal because the aim is to persuade and argue a point by reporting on events which presents minority groups in a negative light. In other words, it presents racist opinions as facts as a way to legitimate racist ideologies.

4   Conclusion

Many classifiers used to detect abusive language are trained on offensive terms. In this study, we aimed to avoid using offensive terms, and instead examined a wide range of functionally-significant grammatical features to identify the main dimensions of functional linguistic variation that occur in racist and sexist Tweets. Although we do not apply our results directly to the task of abusive language detection here, such linguistic co-occurrence patterns could in all likelihood be usefully incorporated into future classification models. Furthermore, the general patterns we have identified in this paper should help to explain why some features work better than others for detecting and distinguishing forms of abusive language online and suggest new directions for feature selection.

In summary, based on the analysis of Waseem and Hovys (2016) data, and using a novel categorical approach to MDA, we have identified 3 dimensions of linguistic variation in racist and sexist Tweets: *interactive*, *antagonistic*, and *attitudinal*. Although there is no absolute distinction between racist and sexist Tweets, by plotting each Tweets dimension coordinates, we have revealed that racist and sexist Tweets do differ functionally in respect to Dimension 2 and Dimension 4, with sexist Tweets tending to be more interactive and attitudinal, perhaps reflecting a somewhat different intent for racist and sexist Tweets. These re-sults suggest that certain features used for classifiers may be biased towards particular types and functions of abusive language. For example, studies selecting the word tri-gram "you are [adjective: offensive word]" (e.g. Chen et al., 2012) are likely to find Tweets that have an interactive and attitudinal function. As a result, other linguistic co-occurrence patterns that represent other functions of abusive language may be missed.

The *antagonistic* and *attitudinal* dimensions are perhaps the most obvious because abusive language is by nature hostile, opinionated and controversial. Nevertheless, we have demonstrated that abusive language can be discussed amongst acquaintances meaning that the function of the interaction changes to be less antagonistic and more collaborative, at least to its immediate audience. Additionally, we have shown that abusive language does not have to be attitudinal as the speakers point of view can be suppressed and the Tweets can function to report on action and provide evidence to such reports.

Without relying on profanity, we have highlighted the value of such research in identifying particular linguistic co-occurrence patterns and functional variation in abusive language. Unfortunately, we have only looked at these particular racist and sexist Tweets and therefore the dimensions could change with more data. However, in the future we aim to gather a larger corpus of different types of abusive language and improve the feature set in order reveal further and more detailed dimensions of linguistic variation of abusive language. Moreover, we aim to validate these dimensions by collecting a corpus of non-abusive language and making comparisons between the two.

References

K. Balci and A. A. Salah. 2015. Automatic analysis and identification of verbal aggression and abusive behaviors for online social games. *Computers in Human Behavior* 53:517–526.

D. Biber. 1988. *Variation across speech and writing.* Cambridge University Press, Cambridge.

D. Biber. 1989. A typology of english texts. *Linguistics* 27:3–43.

M. Bieswanger. 2016. Electronically-mediated englishes: Synchronicity revisited. In L.Squires, editor, *English in Computer-Mediated Communication:*

Variation, Representation, and Change, De Gruyter, Berlin Boston.

P. Burnap and M. L. Williams. 2014. Hate speech, machine classification and statistical modelling of information flows on twitter: Interpretation and communication for policy decision making. In *Proceedings of the Internet, Policy and Politics Conference*. Oxford.

Y. Chen, Y. Zhou, S. Zhu, and H. Xu. 2012. Detecting offensive language in social media to protect adolescent online safety. In *Proceedings of the 2012 ASE/IEEE International Conference on Social Computing and 2012 ASE/IEEE International Conference on Privacy, Security, Risk and Trust*. IEEE Computer Society, Washington, DC, USA, SOCIALCOM-PASSAT '12, pages 71–80. https://doi.org/10.1109/SocialCom-PASSAT.2012.55.

M. Dadvar, D. Trieschnigg, and F. de Jong. 2013. Expert knowledge for automatic detection of bullies in social networks. In *Proceedings of the 25th Benelux Conference on Artificial Intelligence, BNAIC 2013, Delft, the Netherlands*. TU Delft, pages 57–64.

T. Davidson, D. Warmsley, M. Macy, and I. Weber. 2017. Automated hate speech detection and the problem of offensive language. In *In Proceedings of the 11th International AAAI Conference on Web and Social Media ICWSM17*. World Academy of Science, Engineering and Technology. https://arxiv.org/pdf/1703.04009.pdf.

N. Fairclough. 1992. *Discourse and Social Change*. Blackwell Publishing Ltd., Cambridge.

J. Gentry. 2016. Package twitter pages 1–30. https://cran.r-project.org/web/packages/twitteR/twitteR.pdf.

J. Gibbons. 2008. Questioning in common law criminal courts. In J. Gibbons and M. Teresa Turell, editors, *Dimensions of Forensic Linguistics*, John Benjamins Publishing Company, Amsterdam/Philadelphia, pages 115–130.

K. Gimpel, N. Schneider, B. OConnor, D. Das, D. Mills, J. Eisenstein, M Heilman, D Yogatama, J Flanigan, and N. A Smith. 2011. Part-of-speech tagging for twitter: Annotation, features, and experiments. In *Proceedings of the 49th Annual Meeting of the Association for Computational Linguistics: Short Papers*. Association for Computational Linguistics, pages 19–24. www.aclweb.org/anthology/P11-2008.

D. Glynn. 2009. Polysemy, syntax, and variation: A usage-based method for cognitive semantics. In V. Evans and S. Pourcel, editors, *New directions in Cognitive Linguistics*, John Benjamins, Amsterdam, pages 77–106.

D. Glynn. 2014. Correspondence analysis: Exploring data and identifying patterns. In D. Glynn and J. A. Robinson, editors, *Corpus Methods for Semantics: Quantitative studies in polysemy and synonymy*, John Benjamins, Amsterdam, pages 443–485.

J. Grieve, D. Biber, E. Friginal, and T Nekrasova. 2010. Variation among blogs: A multi dimensional analysis. In A. Mehler, S. Sharoff, and M. Santini, editors, *Genres on the web: Computational Models and Empirical Studies*, Springer-Verlag, New York, pages 45–71.

C. Hardaker. 2010. Trolling in asynchronous computer-mediated communication: From user discussions to academic definitions. *Journal of Politeness Research* 6:215–242.

S. Herring, D. A. Johnson, and T. DiBenedetto. 1995. This discussion is going too far! male resistance to female participation on the internet. In K. Hall and M. Bucholtz, editors, *Gender Articulated: Language and the Socially Constructed Self*, Routledge, New York and London, chapter 3, pages 67–96.

G. E. Hine, J. Onaolapo, E. De Cristofaro, N. Kourtellis, I. Leontiadis, R. Samaras, G. Stringhini, and J. Blackburn. 2017. Kek, cucks, and god emperor trump: A measurement study of 4chan's politically incorrect forum and its effects on the web. In *Proceedings of the 11th International AAAI Conference on Web and Social Media (ICWSM-17)*. https://arxiv.org/abs/1610.03452.

F. Husson, J. Josse, S. Le, and J. Mazet. 2017. Factominer: Multivariate exploratory data analysis and data mining pages 1–96. https://cran.r-project.org/web/packages/FactoMineR/FactoMineR.pdf.

F. Husson, S. Lê, and J. Pags. 2010. *Exploratory Multivariate Analysis by Example Using R*. Chapman & Hall CRC, London.

B. Le Roux and H. Rouanet. 2010. *Multiple Correspondence Analysis*. SAGE Publications, Inc., California.

Y. Mehdad and J. Tetreault. 2016. Do characters abuse more than words? In *Proceedings of the 17th Annual Meeting of the Special Interest Group on Discourse and Dialogue*. Association for Computational Linguistics, Los Angeles, pages 299–303. http://www.aclweb.org/anthology/W16-3638.

R. J. Passonneau, N. Ide, S. Su, and J. Stuart. 2014. Biber redux: Reconsidering dimensions of variation in american english. In *COLING 2014, 25th International Conference on Computational Linguistics, Proceedings of the Conference: Technical Papers, August 23-29, 2014, Dublin, Ireland.* pages 565–576. http://aclweb.org/anthology/C/C14/C14-1054.pdf.

G. Tottie. 1983. *Much about not and nothing: a study of the variation between analytic and synthetic negation in contemporary American English.* CWK Gleerup, Lund.

J. Tummers, D. Speelman, and D. Geeraerts. 2012. Multiple correspondence analysis as heuristic tool to unveil confounding variables in corpus linguistics. In *Proceedings of the 11th International Conference on Statistical Analysis of Textual Data.* JADT, pages 923–936.

T. A. van Dijk. 1993. Stories and racism. In D. K. Mumby, editor, *Narrative and Social Control: critical perspectives*, Sage, Newbury Park, CA, chapter 5.

W. Warner and J. Hirschberg. 2012. Detecting hate speech on the world wide web. In *Proceedings of the Workshop on Language and Social Media.* The Association for Computational Linguistics, pages 19–26. https://aclweb.org/anthology/W/W12/W12-21.pdf.

Z. Waseem and D. Hovy. 2016. Hateful symbols or hateful people? predictive features for hate speech detection on twitter. In *Proceedings of Proceedings of NAACL-HLT 2016.* The Association for Computational Linguistics, pages 88–93. https://aclweb.org/anthology/N/N16/N16-2.pdf.

G. Xiang, B. Fan, L. Wang, J. Hong, and C. Rose. 2012. Detecting offensive tweets via topical feature discovery over a large scale twitter corpus. In *Proceedings of the 21st ACM International Conference on Information and Knowledge Management.* ACM, New York, NY, USA, CIKM '12, pages 1980–1984. https://doi.org/10.1145/2396761.2398556.

D. Yin, Z. Xue, L. Hong, B. D. Davison, A. Kontostathis, and L. Edwards. 2009. Detection of harassment on web 2.0. In *Proceedings of the Content Analysis in the WEB.* Dublin City University and Association for Computational Linguistics, pages 1–7. http://www.cse.lehigh.edu/ brian/pubs/2009/CAW2/harassment.pdf.

Constructive Language in News Comments

Varada Kolhatkar
Discourse Processing Lab
Simon Fraser University
Burnaby, Canada
vkolhatk@sfu.ca

Maite Taboada
Discourse Processing Lab
Simon Fraser University
Burnaby, Canada
mtaboada@sfu.ca

Abstract

We discuss the characteristics of constructive news comments, and present methods to identify them. First, we define the notion of *constructiveness*. Second, we annotate a corpus for constructiveness. Third, we explore whether available argumentation corpora can be useful to identify constructiveness in news comments. Our model trained on argumentation corpora achieves a top accuracy of 72.59% (baseline=49.44%) on our crowd-annotated test data. Finally, we examine the relation between constructiveness and toxicity. In our crowd-annotated data, 21.42% of the non-constructive comments and 17.89% of the constructive comments are toxic, suggesting that non-constructive comments are not much more toxic than constructive comments.

1 Introduction

The goal of online news comments is to provide constructive, intelligent and informed remarks that are relevant to the article, often in the form of an exchange with other readers. Many comments, however, do not contribute to achieving this goal. Online comments have a broad range: they can be vacuous, dismissive, abusive, hateful, but also constructive. Below we show two comments on an article about Hillary Clinton's loss in the presidential election in 2016.[1]

(1) I have 3 daughters, and I told them that Mrs. Clinton lost because she did not have a platform. The only message that I got from her was that Mr. Trump is not fit to be in office and that she wanted to be the first female President. I honestly believe that she lost because she offered no hope, or direction, to the average American. Mr. Trump, with all his shortcomings, at least offered change and some hope.

(2) This article was a big disappointment. Thank you Ms Henein. Now women know that wasting their time reading your emotion-based opinion is not an option.

Both comments disagree with the author, but one does it constructively and the other dismissively. Comment (1) treats the article as a genuine starting point for discussion and presents disagreement without denigrating, with reasons for the disagreement. On the other hand, comment (2) is dismissive and probably sarcastic.

Our goal is to understand constructiveness in news comments, which may help in filtering and organizing many kinds of online comments. News comments may be filtered according to different criteria, for example, based on their toxicity and/or constructiveness. Toxic comments may be filtered negatively, i.e., they can be blocked, deleted, or demoted. Constructive comments may be filtered positively, i.e., they can be promoted, as it is done manually for the New York Times Picks (Diakopoulos, 2015). A number of approaches have been proposed for toxicity (e.g., Kwok and Wang, 2013; Waseem and Hovy, 2016; Wulczyn et al., 2016; Nobata et al., 2016; Davidson et al., 2017). A recent example is the effort by Google to identify abusive or toxic comments through the Perspective API.[2] There is, however, not as much research on the constructiveness of individual comments. Niculae and Danescu-Niculescu-Mizil (2016) and Napoles et al. (2017) study constructiveness at the comment thread-level, but not at the comment level.

In this paper, we focus on the constructiveness of individual news comments. First, we define the notion of *constructiveness*. Second, we de-

---

[1] http://www.theglobeandmail.com/opinion/thank-you-hillary-women-now-know-retreat-is-not-an-option/article32803341/

[2] https://www.perspectiveapi.com/

Proceedings of the First Workshop on Abusive Language Online, pages 11–17,
Vancouver, Canada, July 30 - August 4, 2017. ©2017 Association for Computational Linguistics

scribe our annotated corpus of online comments labelled for constructiveness. Third, we explore deep learning approaches for identifying constructive comments. Fourth, we discuss the association between constructiveness and a number of argumentation features. Finally, we examine the relationship between toxicity and constructiveness.

2   Constructiveness: Definition and corpus

We are interested in comments that contribute to the conversation, which construct, build and promote a dialogue. Napoles et al. (2017) define constructive conversations in terms of ERICs— Engaging, Respectful, and/or Informative Conversations. Rather than relying on our intuitions, we posted a survey asking what a constructive comment is. We opened a survey on SurveyMonkey[3], requesting 100 answers. A composite of the answers is: *Constructive comments intend to create a civil dialogue through remarks that are relevant to the article and not intended to merely provoke an emotional response. They are typically targeted to specific points and supported by appropriate evidence.*

In order to study constructiveness in news comments, we crawled 1,121 comments from 10 articles of the Globe and Mail news website[4] covering a variety of subjects: technology, immigration, terrorism, politics, budget, social issues, religion, property, and refugees. We used CrowdFlower[5] as our crowdsourcing annotation platform and annotated the comments for constructiveness. We asked the annotators to first read the relevant article, and then to tell us whether the displayed comment was constructive or not. For quality control, 100 units were marked as gold: Annotators were allowed to continue with the annotation task only when their answers agreed with our answers to the gold questions. As we were interested in the verdict of native speakers of English, we limited the allowed demographic region to English-speaking countries. We asked for three judgments per instance and paid 5 cents per annotation unit. Percentage agreement for the constructiveness question was 87.88%, suggesting that constructiveness can be reliably annotated. Agreement numbers are provided by CrowdFlower, and are calculated on a random sample of 100 annotations. Other measures of agreement, such as kappa, are not easily computed with CrowdFlower data, because many different annotators are involved. Constructiveness seemed to be equally distributed in our dataset: Out of the 1,121 comments, 603 comments (53.79%) were classified as constructive, 517 (46.12%) as non-constructive, and the annotators were not sure in only one case. We use this annotated corpus as the test data in our experiments. We have also made the corpus publicly available.[6]

3   Identifying constructive comments

We take the view that constructiveness is closely related to argumentation. Argumentative texts usually establish a position on a topic and provide reasoning for that particular position. Similarly, a constructive comment provides reasoning for the commenter's point of view. We exploit argumentation-related datasets to train a bidirectional Long Short-Term Memory (biLSTM) model (Hochreiter and Schmidhuber, 1997; Graves and Schmidhuber, 2005) to identify constructive comments. We also explore the association between constructiveness and argumentation features.

3.1   Building a constructiveness classifier

Constructiveness is an interplay between different kinds of linguistic knowledge: lexical, syntactic, semantic and pragmatic knowledge. Lexical and syntactic features, such as use of hedges and modals, sentence structure, readability or text complexity; semantic features, such as the use of personal and emotion words or the sentiment score for the comment; and discourse features, such as cohesion, discourse relations, the comment's topic, or the topic distance from the article, have shown to help in identifying similar phenomena, such as quality of student essays or constructiveness of a comment thread (Pitler and Nenkova, 2008; Brand and Van Der Merwe, 2014; Diakopoulos, 2015; Momeni et al., 2015; Niculae and Danescu-Niculescu-Mizil, 2016). The primary challenge in developing a computational system for constructiveness is the lack of training data from which we can learn about these different aspects of constructiveness.

Training data   Since there is no training data available for constructiveness at the comment

[3] https://www.surveymonkey.com/
[4] http://www.theglobeandmail.com/
[5] https://www.crowdflower.com/

[6] https://github.com/sfu-discourse-lab/Constructiveness_Toxicity_Corpus

level, we gathered annotated data from similar tasks. In particular, we exploit two annotated corpora. The first corpus is the Yahoo News Annotated Corpus (YNC)[7] (Napoles et al., 2017), which contains thread-level constructiveness annotations for Yahoo News comment threads. We are interested in comment-level annotations, and thus assume that a comment from a constructive thread is constructive and vice versa for non-constructive threads. We extracted 33,957 comments from constructive conversations and 26,821 comments from non-constructive conversations from this dataset. Other than constructiveness annotations, the YNC corpus also contains annotations for sub-dialogue type (argumentative, flamewar, off topic, personal stories, positive, respectful, snarky or humorous). We concatenate these annotations to the comments when training.

The second corpus is the Argument Extraction Corpus (AEC)[8] (Swanson et al., 2015). The corpus includes annotations for argument quality on sentences extracted from the topics of gun control, gay marriage, evolution, and death penalty. Our intuition is that sentences with high argument quality are constructive and low argument quality are non-constructive. We extract 2,613 examples with high argumentation quality and 2,761 examples with low argumentation quality. In total, we had 36,570 constructive and 29,582 non-constructive training examples.

Test data   Our test data is our crowd-sourced constructiveness corpus containing 1,121 instances marked for constructiveness. As news comments are not always well written, we carried out some preprocessing of the data, such as word segmentation and spelling correction. For example, in *Climate change has always been a **hoax,as** ...*, our preprocessing will add a space between *hoax,* and *as*.

Model and results   We carry out preliminary experiments to assess whether argumentative comment representations are useful to identify constructive comments. We train biLSTM models with the annotated argumentation corpora. These models are usually used for sequential predictions. The models have *memory* in the sense that the results from the previous predictions can inform future predictions. The model learns what kind of

[7]https://webscope.sandbox.yahoo.com
[8]https://nlds.soe.ucsc.edu/node/29

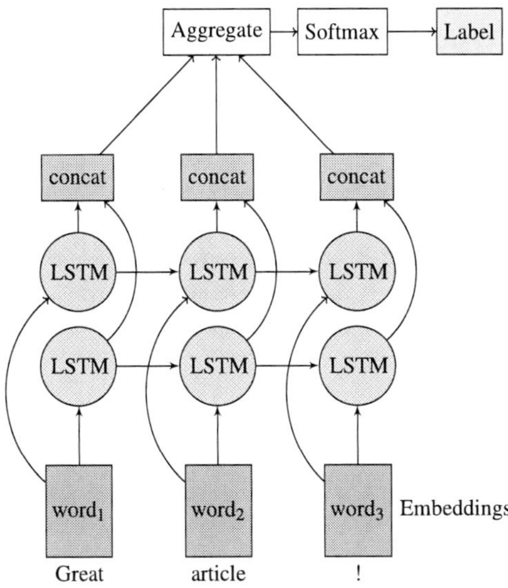

Figure 1: Bidirectional LSTM architecture. Label values: constructive, non-constructive.

memories are important in predicting the output.

Although our task is *not* a sequential prediction task, the primary reason for using biLSTMs is that these models can utilize the expanded paragraph-level contexts and learn paragraph representations directly. In our case, the memory is used not to remember the previous comments' predictions, but to remember the long-distance context within the same comment. Moreover, biLSTMs have been shown to learn better representations of sequences by processing them from left to right and from right to left. They have recently been used in diverse tasks, such as stance detection (Augenstein et al., 2016), sentiment analysis (Teng et al., 2016), and medical event detection (Jagannatha and Yu, 2016).

Figure 1 outlines the general architecture of our model. The words in each comment are mapped to their corresponding word representation using the embedding layer. The embedding layer contains the word vector mapping from words to dense n-dimensional vector representations. We initialize the embedding layer weights with GloVe vectors (Pennington et al., 2014). The word embeddings are fed into the LSTM layer. The LSTM layer has two LSTM chains: one propagating in the forward direction and one propagating in the backward direction. The representations are combined by taking linear combinations of the LSTM outputs. The output is then passed through the Softmax acti-

Training	Validation accuracy (%)	Test accuracy (%)
YNC + AEC	68.43	68.45
YNC	72.76	**72.59**
AEC	69.30	52.54

Table 1: Constructiveness prediction results using argumentation corpora. The test data was our annotated constructiveness data in all cases. Random baseline accuracy = 49.44%.

Feature	OR
Argumentative discourse relations	3.49
Stance adverbials	2.52
Reasoning verbs & modals	2.02
Root clauses	1.37
Conjunctions & connectives	0.82
Abstract nouns	0.51

Table 2: Association of constructiveness with linguistic features in terms of OR (odds ratio).

vation function, which produces a probability-like output for each label type, in our case for the labels constructive and non-constructive.

The network is trained with backpropagation. The embedding vectors are also updated based on the backpropagated errors. We use bidirectional LSTMs as implemented in TensorFlow[9]. We trained with the ADAM stochastic gradient descent for 10 epochs. The important parameter settings are: batch size=512, embedding size=200, drop out=0.5, and learning rate=0.001.

We wanted to examine which argumentation dataset is more effective in identifying constructiveness. So we carried out experiments with different train and test combinations. In each experiment, 1% of the training data was used as the validation set.

Table 1 shows the average validation and test accuracies for three runs with the same parameter settings. Below we note a few observations. First, we achieved the best result when YNC was included in the training set. Second, AEC seems not to have much effect on the test accuracy but YNC does; when we do not have YNC in the training data, the results drop markedly. This might be because the size of the AEC corpus is relatively small and the model was not able to learn any relevant patterns from this data. Finally, the validation and test accuracy is more or less same for the first two rows, when YNC is included in the training data.

3.2 Association with argumentation features

In addition to the classifier described above, we also examine the association between constructiveness and a number of linguistic and discourse features typically found in argumentative texts, based on the extensive literature on argumentation

(Biber, 1988; van Eemeren et al., 2007; Moens et al., 2007; Tseronis, 2011; Becker et al., 2016; Habernal and Gurevych, 2017; Azar, 1999; Peldszus and Stede, 2016). We calculate association in terms of odds ratio (Horwitz, 1979), which tells us the odds of a comment being constructive in the presence of a feature. Results are shown in Table 2. We observed a strong association between constructiveness and occurrence of argumentative discourse relations (Cause, Comparison, Condition, Contrast, Evaluation and Explanation).[10] The odds ratio for argumentative discourse relations is 3.49, which means that constructive texts are 3.49 times more likely to have this feature than non-constructive texts. Other features with strong association with constructiveness are stance adverbials (e.g., *undoubtedly, paradoxically, of course*), and reasoning verbs (e.g., *cause, lead*) and modals. Root clauses (clauses with a matrix verb and an embedded clause, such as *I think that ...*) show a medium association with constructiveness. On the other hand, abstract nouns (e.g., *issue, reason*) and, surprisingly, conjunctions and connectives are not associated with constructive texts. The latter is surprising because many discourse relations contain a connnective.

4 Toxicity in news comments

In the context of filtering news comments, we are also interested in the relationship between constructiveness and toxicity. We propose the label *toxicity* for a range of phenomena, including verbal abuse, offensive comments and hate speech. To better understand the nature of toxicity and its relationship with constructiveness, we extended our CrowdFlower annotation. For the 1,121 comments described in Section 2, we also asked anno-

---

[9]https://www.tensorflow.org/

[10]For this analysis we used the discourse relations given by the discourse parser described in Joty et al. (2015).

tators to identify toxicity. The question posed was: How toxic is the comment? We established four classes: *Very toxic*, *Toxic*, *Mildly toxic* and *Not toxic*. The definition for Very toxic included comments which use harsh, offensive or abusive language; comments which include personal attacks or insults; or which are derogatory or demeaning. Toxic comments were sarcastic, containing ridicule or aggressive disagreement. Mildly toxic comments were described as those which may be considered toxic only by some people, or which express anger and frustration.

The distribution of toxicity levels by constructiveness label is shown in Table 3. The percentage agreement provided by CrowdFlower for this task was 81.82%. The most important result of this annotation experiment is that there were no significant differences in toxicity levels between constructive and non-constructive comments, i.e., constructive comments were as likely to be toxic (in its three categories) as non-constructive comments. For instance, consider Example (3) below. It was labelled as constructive by two out of three annotators, and toxic by all three (two as Toxic, and one as Very toxic). It could be the case, in some situations, that a moderator may allow a somewhat toxic comment if it contributes to the conversation, i.e., if it is constructive.

> (3) If it's wrong to vote AGAINST someone based on their gender,Then surely it is also wrong to vote FOR someone based on their gender.Yet there were many people advocating openly for people to to do just that.I wonder how many votes Clinton got just because she was a woman.

We conclude, then, that constructiveness and toxicity are orthogonal categories. The results also suggest that it is important to consider constructiveness of comments along with toxicity when filtering comments, as aggressive constructive debate might be a good feature of online discussion. Given these results, the classification of constructiveness and toxicity should probably be treated as separate problems.

5   Discussion and conclusion

We have proposed a definition of constructiveness that hinges on argumentative aspects of news comments. We have shown that well-known linguistic indicators of argumentation, such as adverbials and rhetorical relations show an association with constructive comments. Our definition of constructiveness is at the comment level, because it

	C ($n = 603$)	Non-C ($n = 518$)
Not toxic	82.09%	78.57%
Mildly toxic	16.08%	15.44%
Toxic	1.33%	5.21%
Very toxic	0.50%	0.77%
Total	100%	100%

Table 3: Percent distribution of constructive and toxic comments in CrowdFlower annotation. C = Constructive.

is important to identify comments as they come in, rather than waiting for a thread to degenerate (Wulczyn et al., 2016), and because many comments are top-level, i.e., not part of a thread.

We assume that constructive comments contain good argumentation and explored argumentation datasets to train a bidirectional LSTM to identify constructive comments. The highest accuracy of our model was 72.59% (random baseline=49.44%).

Through an annotation experiment, we studied the relationship between constructiveness and toxicity, and found that constructive comments are just as likely to be toxic (or not toxic) as non-constructive comments. In terms of filtering, this poses an interesting question, since some of our toxic comments were also deemed to be constructive by the annotators.

As for future work, our long-term goal is to build a robust system for identifying constructive news comments. We also plan to investigate the relation between toxicity and constructiveness more deeply. We plan to train on more relevant and directly related training data, such as the New York Times Picks, and systematically explore different argumentation features for constructiveness (e.g., readability, cohesion, coherence).

Acknowledgments

We are grateful to Shafiq Joty for running his discourse parser on our data. We would like to thank the members of the Discourse Processing Lab: Hanhan Wu for data collection; Luca Cavasso, Jennifer Fest, Emilie Francis, Emma Mileva and Kazuki Yabe for testing CrowdFlower questions and providing feedback. Thank you also to the reviewers for very constructive suggestions.

References

Isabelle Augenstein, Tim Rocktäschel, Andreas Vlachos, and Kalina Bontcheva. 2016. Stance detection with bidirectional conditional encoding. In *Proceedings of the 2016 Conference on Empirical Methods in Natural Language Processing*. Austin, TX, pages 876–885.

Moshe Azar. 1999. Argumentative text as rhetorical structure: An application of Rhetorical Structure Theory. *Argumentation* 13(1):97–144.

Maria Becker, Alexis Palmer, and Anette Frank. 2016. Clause types and modality in argumentative microtexts. In *Proceedings of the Workshop on Foundations of the Language of Argumentation (in conjunction with COMMA 2016)*. Postdam, pages 1–9.

Douglas Biber. 1988. *Variation across Speech and Writing*. Cambridge University Press, Cambridge.

Dirk Brand and Brink Van Der Merwe. 2014. Comment classification for an online news domain. In *Proceedings of the First International Conference on the use of Mobile Informations and Communication Technology in Africa UMICTA*. Stellenbosch, South Africa, pages 50–56.

Thomas Davidson, Dana Warmsley, Michael Macy, and Ingmar Weber. 2017. Automated hate speech detection and the problem of offensive language. In *Proceedings of the 11th International Conference on Web and Social Media*. Montréal.

Nicholas Diakopoulos. 2015. Picking the NYT Picks: Editorial criteria and automation in the curation of online news comments. *ISOJ Journal* 6(1):147–166.

Alex Graves and Jürgen Schmidhuber. 2005. Framewise phoneme classification with bidirectional LSTM networks. In *Proceedings of the IEEE International Joint Conference on Neural Networks, IJCNN*. volume 4, pages 2047–2052.

Ivan Habernal and Iryna Gurevych. 2017. Argumentation mining in user-generated web discourse. *Computational Linguistics* 43(1):125–179.

Sepp Hochreiter and Jürgen Schmidhuber. 1997. Long Short-Term Memory. *Neural Computation* 9(8):1735–1780.

Ralph I. Horwitz. 1979. A method of estimating comparative rates from clinical data: Applications to cancer of the lung, breast, and cervix: Cornfield J: J Nat Cancer Inst 11: 12691275, 1951. *Journal of Chronic Diseases* 32(1-2):i.

Abhyuday N. Jagannatha and Hong Yu. 2016. Bidirectional RNN for medical event detection in electronic health records. In *Proceedings of the 2016 Conference of the North American Chapter of the Association for Computational Linguistics: Human Language Technologies*. San Diego, CA, pages 473–482.

Shafiq Joty, Giuseppe Carenini, and Raymond Ng. 2015. CODRA: A novel discriminative framework for rhetorical analysis. *Computational Linguistics* 41(3):385–435.

Irene Kwok and Yuzhou Wang. 2013. Locate the hate: Detecting tweets against blacks. In *Proceedings of the Twenty-Seventh AAAI Conference on Artificial Intelligence*. AAAI'13, pages 1621–1622.

Marie-Francine Moens, Erik Boiy, Raquel Mochales Palau, and Chris Reed. 2007. Automatic detection of arguments in legal texts. In *Proceedings of the 11th international conference on Artificial intelligence and law*. ACM, Stanford, California, pages 225–230.

Elaheh Momeni, Claire Cardie, and Nicholas Diakopoulos. 2015. A survey on assessment and ranking methodologies for user-generated content on the web. *ACM Computing Surveys* 48(3):1–49.

Courtney Napoles, Joel Tetreault, Aasish Pappu, Enrica Rosato, and Brian Provenzale. 2017. Finding good conversations online: The Yahoo News Annotated Comments Corpus. In *Proceedings of the 11th Linguistic Annotation Workshop, EACL*. Valencia, pages 13–23.

Vlad Niculae and Cristian Danescu-Niculescu-Mizil. 2016. Conversational markers of constructive discussions. In *Proceedings of the 2016 Conference of the North American Chapter of the Association for Computational Linguistics: Human Language Technologies*. San Diego, pages 568–578.

Chikashi Nobata, Joel Tetreault, Achint Thomas, Yashar Mehdad, and Yi Chang. 2016. Abusive language detection in online user content. In *Proceedings of the 25th International World Wide Web Conference*. Montréal, pages 145–153.

Andreas Peldszus and Manfred Stede. 2016. Rhetorical structure and argumentation structure in monologue text. In *Proceedings of the 3rd Workshop on Argument Mining, ACL*. Berlin, pages 103–112.

Jeffrey Pennington, Richard Socher, and Christopher D. Manning. 2014. GloVe: Global vectors for word representation. In *Proceedings of the Conference on Empirical Methods in Natural Language Processing*. Doha, Qatar, pages 1532–1543.

Emily Pitler and Ani Nenkova. 2008. Revisiting readability: A unified framework for predicting text quality. In *Proceedings of the Conference on Empirical Methods in Natural Language Processing*. Honolulu, HI, pages 186–195.

Reid Swanson, Brian Ecker, and Marilyn Walker. 2015. Argument mining: Extracting arguments from online dialogue. In *Proceedings of the 16th Annual Meeting of the Special Interest Group on Discourse and Dialogue*. Prague, Czech Republic, pages 217–226.

Zhiyang Teng, Duy Tin Vo, and Yue Zhang. 2016. Context-sensitive lexicon features for neural sentiment analysis. In *Proceedings of the 2016 Conference on Empirical Methods in Natural Language Processing*. Association for Computational Linguistics, Austin, Texas, pages 1629–1638.

Assimakis Tseronis. 2011. From connectives to argumentative markers: A quest for markers of argumentative moves and of related aspects of argumentative discourse. *Argumentation* 25(4):427–447.

Frans H. van Eemeren, Peter Houtlosser, and A. Francisca Snoeck Henkemans. 2007. *Argumentative Indicators in Discourse: A pragma-dialectical study*. Springer, Berlin.

Zeerak Waseem and Dirk Hovy. 2016. Hateful symbols or hateful people? Predictive features for hate speech detection on Twitter. In *Proceedings of the 2016 Conference of the North American Chapter of the Association for Computational Linguistics: Human Language Technologies*. San Diego, CA, pages 88–93.

Ellery Wulczyn, Nithum Thain, and Lucas Dixon. 2016. Ex machina: Personal attacks seen at scale. *arXiv:1702.08138v1* .

Rephrasing Profanity in Chinese Text

Hui-Po Su, Zhen-Jie Huang, Hao-Tsung Chang[1] and Chuan-Jie Lin[2]
Department of Computer Science and Engineering
National Taiwan Ocean University
{[1]htchang.cse, [2]cjlin}@mail.ntou.edu.tw

Abstract

This paper proposes a system that can detect and rephrase profanity in Chinese text. Rather than just masking detected profanity, we want to revise the input sentence by using inoffensive words while keeping their original meanings. 29 of such rephrasing rules were invented after observing sentences on real-word social websites. The overall accuracy of the proposed system is 85.56%

1 Introduction

Profanity, or offensive language, is often seen in social media, especially when users can write things anonymously. In nowadays, many social media or chatrooms have policies to detect and mask offensive words in order to reduce web abuse.

Most of the English profanity processing systems maintain a list of offensive words and their substitutions. A simple match-and-replace method can handle most of the cases (Razavi *et al.*, 2010; Vandersmissen, 2012; Xiang *et al.*, 2012; Bretschneider *et al.*, 2014).

However, detecting profanity in Chinese is more complicated than in English. A Chinese character appearing in an offensive word may also appear in a mild word. For example, although the character "幹" means "fxxk" in some context, it also has meanings of "do", "work", and "stem", as its appearances in the words "幹活" (do works) or "枝幹" (tree branches and stems). Simple detection and masking will filter out inoffensive words.

Moreover, our system tries to offer an alternative way to express what a writer wants to say, rather than just applies masking and leave the offensive words there. There are two reasons that we want to rephrase the offensive expressions instead of masking them:

1. Sometimes in Chinese, the masking will make the sentence incomprehensible.

2. Hopefully, it will gradually make the writer to put words more politely.

To our best knowledge, there is no much research work in NLP discussing about detecting and rephrasing profanity in Chinese text. As a preliminary study, we only focused on the most frequent types of offensive words in Traditional Chinese, as well as some Mandarin transliterations in the Southern Min dialect (referred to as Taiwanese hereafter).

We have to apologize that this paper contains a lot of offensive words, both in Chinese and English. We will rewrite these words in the following ways to make them less offensive: a) for a single Chinese character, it will be replaced by an uppercase English letter, such as "F 你"; b) for a multi-character Chinese word, underlines are inserted between characters, such as 賤_人; c) for a phrase, plus signs are inserted between words, such as 你＋奶奶＋的; d) for an English word, some letter will be replaced by 'x', such as "fxxk". We hope the readers can feel less offended with these revisions.

Another challenge in English is to detect abusive languages in articles, including racist, sexual-oriented harassment, bullying, and hateful speech (Ross *et al.*, 2016; Waseem, 2016; Waseem and Hovy, 2016; Wulczyn, *et al.*, 2017). It will be our future work in Chinese.

This paper is organized as follows. Section 2 defines the categories of offensive expressions studied in this paper and explains how to build the experimental dataset. Section 3 describes the rephrasing rules. Section 4 delivers the evaluation and error analysis. Section 5 concludes the paper.

18

Proceedings of the First Workshop on Abusive Language Online, pages 18–24,
Vancouver, Canada, July 30 - August 4, 2017. ©2017 Association for Computational Linguistics

Figure 1. An Example of searching in Twitter

2 Profanity Data Collection

In order to observe all variations of Chinese profanity in real world, we built a data collection from social media. Offensive expressions were annotated and their milder paraphrases were also created by humans. The procedure is described briefly in the section.

2.1 Real-World Profanity Data Collection

Two popular social media, Twitter and PTT (a famous BBS in Taiwan), were chosen as the source websites to collect offensive expressions.

Twitter[1] provides a search tool to find tweets containing submitted keywords. A search example is illustrated in Figure 1. Because Twitter only returns a small set of results for one query, we only collected the top 30 results for study.

PTT[2], on the other hand, does not provide any tool to search posts. We used Google to do the searching by adding the option "site:ptt.cc", which restricts the source website of the search results. We then retrieved the full texts of the posts by visiting the URLs in the search results. At most top 300 results for each query were collected.

Queries were Chinese characters or words commonly used in Chinese profanity. We expanded the query terms with their synonyms in Tongyici Cilin (同義詞詞林, a thesaurus of Chinese synonyms) or well-known substitutions with similar pronunciation. These query terms belong to the following four categories.

1. Terms related to "sexual intercourse"
2. Terms related to sexual organs or substances
3. Terms synonymous to "bxtch"
4. Terms in the pattern of "one's relative's", a special pattern of profanity in Chinese

In case that tweets or posts written in Simplified Chinese were collected, we converted them into Traditional Chinese by three mapping dictionaries developed by Wikipedia with the longest-matching strategy.

We found that not all the search results from PTT were suitable for our research. Some users expressed their anger against some persons, teams or TV programs by changing their names into indelicate characters. These are not common cases thus should be filtered out. In order not to spend too much human effort on filtering, posts from the Gossip Board and the sex-related boards were discarded. The source board of a post can be determined from its URL.

There are totally 9,557 sentences in the test set.

2.2 Data Annotation

The main purpose of our system is to rephrase profanity into another meaningful text. It is important to find suitable substitutions so that the rephrased text is fluent and has the same (or similar) meaning of the original text. Therefore, we built a develop set as gold standard for observation.

Two annotators (college students) were asked to browse the posts collected from Twitter or PTT, extract the sentences containing profanity, and provide possible paraphrases. Besides, if they saw a sentence containing obscene keywords but was not offensive, they would tag the sentence as "no need to change".

Moreover, if two annotators had different opinions on the same sentence, the authors would discuss and make decisions. Most of the disagreements were about the determination of indelicate text. Some found a text offensive while the other could tolerate it.

3 Detection and Rephrasing Rules

The main purpose of this paper is to develop a system which can detect and rephrase profanity in a given input. This system can be integrated with social media. After a user writes down some words, our system can provide a more decent way to express the same thing before the message is submitted. An example is shown in Figure 2 when integrating with Facebook.

---

[1] https://twitter.com/

[2] https://www.ptt.cc/bbs/

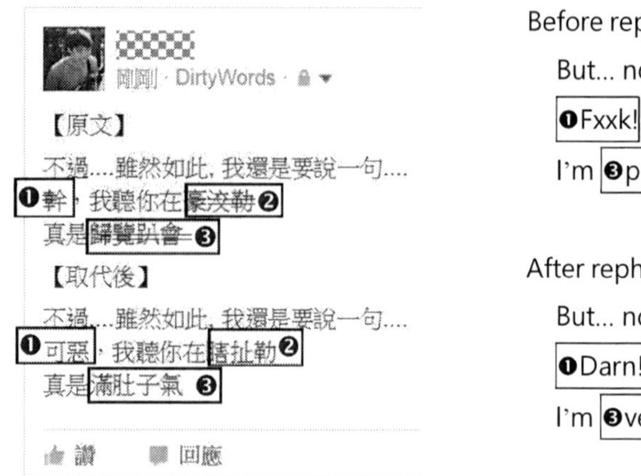

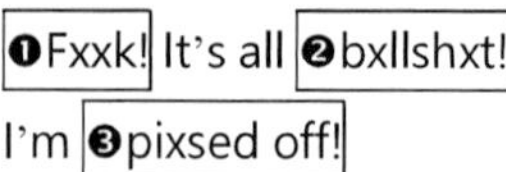

Figure 2. An example of profanity rephrasing on Facebook

After observing the real-world indelicate texts and their paraphrases, we invented 29 sets of detection patterns and rephrasing rules. Detection patterns consist of surface strings, word sets, and preconditions to apply the rules. Appendix A lists all the detection patterns and rephrasing rules. The following subsections explain the definitions and the challenges of the five major categories.

3.1 Phrases with F-words

The direct Chinese translation of "fxxk" is "幹" (masked by **F** hereafter in this paper). Appendix A also lists 3 other synonymous characters. Such characters have several usages.

1. It can be used as a verb as a swear word as in the phrase "**F** 你老師" ("fxxk your teacher"). The writer only wants to express his or her anger, so it can be replaced by "darn" or "oh no" (Rule #1).
   Note that the object of such a verb is often a relative or a close person to the hearer (such as mother or teacher).
2. A single word can form an exclamatory sentence "**F**!" ("Fxxk!"). It has the same meaning as the first case (Rule #2).
3. It can be used as an adjective as in the phrase "覺得很 **F**" ("feeling really fxxked"). Most of the time there will be an adverb preceding it. It can be replaced by an adjective synonymous to "angry" (Rule #3).
4. It can be used as a sentence opener as in the sentence "**F** 昨天忘了買鞋" ("Fxxk I forgot to buy shoes yesterday"). Replacing it with "oh no" is OK (Rule #4).
5. It may appear in an inoffensive word such as "幹活" (do works) or "操作" (operate). A list of formal words containing these offensive characters is maintained. Words in this list will remain unchanged in the input text (Rule #27).

3.2 Phrases Containing Relatives

The original phrase in this category is "他＋媽＋的" ("to his mother" / "his mother's"). Due to the explosion of social media, many similar phrases have been invented. They are all in the pattern of **Pronoun + RL + 的**, where **Pronoun** is a 2nd- or 3rd-person singular pronoun and **RL** is a relative title such as "奶奶" (grandma) or "妹妹" (sister). Note that "的" is a particle and carries no content information.

Such a phrase can also be used as a possessive form in a formal text, such as "他奶奶的拿手菜" ("his grandmother's specialty dish"). But when it is used alone, it becomes offensive (Rule #29).

3.3 Words Synonymous to "Bxtch"

Words in this category are used to scold somebody, so they can be replaced by phrases like "bad person" (Rules #5 ～ #7) which is less offensive.

3.4 Phrases with the Word "Semen"

The word "semen" has more than one translation in Chinese. Its formal term is "精液" and its obscene term is "洨" (siao2, Mandarin transliteration of Taiwanese dialect; masked by **X** hereafter).

Because the obscene term comes from Taiwanese, a lot of Taiwanese profanities are written down in many different ways of Mandarin transliterations, as shown in Appendix A. Their meanings are explained as follows.

1. The Taiwanese word "hau-siau5" means "exaggerating" or "trash talking". Its second character has no corresponding Chinese character therefore is usually written as **X** in text (Rules #12 and #13).

2. The Taiwanese phrase "jia7 siau5" means "eat shxt" and its second character is indeed **X**. We suggest a milder term to expression the same feeling (Rule #14).

3. The Taiwanese phrase "siaN2 siau5" means "what the hxll" and its second character is indeed **X**. We suggest a milder term to express the same feeling (Rule #15).

   Note that "三小" (san-siao3, three + little, what the hxll) is one of the expressions in this category. However, the string may also appear in a common phrase such as "三小時" (three hours). It is rephrased only when it follows a verb (Rule #11).

4. The Taiwanese word "lu5-siau5" means "annoying". Its second character has no corresponding Chinese character therefore is usually written as **X** in text (Rule #17).

5. If the term really means "semen", it should be replaced with its formal term (Rule #16).

6. The character **X** can also be used to replace any character with a sound similar to "siao3" when haters write person names or show names. It is not easy to recover the correct characters in the names. The proposed rule is a baseline rule (Rule #18).

3.5 Phrases Containing Sex Organs

Sex organs often have several names in Chinese. Their obscene terms 屄 (female genital, masked as **B** hereafter), 屌 (male genital, masked as **D** hereafter), and the Taiwanese word "lam7-pha" (scrotum, masked as **LP** hereafter) have developed different meanings in the Internet as listed here.

1. The word "牛 **B**" and the character **D** itself mean "awesome" in some context (Rules #19 and #23).

2. The word "傻 **B**" means "fool" (Rule #20).

3. The character **D** can be an adverb meaning "greatly" as in the phrase "**D** 打" (to defeat greatly) (Rule #24).

4. The character **D** can also be a verb meaning "to pay attention" as in the phrase "**D** 你" (to pay attention to you) (Rule #25).

Rule	Y	N	Acc	Rule	Y	N	Acc
1	85	15	0.85	16	39	5	0.89
2	91	9	0.91	17	98	2	0.98
3	98	0	1.00	18	78	22	0.78
4	76	24	0.76	19	56	44	0.56
5	98	2	0.98	20	99	1	0.99
6	97	3	0.97	21	30	11	0.73
7	70	30	0.70	22	47	53	0.47
8	93	5	0.95	23	98	2	0.98
9	81	19	0.81	24	93	1	0.99
10	88	12	0.88	25	30	14	0.68
11	2	0	1.00	26	68	32	0.68
12	12	0	1.00	27	93	7	0.93
13	96	4	0.96	28	10	0	1.00
14	42	4	0.91	29	86	14	0.86
15	90	10	0.90	**Total**	2044	345	0.86

Table 1. Evaluation results of rephrasing rules

5. The Taiwanese phrase "gui **LP** hoe2" (all + scrotum + fire) means "being pixsed off" or "very angry" (Rule #8).

6. If a word **B**, **D**, or **LP** really refers to "genital", a more decent expression is provided (Rules #9, #21, #22, and #26).

4 Evaluation

As a preliminary experiment, we evaluated our system in a small test set constructed by the following steps. For each of the 29 rephrasing rules, we randomly selected at most 100 sentences containing corresponding keywords to do the evaluation. Note that some groups were infrequent so we only had less than 100 sentences. There are totally 2,389 sentences in the test set.

Each rephrased (or detected but remain unchanged) part was assessed by two assessors in terms of both correct and fluent. The evaluation metric is the ratio of the correctness of the processing by the rephrasing rules. Note that if two or more parts in a sentence were detected, they were assessed separately.

The evaluation result is shown in Table 1, where Acc denotes accuracy. We can see that 15 of 29 groups of rules achieved accuracy above 90% and only 4 groups did not achieved accuracy better than 70%. The overall accuracy was 85.56%.

The main error types are discussed as follows.

1. Out-of-vocabulary problem
    Although we have tried to collect as many variants as possible, there are still newly invented ways to transliterate Taiwanese profanity. For example, "**F** 0 糧" has similar sound to "**F** 您_娘" (fxxk your mother) but does not appear in our dictionary. It is the major error of Rules #4 and #7.

2. Similar sound substitution
    Haters usually like to disparage the targets whom they are criticizing by replacing characters in the names with profane characters **B**, **D**, or **X**. It is not easy to recover the original names and becomes the major errors of Rules #18, #22, and #26.

3. Proper names containing obscene words
    There is a hamburger restaurant in Taiwan whose name is "牛逼洋行". The term "牛逼" inside its name should not be changed by Rule #19. The accuracy of Rule #19 becomes 94% if our system can recognize this name.

4. Sentence segmentation
    Some writers are too lazy to use punctuation marks to separate sentences. Words in different sentences are incorrectly adjoined and matched with wrong rephrasing rules. For example, "你 **D**" should be rephrased into "你屬害" (you are awesome). But "你 **D** 你 **D** 你 **D**…" matches Rule #25 and is incorrectly rephrased as "你理你理你…" (you notice you notice you…).

5 Conclusion

This paper proposes a system to deal with profanity in Chinese text. The system does not only detect profanity, but also provide rephrased text which is less offensive.

Nearly ten thousand sentences containing Chinese profanity were collected from real-world social websites. After human annotation, 29 groups of detection and rephrasing rules were invented. The overall accuracy of our system was 85.56% when evaluating on a test set of 2,389 sentences.

Now we have handled five main types of Chinese profanity. We need to look for a larger dataset in order to expand our rephrasing rules and find more types of profanities in the future.

Moreover, the proposed rephrasing rules were hand-crafted. We should try to discover more rules by machine learning.

References

Uwe Bretschneider, Thomas Wöhner, and Ralf Peters. 2014. Detecting Online Harassment in Social Networks. In *Proceedings of the Thirty Fifth International Conference on Information Systems*, pages 1-14. http://aisel.aisnet.org/icis2014/proceedings/ConferenceTheme/2/

Amir H. Razavi, Diana Inkpen, Sasha Uritsky, and Stan Matwin. 2010. Offensive Language Detection Using Multi-level Classification. In *Proceedings of Advances in Artificial Intelligence (AI 2010). Lecture Notes in Computer Science*, 6085. http://link.springer.com/chapter/10.1007/978-3-642-13059-5_5

Björn Ross, Michael Rist, Guillermo Carbonell, Benjamin Cabrera, Nils Kurowsky, and Michael Wojatzki. 2016. Measuring the Reliability of Hate Speech Annotations: The Case of the European Refugee Crisis. In *Proceedings of NLP4CMC III: 3rd Workshop on Natural Language Processing for Computer-Mediated Communication. Bochumer Linguistische Arbeitsberichte*, 17:6-9. https://www.linguistics.ruhr-uni-bochum.de/bla/nlp4cmc2016/ross.pdf

Baptist Vandersmissen. 2012. *Automated detection of offensive language behavior on social networking sites.* Master Thesis, Universiteit Gent. http://lib.ugent.be/catalog/rug01:001887239

Zeerak Waseem. 2016. Are You a Racist or Am I Seeing Things? Annotator Influence on Hate Speech Detection on Twitter. In *Proceedings of the First Workshop on NLP and Computational Social Science. Association for Computational Linguistics*, pages 138-142. http://aclweb.org/anthology/W16-5618.

Zeerak Waseem and Dirk Hovy. 2016. Hateful Symbols or Hateful People? Predictive Features for Hate Speech Detection on Twitter. In *Proceedings of the NAACL Student Research Workshop. Association for Computational Linguistics*, pages 88-93. http://www.aclweb.org/anthology/N16-2013.

Ellery Wulczyn, Nithum Thain, and Lucas Dixon. 2017. Ex Machina: Personal Attacks Seen at Scale. To appear in *Proceedings of the 26th International Conference on World Wide Web – WWW 2017.*

Guang Xiang, Bin Fan, Ling Wang, Jason I. Hong, and Carolyn P. Rose. 2012. Detecting Offensive Tweets via Topical Feature Discovery over a Large Scale Twitter Corpus. In *Proceedings of the 21st ACM international conference on Information and knowledge management (CIKM 2012)*, pages 1980-1984. https://doi.org/10.1145/2396761.2398556

Appendix A. Chinese Profanity Detection and Rephrasing Rules

#	Detection Patterns	Example	Rephrasing Rules
1	**F** (*fxxk*) + Pronoun + **RL** (*relative title*) + [老 (*old*)] + [的 ('*s*)] + [**JB** (*genital*)]	**F** 你娘 (*fxxk your mother*)	真是可惡 (*Darn*)
2	**F** (single word in one sentence)		可惡 (*Oh no*)
3	Adverb + **F**	很 **F** (*really fxxked*)	Adverb + 可惡
4	**F** (in the beginning of a sentence)	**F** 我今天… (*Fxxk! Today I…*)	可惡
29	他 + **RL** (*relative title*) + 的 你 + **RL** (*relative title*) + 的	他_媽_的 (*to his mother*) 你_媽_的 (*to your mother*)	Removed 你的 (*your*)
5	**BW** (*bxtchy whxre*)		壞女人 (*bad woman*)
6	賤_人 (*bxtch*)		壞人 (*bad person*)
7	**BT** (*bxtchy*)		機車 (a mild term)
11	Verb + 三小 (*what the hxll*)	你在講三小 (*what the hxll are you talking about*)	Verb + 什麼 (*what*)
12	在 (*be*) + **H** (*to lie*) + **X** (*semen*)	在_豪_洨 (*is shxt talking*)	在 + 瞎扯 (*trash talking*)
13	**H** + **X**	豪洨的劇情 (*ridiculous plot*)	唬人 (*to bluff* or *to lie*)
14	**J** (*to eat*) + **X** (*semen*)	你_甲_洨_啦 (*Eat shxt!*)	撞牆 (*run into the wall*)
15	**S** (*what*) + **X** (*semen*)	我到底在玩三_洨 (*what the hxll am I playing at all*)	什麼 (*what*)
16	的 (Chinese particle) + **X** (*semen*) (at the end of a sentence)		的 + 精液 (formal term)
17	**L** (*annoy*) + **X** (*semen*) **L** + **X** + **X**	魯_洨 (*to annoy*) 魯_洨_洨 (*annoying person*)	糾纏 (*to annoy*) 煩人精 (*annoyer*)
18	**X** (siao2, not the cases above)	洨_明 (*Little Min*, a name)	小 (siao3, *little*)

Synonym sets:

　　F = 幹, 操, 肏, (Taiwanese) 賽

　　RL = 娘 (*mother*), 祖母 (*grandma*), 老師 (*teacher*), 全家 (*whole family*)…

　　JB = 機_掰, 雞_掰

　　BW = 賤_婊, 婊_子, 破_麻, 賤_婊_子, 淫_蕩, 淫_娃, 賤_貨, 賤_女人

　　BT = **JB**, 機_八, 雞_八, 機_歪, 雞_歪, 機機_歪歪, 雞雞_歪歪

　　X = (Taiwanese) 洨

　　H = (Taiwanese) 豪, 唬, 虎, 毫

　　J = (Taiwanese) 甲, 假, 呷

　　S = (Taiwanese) 三, 撒, 殺, 啥, 沙

　　L = (Taiwanese) 魯, 盧, 嚕

Format:

　　SET (transliteration, *English meaning*, condition or note) [optional]

Appendix A. Chinese Profanity Detection and Rephrasing Rules (*Cont.*)

#	Detection Patterns	Example	Rephrasing Rules
8	**ALL** + **LP** (*scrotum*) + **FIRE** **LP** (*scrotum*) + **FIRE**	歸_覽_趴_會 (*fire full of my scrotum; pixsed off*)	滿肚子氣 一肚子氣 (*very angry*)
9	**PN** (*pxnis*) **LP** (*scrotum*)		那話兒 (*a mild term*)
10	去死 (*to go to hxll*)		去撞牆 (*to go to bump into the wall; to punish yourself*)
19	牛 (*cow*) + **B** (*puxs*)	牛_屄	厲害 (*awesome*)
20	傻 (*stupid*) + **B** (*puxs*)	傻_屄	傻子 (*fool*)
21	臭 (*stinky*) + **B** (*puxs*)	臭_屄	臭 + 下體 (*private part*)
22	**B** (not the cases above)		女生下體 (*female genital*)
23	Adverb + **D** (*dxck*)	特_屌 (*very impressive*)	Adverb + 厲害 (*awesome*)
24	**D** (*dxck*) + 打 (*to beat*)	屌_打 (*to defeat*)	打爆 (*a mild term*)
25	**D** (*dxck*) + Pronoun	不_屌_你 (*don't give you a shxt*)	理 (*to notice*) + Pronoun
26	**D** (not the cases above)		那話兒 (*a mild term*)
27	Formal words containing in-decent characters	幹部 (*manager*) 幹活 (*do work*)	Unchanged
28	A list of direct mappings	怪淡 睡懶覺	怪咖 (*weirdo*) 睡覺 (*to sleep*)

Synonym sets:

    ALL = (Taiwanese) 歸, 規, 龜

    LP = (Taiwanese) 覽_趴, 懶_趴, 攬_趴

    FIRE = 火, (Taiwanese) 會

    PN = (Taiwanese) 懶_覺, 懶_較, 覽_覺, 覽_較

    B = 屄, 逼

    D = 屌

Deep Learning for User Comment Moderation

John Pavlopoulos
StrainTek
Athens, Greece
ip@straintek.com

Prodromos Malakasiotis
StrainTek
Athens, Greece
mm@straintek.com

Ion Androutsopoulos
Department of Informatics
Athens University of Economics
and Business, Greece
ion@aueb.gr

Abstract

Experimenting with a new dataset of 1.6M user comments from a Greek news portal and existing datasets of English Wikipedia comments, we show that an RNN outperforms the previous state of the art in moderation. A deep, classification-specific attention mechanism improves further the overall performance of the RNN. We also compare against a CNN and a word-list baseline, considering both fully automatic and semi-automatic moderation.

1 Introduction

User comments play a central role in social media and online discussion fora. News portals and blogs often also allow their readers to comment in order to get feedback, engage their readers, and build customer loyalty. User comments, however, and more generally user content can also be abusive (e.g., bullying, profanity, hate speech). Social media are increasingly under pressure to combat abusive content. News portals also suffer from abusive user comments, which damage their reputation and make them liable to fines, e.g., when hosting comments encouraging illegal actions. They often employ moderators, who are frequently overwhelmed by the volume of comments. Readers are disappointed when non-abusive comments do not appear quickly online because of moderation delays. Smaller news portals may be unable to employ moderators, and some are forced to shut down their comments sections entirely.[1]

We examine how deep learning (Goodfellow et al., 2016; Goldberg, 2016) can be used to moderate user comments. We experiment with a new dataset of approx. 1.6M manually moderated user

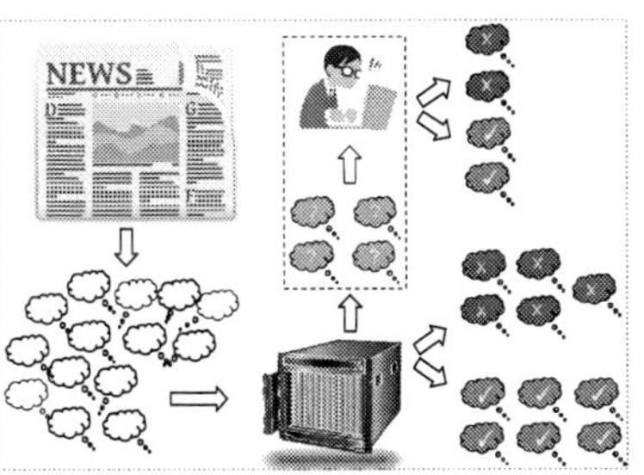

Figure 1: Semi-automatic moderation.

comments from a Greek sports portal (Gazzetta), which we make publicly available.[2] Furthermore, we provide word embeddings pre-trained on 5.2M comments from the same portal. We also experiment on the datasets of Wulczyn et al. (2017), which contain English Wikipedia comments labeled for personal attacks, aggression, toxicity.

In a fully automatic scenario, a system directly accepts or rejects comments. Although this scenario may be the only available one, e.g., when portals cannot afford moderators, it is unrealistic to expect that fully automatic moderation will be perfect, because abusive comments may involve irony, sarcasm, harassment without profanity etc., which are particularly difficult for machines to handle. When moderators are available, it is more realistic to develop semi-automatic systems to assist rather than replace them, a scenario that has not been considered in previous work. Comments for which the system is uncertain (Fig. 1) are shown to a moderator to decide; all other comments are accepted or rejected by the system. We discuss how moderation systems can be tuned, depending on the availability and workload of moderators. We also introduce additional evaluation

---

[1] See, for example, http://niemanreports.org/articles/the-future-of-comments/.

[2] The portal is http://www.gazzetta.gr/. Instructions to obtain the Gazzetta data will be posted at http://nlp.cs.aueb.gr/software.html.

25

Proceedings of the First Workshop on Abusive Language Online, pages 25–35,
Vancouver, Canada, July 30 - August 4, 2017. ©2017 Association for Computational Linguistics

Dataset/Split	Accepted	Rejected	Total
G-TRAIN-L	960,378 (66%)	489,222 (34%)	1,45M
G-TRAIN-S	67,828 (68%)	32,172 (32%)	100,000
G-DEV	20,236 (68%)	9,464 (32%)	29,700
G-TEST-L	20,064 (68%)	9,636 (32%)	29,700
G-TEST-S	1,068 (71%)	432 (29%)	1,500
G-TEST-S-R	1,174 (78%)	326 (22%)	1,500
W-ATT-TRAIN	61,447 (88%)	8,079 (12%)	69,526
W-ATT-DEV	20,405 (88%)	2,755 (12%)	23,160
W-ATT-TEST	20,422 (88%)	2,756 (12%)	23,178
W-TOX-TRAIN	86,447 (90%)	9,245 (10%)	95,692
W-TOX-DEV	29,059 (90%)	3,069 (10%)	32,128
W-TOX-TEST	28,818 (90%)	3,048 (10%)	31,866

Table 1: Statistics of the datasets used.

measures for the semi-automatic scenario.

On both Gazzetta and Wikipedia comments and for both scenarios (automatic, semi-automatic), we show that a recursive neural network (RNN) outperforms the system of Wulczyn et al. (2017), the previous state of the art for comment moderation, which employed logistic regression (LR) or a multi-layered Perceptron (MLP). We also propose an attention mechanism that improves the overall performance of the RNN. Our attention differs from most previous ones (Bahdanau et al., 2015; Luong et al., 2015) in that it is used in text classification, where there is no previously generated output subsequence to drive the attention, unlike sequence-to-sequence models (Sutskever et al., 2014). In effect, our attention mechanism detects the words of a comment that affect mostly the classification decision (accept, reject), by examining them in the context of the particular comment.

Our main contributions are: (i) We release a new dataset of 1.6M moderated user comments. (ii) We are among the first to apply deep learning to user comment moderation, and we show that an RNN with a novel classification-specific attention mechanism outperforms the previous state of the art. (iii) Unlike previous work, we also consider a semi-automatic scenario, along with threshold tuning and evaluation measures for it.

2   Datasets

We first discuss the datasets we used, to help acquaint the reader with the problem.

2.1   Gazzetta dataset

There are approx. 1.45M training comments (covering Jan. 1, 2015 to Oct. 6, 2016) in the Gazzetta dataset; we call them G-TRAIN-L (Table 1). Some experiments use only the first 100K comments of

G-TRAIN-L, called G-TRAIN-S. An additional set of 60,900 comments (Oct. 7 to Nov. 11, 2016) was split to development (G-DEV, 29,700 comments), large test (G-TEST-L, 29,700), and small test set (G-TEST-S, 1,500). Gazzetta's moderators (2 full-time, plus journalists occasionally helping) are occasionally instructed to be stricter (e.g., during violent events). To get a more accurate view of performance in normal situations, we manually re-moderated (labeled as 'accept' or 'reject') the comments of G-TEST-S, producing G-TEST-S-R. The reject ratio is approximately 30% in all subsets, except for G-TEST-S-R where it drops to 22%, because there are no occasions where the moderators were instructed to be stricter in G-TEST-S-R.

Each G-TEST-S-R comment was re-moderated by 5 annotators. Krippendorff's (2004) alpha was 0.4762, close to the value (0.45) reported by Wulczyn et al. (2017) for Wikipedia comments. Using Cohen's Kappa (Cohen, 1960), the mean pairwise agreement was 0.4749. The mean pairwise percentage of agreement (% of comments each pair of annotators agreed on) was 81.33%. Cohen's Kappa and Krippendorff's alpha lead to moderate scores, because they account for agreement by chance, which is high when there is class imbalance (22% reject, 78% accept in G-TEST-S-R).

We also provide 300-dimensional word embeddings, pre-trained on approx. 5.2M comments (268M tokens) from Gazzetta using WORD2VEC (Mikolov et al., 2013a,b).[3] This larger dataset cannot be used to train classifiers, because most of its comments are from a period (before 2015) when Gazzetta did not employ moderators.

2.2   Wikipedia datasets

Wulczyn et al. (2017) created three datasets containing English Wikipedia talk page comments.

Attacks dataset: This dataset contains approx. 115K comments, which were labeled as personal attacks (reject) or not (accept) using crowdsourcing. Each comment was labeled by at least 10 annotators. Inter-annotator agreement, measured on a random sample of 1K comments using Krippendorff's (2004) alpha, was 0.45. The gold label of each comment is determined by the majority of annotators, leading to *binary labels* (accept, reject). Alternatively, the gold label is the percentage of annotators that labeled the comment as 'accept'

---

[3] We used CBOW, window size 5, min. term freq. 5, negative sampling, obtaining a vocabulary size of approx. 478K.

(or 'reject'), leading to *probabilistic labels*.[4] The dataset is split in three parts (Table 1): training (W-ATT-TRAIN, 69,526 comments), development (W-ATT-DEV, 23,160), and test (W-ATT-TEST, 23,178 comments). In all three parts, the rejected comments are 12%, but this ratio is artificial (in effect, Wulczyn et al. oversampled comments posted by banned users), unlike Gazzetta subsets where the truly observed accept/reject ratios are used.

Toxicity dataset: This dataset was created like the previous one, but contains more comments (159,686), now labeled as toxic (reject) or not (accept). Inter-annotator agreement was not reported. Again, binary or probabilistic gold labels can be used. The dataset is split in three parts (Table 1): training (W-TOX-TRAIN, 95,692 comments), development (W-TOX-DEV, 32,128), and test (W-TOX-TEST, 31,866). In all three parts, the rejected (toxic) comments are 10%, again an artificial ratio.

Wikipedia comments are longer (median 38 and 39 tokens for attacks, toxicity) compared to Gazzetta's (median 25). Wulczyn et al. (2017) also created an 'aggression' dataset containing the same comments as the personal attacks one, but now labeled as aggressive or not. The (probabilistic) labels of the two datasets are very highly correlated (0.8992 Spearman, 0.9718 Pearson) and we do not consider the aggression dataset further.

3 Methods

We experimented with an RNN operating on word embeddings, the same RNN enhanced with our attention mechanism (a-RNN), several variants of a-RNN, a vanilla convolutional neural network (CNN) also operating on word embeddings, the DETOX system of Wulczyn et al. (2017), and a baseline that uses word lists with precision scores.

3.1 DETOX

DETOX (Wulczyn et al., 2017) was the previous state of the art in comment moderation, in the sense that it had the best reported results on the Wikipedia datasets (Section 2.2), the largest previous publicly available datasets of moderated user comments.[5] DETOX represents each comment as a

bag of word n-grams ($n \leq 2$, each comment becomes a bag containing its 1-grams and 2-grams) or a bag of character n-grams ($n \leq 5$, each comment becomes a bag containing character 1-grams, ..., 5-grams). DETOX can rely on a logistic regression (LR) or multi-layer Perceptron (MLP) classifier, and use binary or probabilistic gold labels (Section 2.2) during training. We used the DETOX implementation of Wulczyn et al. and the same grid search to tune the hyper-parameters that select word or character n-grams, classifier (LR or MLP), and gold labels (binary or probabilistic). For Gazzetta, only binary gold labels were possible, since G-TRAIN-L and G-TRAIN-S have a single gold label per comment. Unlike Wulczyn et al., we tuned the hyper-parameters by evaluating (computing AUC and Spearman, Section 4) on a random 2% of held-out comments of W-ATT-TRAIN, W-TOX-TRAIN, or G-TRAIN-S, instead of the development subsets, to be able to obtain more realistic results from the development sets while developing the methods. The tuning always selected character n-grams, as in the work of Wulczyn et al., and LR to MLP, whereas Wulczyn et al. reported slightly higher performance for the MLP on W-ATT-DEV.[6] The tuning also selected probabilistic labels when available (Wikipedia datasets), as in the work of Wulczyn et al.

3.2 RNN-based methods

RNN: The RNN method is a chain of GRU cells (Cho et al., 2014) that transforms the tokens $w_1 \ldots, w_k$ of each comment to hidden states $h_1 \ldots, h_k$, followed by an LR layer that uses h_k to classify the comment (accept, reject). Formally, given the vocabulary V, a matrix $E \in \mathbb{R}^{d \times |V|}$ containing d-dimensional word embeddings, an initial h_0, and a comment $c = \langle w_1, \ldots, w_k \rangle$, the RNN computes $h_1, \ldots, h_k$ as follows ($h_t \in \mathbb{R}^m$):

$$
\begin{aligned}
\tilde{h}_t &= \tanh(W_h x_t + U_h(r_t \odot h_{t-1}) + b_h) \\
h_t &= (1 - z_t) \odot h_{t-1} + z_t \odot \tilde{h}_t \\
z_t &= \sigma(W_z x_t + U_z h_{t-1} + b_z) \\
r_t &= \sigma(W_r x_t + U_r h_{t-1} + b_r)
\end{aligned}
$$

where $\tilde{h}_t \in \mathbb{R}^m$ is the proposed hidden state at position t, obtained by considering the word embedding x_t of token w_t and the previous hidden state

---

[4]We also construct probabilistic gold labels (in addition to binary ones) for G-TEST-S-R, where there are 5 annotators.

[5]Two of the co-authors of Wulczyn et al. (2017) are with Jigsaw, who recently announced Perspective, a system to detect 'toxic' comments. Perspective is not the same as DETOX (personal communication), but we were unable to obtain scientific articles describing it. We have applied for access to its

API (http://www.perspectiveapi.com/).

[6]Wulczyn et al. (2017) report results only on W-ATT-DEV. We repeated the tuning by evaluating on W-ATT-DEV, and again character n-grams with LR were selected.

h_{t-1}; $\odot$ denotes element-wise multiplication; $r_t \in \mathbb{R}^m$ is the reset gate (for r_t all zeros, it allows the RNN to forget the previous state h_{t-1}); $z_t \in \mathbb{R}^m$ is the update gate (for z_t all zeros, it allows the RNN to ignore the new proposed $\tilde{h}_t$, hence also x_t, and copy h_{t-1} as h_t); σ is the sigmoid function; $W_h, W_z, W_r \in \mathbb{R}^{m \times d}$; $U_h, U_z, U_r \in \mathbb{R}^{m \times m}$; $b_h, b_z, b_r \in \mathbb{R}^m$. Once h_k has been computed, the LR layer estimates the probability that comment c should be rejected, with $W_p \in \mathbb{R}^{1 \times m}, b_p \in \mathbb{R}$:

$$P_{\mathrm{RNN}}(reject|c) = \sigma(W_p h_k + b_p)$$

a-RNN: When the attention mechanism is added, the LR layer considers the weighted sum h_{sum} of all the hidden states, instead of just h_k (Fig. 2):

$$h_{sum} = \sum_{t=1}^{k} a_t h_t \qquad (1)$$

$$P_{a-\mathrm{RNN}}(reject|c) = \sigma(W_p h_{sum} + b_p)$$

The weights a_t are produced by an attention mechanism, which is an MLP with l layers:

$$a_t^{(1)} = \mathrm{ReLU}(W^{(1)} h_t + b^{(1)}) \qquad (2)$$

$$\dots$$

$$a_t^{(l-1)} = \mathrm{ReLU}(W^{(l-1)} a_t^{(l-2)} + b^{(l-1)})$$
$$a_t^{(l)} = W^{(l)} a_t^{(l-1)} + b^{(l)}$$
$$a_t = \mathrm{softmax}(a_t^{(l)}; a_1^{(l)}, \dots, a_k^{(l)})$$

where $a_t^{(1)}, \dots, a_t^{(l-1)} \in \mathbb{R}^r, a_t^{(l)}, a_t \in \mathbb{R}, W^{(1)} \in \mathbb{R}^{r \times m}, W^{(2)}, \dots, W^{(l-1)} \in \mathbb{R}^{r \times r}, W^{(l)} \in \mathbb{R}^{1 \times r}, b^{(1)}, \dots, b^{(l-1)} \in \mathbb{R}^r, b^{(l)} \in \mathbb{R}$. The $\mathrm{softmax}$ operates across all the $a_t^{(l)}$ ($t = 1, \dots, k$), making the attention weights a_t sum to 1. Our attention mechanism differs from most previous ones (Mnih et al., 2014; Bahdanau et al., 2015; Xu et al., 2015; Luong et al., 2015) in that it is used in a classification setting, where there is no previously generated output subsequence (e.g., partly generated translation) to drive the attention (e.g., assign more weight to source words to translate next), unlike seq2seq models (Sutskever et al., 2014). It assigns larger weights a_t to hidden states h_t corresponding to positions where there is more evidence that the comment should be accepted or rejected.

Yang et al. (2016) use a similar attention mechanism, but ours is deeper. In effect they always set $l = 2$, whereas we allow l to be larger (tuning selects $l = 4$).[7] On the other hand, the attention

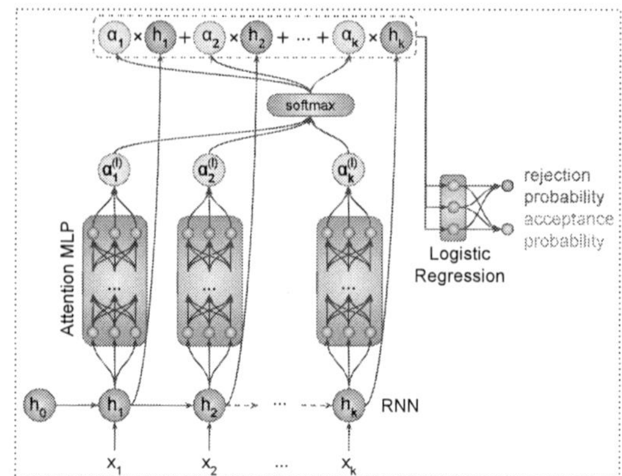

Figure 2: Illustration of a-RNN.

mechanism of Yang et al. is part of a classification method for longer texts (e.g., product reviews). Their method uses two GRU RNNs, both bidirectional (Schuster and Paliwal, 1997), one turning the word embeddings of each sentence to a sentence embedding, and one turning the sentence embeddings to a document embedding, which is then fed to an LR layer. Yang et al. use their attention mechanism in both RNNs, to assign attention scores to words and sentences. We consider shorter texts (comments), we have a single RNN, and we assign attention scores to words only.[8]

da-RNN: In a variant of a-RNN, called da-RNN (direct attention), the input to the first layer of the attention mechanism is the embedding x_t of word w_t, rather than h_t (cf. Eq. 2; $W^{(1,x)} \in \mathbb{R}^{r \times d}$):

$$a_t^{(1)} = \mathrm{ReLU}(W^{(1,x)} x_t + b^{(1)}) \qquad (3)$$

Intuitively, the attention of a-RNN considers each word embedding x_t in its (left) context, modelled by h_t, whereas the attention of da-RNN considers directly x_t without its context, but h_{sum} is still the weighted sum of the hidden states (Eq. 1).

eq-RNN: In another variant of a-RNN, called eq-RNN, we assign equal attention to all the hidden states. The feature vector of the LR layer is now the average $h_{sum} = \frac{1}{k} \sum_{t=1}^{k} h_t$ (cf. Eq. 1).

da-CENT: For ablation testing, we also experiment with a variant, called da-CENT, that does not use the hidden states of the RNN. The input to the attention mechanism is now directly the embedding x_t instead of h_t (as in da-RNN, Eq. 3), and

---

[7]Yang et al. use tanh instead of ReLU in Eq. 2, which works worse in our case, and no bias $b^{(l)}$ in the l-th layer.

[8]We tried a bidirectional instead of unidirectional GRU chain in our methods, also replacing the LR layer by a deeper classification MLP, but there were no improvements.

h_{sum} is the weighted average (centroid) of word embeddings $h_{sum} = \sum_{t=1}^{k} a_t x_t$ (cf. Eq. 1).[9]

***eq*-CENT:** For further ablation, we also experiment with *eq*-CENT, which uses neither the RNN nor the attention mechanism. The feature vector of the LR layer is now simply the average of word embeddings $h_{sum} = \frac{1}{k} \sum_{t=1}^{k} x_t$ (cf. Eq. 1).

We set $l = 4, d = 300, m = r = 128$, having tuned the hyper-parameters of RNN and *a*-RNN on the same 2% held-out training comments used to tune DETOX; *da*-RNN, *eq*-RNN, *da*-CENT, and *eq*-CENT use the same hyper-parameter values as *a*-RNN, to make their results more directly comparable and save time. We use Glorot initialization (Glorot and Bengio, 2010), cross-entropy loss, and Adam (Kingma and Ba, 2015).[10] Early stopping evaluates on the same held-out subsets. For Gazzetta, word embeddings are initialized to the WORD2VEC embeddings we provide (Section 2.1). For the Wikipedia datasets, they are initialized to GLOVE embeddings (Pennington et al., 2014).[11] In both cases, the embeddings are updated during backpropagation. Out of vocabulary (OOV) words, meaning words not encountered in the training set and/or words we have no initial embeddings for, are mapped (during training and testing) to a single randomly initialized embedding, which is also updated during training.[12]

3.3 CNN

We also compare against a vanilla CNN operating on word embeddings. We describe the CNN only briefly, because it is very similar to that of of Kim (2014); see also Goldberg (2016) for an introduction to CNNs, and Zhang and Wallace (2015).

For Wikipedia comments, we use a 'narrow' convolution layer, with kernels sliding (stride 1) over (entire) embeddings of word n-grams of sizes $n = 1, \ldots, 4$. We use 300 kernels for each n value, a total of 1,200 kernels. The outputs of each kernel, obtained by applying the kernel to the different n-grams of a comment c, are then max-pooled, leading to a single output per kernel. The resulting feature vector (1,200 max-

---

[9]We also tried *tf-idf* scores in the h_{sum} of *da*-CENT, instead of attention scores, but preliminary results were poor.

[10]We used Keras (`http://keras.io/`) with the TensorFlow back-end (`http://www.tensorflow.org/`).

[11]See `https://nlp.stanford.edu/projects/glove/`. We use 'Common Crawl' (840B tokens).

[12]For Gazzetta, words encountered only once in the training set (G-TRAIN-L or G-TRAIN-S) are also treated as OOV.

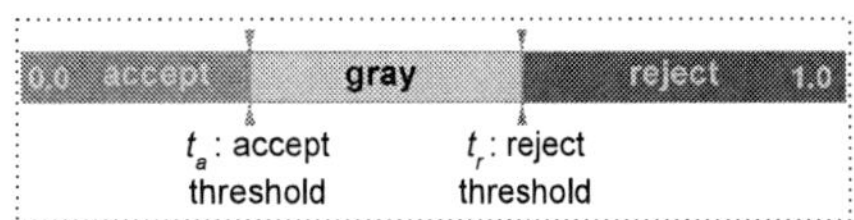

Figure 3: Illustration of threshold tuning.

pooled outputs) goes through a dropout layer (Hinton et al., 2012) ($p = 0.5$), and then to an LR layer, which provides $P_{\text{CNN}}(reject|c)$. For Gazzetta, the CNN is the same, except that $n = 1, \ldots, 5$, leading to 1,500 features per comment. All hyper-parameters were tuned on the 2% held-out training comments used to tune the other methods. Again, we use 300-dimensional word embeddings, which are now randomly initialized, since tuning indicated this was better than initializing to pre-trained embeddings. OOV words are treated as in the RNN-based methods. All embeddings are updated. Early stopping evaluates on the held-out subsets. Again, we use Glorot initialization, cross-entropy loss, and Adam.[13]

3.4 LIST baseline

A baseline, called LIST, collects every word w that occurs in more than 10 (for W-ATT-TRAIN, W-TOX-TRAIN, G-TRAIN-S) or 100 comments (for G-TRAIN-L) in the training set, along with the precision of w, i.e., the ratio of rejected training comments containing w divided by the total number of training comments containing w. The resulting lists contain 10,423, 11,360, 16,864, and 21,940 word types, when using W-ATT-TRAIN, W-TOX-TRAIN, G-TRAIN-S, G-TRAIN-L, respectively. For a comment c, $P_{\text{LIST}}(reject|c)$ is the maximum precision of all the words in c.

3.5 Tuning thresholds

All methods produce a $p = P(reject|c)$ per comment c. In semi-automatic moderation (Fig. 1), a comment is directly rejected if its p is above a rejection threshold t_r, it is directly accepted if p is below an acceptance threshold t_a, and it is shown to a moderator if $t_a \leq p \leq t_r$ (gray zone of Fig. 3).

In our experience, moderators (or their employers) can easily specify the approximate percentage of comments they can afford to check manually (e.g., 20% daily) or, equivalently, the approximate percentage of comments the system should handle automatically. We call *coverage* the latter percentage; hence, $1 - coverage$ is the approximate

---

[13]We implemented the CNN directly in TensorFlow.

percentage of comments to be checked manually. By contrast, moderators are baffled when asked to tune t_r and t_a directly. Consequently, we ask them to specify the approximate desired coverage. We then sort the comments of the development set (G-DEV, W-ATT-DEV, W-TOX-DEV) by p, and slide t_a from 0.0 to 1.0 (Fig. 3). For each t_a value, we set t_r to the value that leaves a $1 - coverage$ percentage of development comments in the gray zone ($t_a \leq p \leq t_r$). We then select the t_a (and t_r) that maximizes the weighted harmonic mean $F_\beta(P_{reject}, P_{accept})$ on the development set:

$$F_\beta(P_{reject}, P_{accept}) = \frac{(1 + \beta^2) \cdot P_{reject} \cdot P_{accept}}{\beta^2 \cdot P_{reject} + P_{accept}}$$

where P_{reject} is the *rejection precision* (correctly rejected comments divided by rejected comments) and P_{accept} is the *acceptance precision* (correctly accepted divided by accepted). Intuitively, coverage sets the width of the gray zone, whereas P_{reject} and P_{accept} show how certain we can be that the red (reject) and green (accept) zones are free of misclassified comments. We set $\beta = 2$, emphasizing P_{accept}, because moderators are more worried about wrongly accepting abusive comments than wrongly rejecting non-abusive ones.[14] The selected t_a, t_r (tuned on development data) are then used in experiments on test data. In fully automatic moderation, $coverage = 100\%$ and $t_a = t_r$; otherwise, threshold tuning is identical.

4 Experimental results

Following Wulczyn et al. (2017), we report in Tables 2–3 AUC scores (area under ROC curve), along with Spearman correlations between system-generated probabilities $P(accept|c)$ and human probabilistic gold labels (Section 2.2) when probabilistic gold labels are available.[15]

A first observation is that increasing the size of the Gazzetta training set (G-TRAIN-S to G-TRAIN-L, Table 2) significantly improves the performance of all methods; we do not report DETOX results for G-TRAIN-L, because its implementation could not handle the size of G-TRAIN-L. Tables 2–3

[14]More precisely, when computing F_β, we reorder the development comments by time posted, and split them into batches of 100. For each t_a (and t_r) value, we compute F_β per batch and macro-average across batches. The resulting thresholds lead to F_β scores that are more stable over time.

[15]When computing AUC, the gold label is the majority label of the annotators. When computing Spearman, the gold label is probabilistic (% of annotators that accepted the comment). The decisions of the systems are always probabilistic.

Training dataset: G-TRAIN-S					
System	G-DEV	G-TEST-L	G-TEST-S	G-TEST-S-R	
	AUC	AUC	AUC	AUC	Spearman
RNN	75.75	75.10	74.40	80.27	51.89
a-RNN	**76.19**	**76.15**	**75.83**	**80.41**	**52.51**
da-RNN	75.96	75.90	74.25	80.05	52.49
eq-RNN	74.31	74.01	73.28	77.73	45.77
da-CENT	75.09	74.96	74.20	79.92	51.04
eq-CENT	73.93	73.82	73.80	78.45	48.14
CNN	70.97	71.34	70.88	76.03	42.88
DETOX	72.50	72.06	71.59	75.67	43.80
LIST	61.47	61.59	61.26	64.19	24.33
Training dataset: G-TRAIN-L					
System	G-DEV	G-TEST-L	G-TEST-S	G-TEST-S-R	
	AUC	AUC	AUC	AUC	Spearman
RNN	79.50	79.41	79.23	84.17	59.31
a-RNN	**79.64**	**79.58**	**79.67**	**84.69**	**60.87**
da-RNN	79.60	79.56	79.38	84.40	60.83
eq-RNN	77.45	77.76	77.28	82.11	55.01
da-CENT	78.73	78.64	78.62	83.53	57.82
eq-CENT	76.76	76.85	76.30	82.38	53.28
CNN	77.57	77.35	78.16	83.98	55.90
DETOX	–	–	–	–	–
LIST	67.04	67.06	66.17	69.51	33.61

Table 2: Results on Gazzetta comments.

also show that RNN is always better than CNN and DETOX; there is no clear winner between CNN and DETOX. Furthermore, *a*-RNN is always better than RNN on Gazzetta comments (Table 2), but not always on Wikipedia comments (Table 3). Another observation is that *da*-RNN is always worse than *a*-RNN (Tables 2–3), confirming that the hidden states of the RNN are a better input to the attention mechanism than word embeddings. The performance of *da*-RNN deteriorates further when equal attention is assigned to the hidden states (*eq*-RNN), when the weighted sum of hidden states (h_{sum}) is replaced by the weighted sum of word embeddings (*da*-CENT), or both (*eq*-CENT). Also, *da*-CENT outperforms *eq*-CENT, indicating that the attention mechanism improves the performance of simply averaging word embeddings. The Wikipedia subsets are easier (all methods perform better on Wikipedia subsets, compared to Gazzetta).

Figure 4 shows $F_2(P_{reject}, P_{accept})$ on G-TEST-L, G-TEST-S, W-ATT-TEST, W-TOX-TEST, when t_a, t_r are tuned on the corresponding development tests for varying coverage. For the Gazzetta datasets, we show results training on G-TRAIN-S (solid lines) and G-TRAIN-L (dashed). The differences between RNN and *a*-RNN are again small, but it is now easier to see that *a*-RNN is overall better. Again, *a*-RNN and RNN are better than CNN and DETOX, and the results improve with a larger training set (dashed). On W-ATT-TEST and W-

Training dataset: W-ATT-TRAIN				
System	W-ATT-DEV		W-ATT-TEST	
	AUC	Spearman	AUC	Spearman
RNN	97.39	**71.92**	**97.71**	**72.79**
a-RNN	**97.46**	71.59	97.68	72.32
da-RNN	97.02	71.49	97.31	72.11
eq-RNN	92.66	60.77	92.85	60.16
da-CENT	96.73	70.13	97.06	71.08
eq-CENT	92.30	57.21	92.81	56.33
CNN	96.91	70.06	97.07	70.21
DETOX	96.26	67.75	96.71	68.09
LIST	93.05	55.39	92.91	54.55
Training dataset: W-TOX-TRAIN				
System	W-TOX-DEV		W-TOX-TEST	
	AUC	Spearman	AUC	Spearman
RNN	98.20	68.84	**98.42**	68.89
a-RNN	**98.22**	**68.95**	98.38	**68.90**
da-RNN	98.05	68.59	98.28	68.55
eq-RNN	94.72	55.48	95.04	55.86
da-CENT	97.83	67.86	97.94	67.74
eq-CENT	94.31	53.35	94.61	52.93
CNN	97.76	65.50	97.86	65.56
DETOX	97.16	63.57	97.13	63.24
LIST	93.96	51.35	93.95	51.18

Table 3: Results on Wikipedia comments.

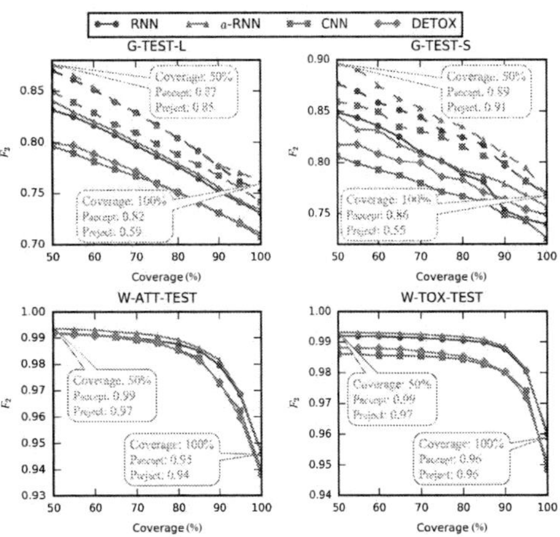

Figure 4: F_2 scores for varying coverage. Dashed lines were obtained using a larger training set.

TOX-TEST, *a*-RNN obtains $P_{accept}, P_{reject} \geq 0.94$ for all coverages (Fig. 4, call-outs). On the more difficult Gazzetta datasets, *a*-RNN still obtains $P_{accept}, P_{reject} \geq 0.85$ when tuned for 50% coverage. When tuned for 100% coverage, comments for which the system is uncertain (gray zone) cannot be avoided and there are inevitably more misclassifications; the use of F_2 during threshold tuning places more emphasis on avoiding wrongly accepted comments, leading to high P_{accept} (≥ 0.82), at the expense of wrongly rejected comments, i.e., sacrificing P_{reject} (≥ 0.56). On the re-moderated G-TEST-S-R (similar diagrams, not shown), P_{accept}, P_{reject} become 0.96, 0.88 for coverage 50%, and 0.92, 0.48 for coverage 100%.

5 Related work

Napoles et al. (2017b) developed an annotation scheme for online conversations, with 6 dimensions for comments (e.g., sentiment, tone, off-topic) and 3 dimensions for threads. The scheme was used to label a dataset, called YNACC, of 9.2K comments (2.4K threads) from Yahoo News and 16.6K comments (1K threads) from the Internet Argument Corpus (Walker et al., 2012; Abbott et al., 2016). Abusive comments were filtered out, hence YNACC cannot be used for our purposes, but it may be possible to extend the annotation scheme for abusive comments, to predict more fine-grained labels, instead of 'accept' or 're-ject'. Napoles et al. also reported that up/down votes, a form of social filtering, are inappropriate proxies for comment and thread quality. Lee et al. (2014) discuss social filtering in detail and propose features (e.g., thread depth, no. of revisiting users) to assess the quality of a thread without processing the texts of its comments. Diakopoulos (2015) discusses how editors select high quality comments.

In further work, Napoles et al. (2017a) aimed to identify high quality threads. Their best method converts each comment to a comment embedding using DOC2VEC (Le and Mikolov, 2014). An ensemble of Conditional Random Fields (CRFs) (Lafferty et al., 2001) assigns labels (from their annotation scheme, e.g., for sentiment, off-topic) to the comments of each thread, viewing each thread as a sequence of DOC2VEC embeddings. The decisions of the CRFs are then used to convert each thread to a feature vector (total count and mean marginal probability of each label in the thread), which is passed on to an LR classifier. Further improvements were observed when additional features were added, BOW counts and POS n-grams being the most important ones. Napoles et al. (2017a) also experimented with a CNN, similar to that of Section 3.3, which was not however a top-performer, presumably because of the small size of the training set (2.1K YNACC threads).

Djuric et al. (2015) experimented with 952K manually moderated comments from Yahoo Finance, but their dataset is not publicly available. They convert each comment to a DOC2VEC embedding, which is fed to an LR classifier. Nobata et al. (2016) experimented with approx. 3.3M manually moderated comments from Yahoo Finance and News; their data are also not available.[16] They used Vowpal Wabbit[17] with character n-grams ($n = 3, \ldots, 5$) and word n-grams ($n = 1, 2$), hand-crafted features (e.g., comment length, number of capitalized or black-listed words), features based on dependency trees, averages of WORD2VEC embeddings, and DOC2VEC-like embeddings. Character n-grams were the best, on their own outperforming Djuric et al. (2015). The best results, however, were obtained using all features. By contrast, we use no hand-crafted features and parsers, making our methods easily portable to other domains and languages.

Wulczyn et al. (2017) experimented with character and word n-grams, based on the findings of Nobata et al. (2016). We included their dataset and moderation system (DETOX) in our experiments. Wulczyn et al. also used DETOX (trained on W-ATT-TRAIN) as a proxy (instead of human annotators) to automatically classify 63M Wikipedia comments, which were then used to study the problem of personal attacks (e.g., the effect of allowing anonymous comments, how often personal attacks were followed by moderation actions). Our methods could replace DETOX in studies of this kind, since they perform better.

Waseem et al. (2016) used approx. 17K tweets annotated for hate speech. Their best method was an LR classifier with character n-grams ($n = 1, \ldots, 4$) and a gender feature. Badjatiya et al. (2017) experimented with the same dataset using LR, SVMs (Cortes and Vapnik, 1995), Random Forests (Ho, 1995), Gradient Boosted Decision Trees (GBDT) (Friedman, 2002), CNN (similar to that of Section 3.3), LSTM (Greff et al., 2015), FastText (Joulin et al., 2017). They also considered alternative feature sets: character n-grams, *tf-idf* vectors, word embeddings, averaged word embeddings. Their best results were obained using GBDT with averaged word embeddings learned by the LSTM, starting from random embeddings.

Warner and Hirschberg (2012) aimed to detect anti-semitic speech, experimenting with 9K paragraphs and a linear SVM. Their features consider windows of up to 5 tokens, the tokens of each window, their order, POS tags, Brown clusters etc., following Yarowsky (1994).

Cheng et al. (2015) predict which users would be banned from on-line communities. Their best system uses a Random Forest or LR classifier, with features examining readability, activity (e.g., number of posts daily), community and moderator reactions (e.g., up-votes, number of deleted posts).

Lukin and Walker (2013) experimented with 5.5K utterances from the Internet Argument Corpus (Walker et al., 2012; Abbott et al., 2016) annotated with nastiness scores, and 9.9K utterances from the same corpus annotated for sarcasm.[18] In a bootstrapping manner, they manually identified cue words and phrases (indicative of nastiness or sarcasm), used the cue words to obtain training comments, and extracted patterns from the training comments. Xiang et al. (2012) also employed bootstrapping to identify users whose tweets frequently or never contain profane words, and collected 381M tweets from the two user types. They trained decision tree, Random Forest, or LR classifiers to distinguish between tweets from the two user types, testing on 4K tweets manually labeled as containing profanity or not. The classifiers used topical features, obtained via LDA (Blei et al., 2003), and a feature indicating the presence of at least one of approx. 330 known profane words.

Sood et al. (2012a; 2012b) experimented with 6.5K comments from Yahoo Buzz, moderated via crowdsourcing. They showed that a linear SVM, representing each comment as a bag of word bigrams and stems, performs better than word lists. Their best results were obtained by combining the SVM with a word list and edit distance.

Yin et al. (2009) used posts from chat rooms and discussion fora ($<$15K posts in total) to train an SVM to detect online harassment. They used TF-IDF, sentiment, and context features (e.g., similarity to other posts in a thread).[19] Our methods might also benefit by considering threads, rather than individual comments. Yin et al. point out that unlike other abusive content, spam in comments or discussion fora (Mishne et al., 2005; Niu et al., 2007) is off-topic and serves a commercial purpose. Spam is unlikely in Wikipedia discussions and extremely rare so far in Gazzetta comments.

Mihaylov and Nakov (2016) identify comments posted by opinion manipulation trolls. Dinakar et

---

[16]According to Nobata et al., their clean test dataset (2K comments) would be made available, but it is currently not.

[17]See `http://hunch.net/~vw/`.

[18]For sarcasm, see Davidov et al. (2010), Gonzalez-Ibanez et al. (2011), Joshi et al. (2015), Oraby et al. (2016).

[19]Sentiment features have been used by several methods, but sentiment analysis (Pang and Lee, 2008; Liu, 2015) is typically not directly concerned with abusive content.

al. (2011) and Dadvar et al. (2013) detect cyber-bullying. Chandrinos et al. (2000) detect pornographic web pages, using a Naive Bayes classifier with text and image features. Spertus (1997) flag flame messages in Web feedback forms, using decision trees and hand-crafted features. A Kaggle dataset for insult detection is also available.[20] It contains 6.6K comments (3,947 train, 2,647 test) labeled as insults or not. However, abusive comments that do not directly insult other participants of the same discussion are not classified as insults, even if they contain profanity, hate speech, insults to third persons etc.

6   Conclusions

We experimented with a new publicly available dataset of 1.6M moderated user comments from a Greek sports news portal and two existing datasets of English Wikipedia talk page comments. We showed that a GRU RNN operating on word embeddings outperforms the previous state of the art, which used an LR or MLP classifier with character or word n-gram features. It also outperforms a vanilla CNN operating on word embeddings, and a baseline that uses an automatically constructed word list with precision scores. A novel, deep, classification-specific attention mechanism improves further the overall results of the RNN. The attention mechanism also improves the results of a simpler method that averages word embeddings. We considered both fully automatic and semi-automatic moderation, along with threshold tuning and evaluation measures for both.

We plan to consider user-specific information (e.g., ratio of comments rejected in the past) and thread statistics (e.g., thread depth, number of revisiting users) (Dadvar et al., 2013; Lee et al., 2014; Cheng et al., 2015; Waseem and Hovy, 2016). We also plan to explore character-level RNNs or CNNs (Zhang et al., 2015), for example to produce embeddings of unknown or obfuscated words from characters (dos Santos and Zadrozny, 2014; Ling et al., 2015). We are also exploring how the attention scores of a-RNN can be used to highlight 'suspicious' words or phrases when showing gray comments to moderators.

Acknowledgments

This work was funded by Google's Digital News Initiative (project ML2P, contract 362826).[21] We are grateful to Gazzetta for the data they provided. We also thank Gazzetta's moderators for their feedback, insights, and advice.

References

R. Abbott, B. Ecker, P. Anand, and M. A. Walker. 2016. Internet Argument Corpus 2.0: An SQL schema for dialogic social media and the corpora to go with it. In *LREC*. Portoroz, Slovenia.

P. Badjatiya, S. Gupta, M. Gupta, and V. Varma. 2017. Deep learning for hate speech detection in tweets. In *WWW (Companion)*. Perth, Australia, pages 759–760.

D. Bahdanau, K. Cho, and Y. Bengio. 2015. Neural machine translation by jointly learning to align and translate. In *ICLR*. San Diego, CA.

D. M. Blei, A. Y. Ng, and M. I. Jordan. 2003. Latent Dirichlet Allocation. *Journal of Machine Learning Research* 3:993–1022.

K.V. Chandrinos, I. Androutsopoulos, G. Paliouras, and C.D. Spyropoulos. 2000. Automatic Web rating: Filtering obscene content on the Web. In *Proc. of the 4th European Conference on Research and Advanced Technology for Digital Libraries*. Lisbon, Portugal, pages 403–406.

J. Cheng, C. Danescu-Niculescu-Mizil, and J. Leskovec. 2015. Antisocial behavior in online discussion communities. In *Proc. of the International AAAI Conference on Web and Social Media*. Oxford University, England, pages 61–70.

K. Cho, B. van Merrienboer, C. Gulcehre, D. Bahdanau, F. Bougares, H. Schwenk, and Y. Bengio. 2014. Learning phrase representations using RNN encoder–decoder for statistical machine translation. In *EMNLP*. Doha, Qatar, pages 1724–1734.

J. Cohen. 1960. A coefficient of agreement for nominal scales. *Educational and Psychological Measurement* 20(1):37–46.

C. Cortes and Vladimir Vapnik. 1995. Support-Vector Networks. *Machine Learning* 20(3):273–297.

M. Dadvar, D. Trieschnigg, R. Ordelman, and F. de Jong. 2013. Improving cyberbullying detection with user context. In *ECIR*. Moscow, Russia, pages 693–696.

D. Davidov, O. Tsur, and A. Rappoport. 2010. Semisupervised recognition of sarcastic sentences in Twitter and Amazon. In *CoNLL*. Uppsala, Sweden, pages 107–116.

---

[20]See http://www.kaggle.com/, data description of the competition 'Detecting Insults in Social Commentary'.

[21]See https://digitalnewsinitiative.com/.

N. Diakopoulos. 2015. Picking the NYT picks: Editorial criteria and automation in the curation of online news comments. *Journal of the International Symposium on Online Journalism* 5:147–166.

K. Dinakar, R. Reichart, and H. Lieberman. 2011. Modeling the detection of textual cyberbullying. In *The Social Mobile Web*. Barcelona, Spain, volume WS-11-02 of *AAAI Workshops*, pages 11–17.

N. Djuric, J. Zhou, R. Morris, M. Grbovic, V. Radosavljevic, and N. Bhamidipati. 2015. Hate speech detection with comment embeddings. In *WWW*. Florence, Italy, pages 29–30.

C. N. dos Santos and B. Zadrozny. 2014. Learning character-level representations for part-of-speech tagging. In *ICML*. Beijing, China, pages 1818–1826.

J.H. Friedman. 2002. Stochastic gradient boosting. *Computational Statistics and Data Analysis* 38(4):367–378.

X. Glorot and Y. Bengio. 2010. Understanding the difficulty of training deep feedforward neural networks. In *Proc. of the International Conference on Artificial Intelligence and Statistics*. Sardinia, Italy, pages 249–256.

Y. Goldberg. 2016. A primer on neural network models for natural language processing. *Journal of Artificial Intelligence Research* 57:345–420.

R. I. González-Ibáñez, S. Muresan, and N. Wacholder. 2011. Identifying sarcasm in Twitter: A closer look. In *ACL*. Portland, Oregon, pages 581–586.

I. Goodfellow, Y. Bengio, and A. Courville. 2016. *Deep Learning*. MIT Press.

K. Greff, R.K. Srivastava, J. Koutník, B.R. Steunebrink, and J. Schmidhuber. 2015. LSTM: A search space Odyssey. *CoRR* abs/1503.04069.

G. E. Hinton, N. Srivastava, A. Krizhevsky, I. Sutskever, and R. Salakhutdinov. 2012. Improving neural networks by preventing co-adaptation of feature detectors. *CoRR* abs/1207.0580.

T.K. Ho. 1995. Random Decision Forests. In *Proc. of the 3rd International Conference on Document Analysis and Recognition*. Montreal, Canada, volume 1, pages 278–282.

A. Joshi, V. Sharma, and P. Bhattacharyya. 2015. Harnessing context incongruity for sarcasm detection. In *ACL*. Beijing, China, pages 757–762.

A. Joulin, E. Grave, P. Bojanowski, and T. Mikolov. 2017. Bag of tricks for efficient text classification. In *EACL (short papers)*. Valencia, Spain, pages 427–431.

Y. Kim. 2014. Convolutional neural networks for sentence classification. In *EMNLP*. Doha, Qatar, pages 1746–1751.

D. P. Kingma and J. Ba. 2015. Adam: A method for stochastic optimization. In *ICLR*. San Diego, CA.

K. Krippendorff. 2004. *Content Analysis: An Introduction to Its Methodology (2nd edition)*. Sage Publications.

J. D. Lafferty, A. McCallum, and F. C. N. Pereira. 2001. Conditional Random Fields: Probabilistic models for segmenting and labeling sequence data. In *ICML*. Williamstown, MA, pages 282–289.

Q. V. Le and T. Mikolov. 2014. Distributed representations of sentences and documents. In *ICML*. Beijing, China, pages 1188–1196.

J.-T. Lee, M.-C. Yang, and H.-C. Rim. 2014. Discovering high-quality threaded discussions in online forums. *Journal of Computer Science and Technology* 29(3):519–531.

W. Ling, C. Dyer, A. W. Black, I. Trancoso, R. Fermandez, S. Amir, L. Marujo, and T. Luís. 2015. Finding function in form: Compositional character models for open vocabulary word representation. In *EMNLP*. Lisbon, Portugal, pages 1520–1530.

B. Liu. 2015. *Sentiment Analysis – Mining Opinions, Sentiments, and Emotions*. Cambridge University Press.

S. Lukin and M. Walker. 2013. Really? well. apparently bootstrapping improves the performance of sarcasm and nastiness classifiers for online dialogue. In *Proc. of the Workshop on Language in Social Media*. Atlanta, Georgia, pages 30–40.

T. Luong, H. Pham, and C. D. Manning. 2015. Effective approaches to attention-based neural machine translation. In *EMNLP*. Lisbon, Portugal, pages 1412–1421.

T. Mihaylov and P. Nakov. 2016. Hunting for troll comments in news community forums. In *ACL*. Berlin, Germany, pages 399–405.

T. Mikolov, K. Chen, G. Corrado, and J. Dean. 2013a. Efficient estimation of word representations in vector space. In *ICLR*. Scottsdale, AZ.

T. Mikolov, W.-t. Yih, and G. Zweig. 2013b. Linguistic regularities in continuous space word representations. In *NAACL-HLT*. Atlanta, GA, pages 746–751.

G. Mishne, D. Carmel, and R. Lempel. 2005. Blocking blog spam with language model disagreement. In *Proc. of the International Workshop on Adversarial Information Retrieval on the Web*. Chiba, Japan.

V. Mnih, N. Heess, A. Graves, and K. Kavukcuoglu. 2014. Recurrent models of visual attention. In *NIPS*. Montreal, Canada, pages 2204–2212.

C. Napoles, A. Pappu, and J. Tetreault. 2017a. Automatically identifying good conversations online (yes, they do exist!). In *Proc. of the International AAAI Conference on Web and Social Media*.

C. Napoles, J. Tetreault, E. Rosato, B. Provenzale, and A. Pappu. 2017b. Finding good conversations online: The Yahoo News annotated comments corpus. In *Proc. of the Linguistic Annotation Workshop*. Valencia, Spain, pages 13–23.

Y. Niu, Y.-M. Wang, H. Chen, M. Ma, and F. Hsu. 2007. A quantitative study of forum spamming using context-based analysis. In *Proc. of the Annual Network and Distributed System Security Symposium*. San Diego, CA, pages 79–92.

C. Nobata, J. Tetreault, A. Thomas, Y. Mehdad, and Y. Chang. 2016. Abusive language detection in online user content. In *WWW*. Montreal, Canada, pages 145–153.

S. Oraby, V. Harrison, L. Reed, E. Hernandez, E. Riloff, and M. A. Walker. 2016. Creating and characterizing a diverse corpus of sarcasm in dialogue. In *SIGDial*. Los Angeles, CA, pages 31–41.

B. Pang and L. Lee. 2008. Opinion mining and sentiment analysis. *Foundations and Trends in Information Retrieval* 2(1-2):1–135.

J. Pennington, R. Socher, and C. Manning. 2014. GloVe: Global vectors for word representation. In *EMNLP*. Doha, Qatar, pages 1532–1543.

M. Schuster and K. K. Paliwal. 1997. Bidirectional recurrent neural networks. *IEEE Transacions of Signal Processing* 45(11):2673–2681.

S. Sood, J. Antin, and E. F. Churchill. 2012a. Profanity use in online communities. In *SIGCHI*. Austin, TX, pages 1481–1490.

S. Sood, J. Antin, and E. F. Churchill. 2012b. Using crowdsourcing to improve profanity detection. In *AAAI Spring Symposium: Wisdom of the Crowd*. Stanford, CA, pages 69–74.

E. Spertus. 1997. Smokey: Automatic recognition of hostile messages. In *Proc. of the National Conference on Artificial Intelligence and the Innovative Applications of Artificial Intelligence Conference*. Providence, Rhode Island, pages 1058–1065.

I. Sutskever, O. Vinyals, and Q. V. Le. 2014. Sequence to sequence learning with neural networks. In *NIPS*. Montreal, Canada, pages 3104–3112.

M. A. Walker, J. E. Fox Tree, P. Anand, R. Abbott, and J. King. 2012. A corpus for research on deliberation and debate. In *LREC*. Istanbul, Turkey, pages 4445–4452.

W. Warner and J. Hirschberg. 2012. Detecting hate speech on the World Wide Web. In *Proc. of the 2nd Workshop on Language in Social Media*. Montreal, Canada, pages 19–26.

Z. Waseem and D. Hovy. 2016. Hateful symbols or hateful people? Predictive features for hate speech detection on Twitter. In *Proc. of the NAACL Student Research Workshop*. San Diego, CA, pages 88–93.

E. Wulczyn, N. Thain, and L. Dixon. 2017. Ex machina: Personal attacks seen at scale. In *WWW*. Perth, Australia, pages 1391–1399.

G. Xiang, B. Fan, L. Wang, J. Hong, and C. Rose. 2012. Detecting offensive tweets via topical feature discovery over a large scale twitter corpus. In *CIKM*. Maui, Hawaii, pages 1980–1984.

K. Xu, J. Ba, J.R. Kiros, K. Cho, A.C. Courville, R. Salakhutdinov, R.S. Zemel, and Y. Bengio. 2015. Show, attend and tell: Neural image caption generation with visual attention. In *ICML*. Lille, France, pages 2048–2057.

Z. Yang, D. Yang, C. Dyer, X. He, A. Smola, and E. Hovy. 2016. Hierarchical attention networks for document classification. In *NAACL-HLT*. San Diego, CA, pages 1480–1489.

D. Yarowsky. 1994. Decision lists for lexical ambiguity resolution: Application to accent restoration in Spanish and French. In *ACL*. Las Cruces, NM, pages 88–95.

D. Yin, Z. Xue, L. Hong, B. D. Davison, A. Kontostathis, and L. Edwards. 2009. Detection of harassment on Web 2.0. In *Proc. of the WWW workshop on Content Analysis in the Web 2.0*. Madrid, Spain.

X. Zhang, J. Zhao, and Y. LeCun. 2015. Character-level convolutional networks for text classification. In *NIPS*. Montreal, Canada, pages 649–657.

Y. Zhang and B. C. Wallace. 2015. A sensitivity analysis of (and practitioners' guide to) convolutional neural networks for sentence classification. *CoRR* abs/1510.03820.

Class-based Prediction Errors to Detect Hate Speech with Out-of-vocabulary Words

Joan Serrà
Telefónica Research,
Barcelona, Spain

Ilias Leontiadis
Telefónica Research,
Barcelona, Spain

Dimitris Spathis
Aristotle University,
Thessaloniki, Greece

Gianluca Stringhini
University College London,
United Kingdom

Jeremy Blackburn
Telefónica Research,
Barcelona, Spain

Athena Vakali
Aristotle University,
Thessaloniki, Greece

Abstract

Common approaches to text categorization essentially rely either on n-gram counts or on word embeddings. This presents important difficulties in highly dynamic or quickly-interacting environments, where the appearance of new words and/or varied misspellings is the norm. A paradigmatic example of this situation is abusive online behavior, with social networks and media platforms struggling to effectively combat uncommon or non-blacklisted hate words. To better deal with these issues in those fast-paced environments, we propose using the error signal of class-based language models as input to text classification algorithms. In particular, we train a next-character prediction model for any given class, and then exploit the error of such class-based models to inform a neural network classifier. This way, we shift from the ability to describe seen documents to the ability to predict unseen content. Preliminary studies using out-of-vocabulary splits from abusive tweet data show promising results, outperforming competitive text categorization strategies by 4–11%.

1 Introduction

The first steps in automatic text categorization rely on the description of the document content. Typically, such content is characterized by some sort of word, stem, and/or n-gram counts (e.g. Wang and Manning, 2012) or, more recently, by unsupervised or semi-supervised word/sentence/paragraph embeddings (e.g. Arora et al., 2017). While the common pipeline performs well for a myriad of tasks, there are a number of situations where a large ratio of seen vs. unseen tokens threatens the performance of the classifier. This is the case, for instance, with abusive language in online user content or microblogging sites (Nobata et al., 2016; Mehdad and Tetreault, 2016). In such cases, the volume of annotated data is not massive, and the vocabulary changes rapidly and non-consistently across sites and user communities. Sometimes these changes and inconsistencies are intentional, so as to hide the real meaning from traditional automatic detectors using hate-word dictionaries or blacklists. For example, the notorious online community *4chan* launched "Operation Google", which aimed to replace racial slurs on social media with the names of prominent tech companies in a sort of adversarial attack on Google's Jigsaw project (Hine et al., 2017).

To avoid relying on specific tokens, existing text classification approaches can incorporate so-called linguistic features (Brody and Diakopoulos, 2011), such as number of tokens, length of tokens, number of punctuations, and so on, or syntactic features (Nobata et al., 2016), based on part-of-speech tags, dependency relations, and sentence structure. Distributional representations (Le and Mikolov, 2014) and recurrent neural network (RNN) language models (Mikolov, 2012) are also used, together with more classical approaches involving word or character n-grams (Wang and Manning, 2012).

The task of automatic hate speech detection is usually framed as a supervised learning problem. Surface-level features like bag-of-words and embeddings systematically produce reasonable clas-

Proceedings of the First Workshop on Abusive Language Online, pages 36–40,
Vancouver, Canada, July 30 - August 4, 2017. ©2017 Association for Computational Linguistics

sification results (Chen et al., 2012; Nobata et al., 2016). Character-level approaches perform better than token-level ones, since the rare spelling variations of slang and swear words will result in unknown tokens (Mehdad and Tetreault, 2016). More complex features like dependency-parse information or specific linguistic attributes like politeness-imperatives have been effective (Chen et al., 2012). Also lexical resources like lists of slurs, are proven effective but only in combination with other features (Schmidt and Wiegand, 2017).

2 Proposed approach

We propose to perform text categorization following a two step approach (Fig. 1). Firstly, a language model for next-character prediction is trained with the data corresponding to each single category. Secondly, we use a normalized, sequential measurement of the performance of those language models as input to a neural network classifier. In a sense, we aim to shift from 'what is said' (ability to describe) to 'the way of saying' (ability to predict). The idea is that the language model should be tailored to a given category, but without developing a strong dependence on particular characters that are frequent or representative for that category.

The concept of class-based errors is reminiscent of universal background models in speaker verification (Reynolds et al., 2000) and a few document attribution strategies in information retrieval (Serrà et al., 2012). Using error signals for classification also relates to derivative-based similarity and classification in time series (Keogh and Pazzani, 2001).

2.1 Class-conditioned language model

For the class-conditioned language model we use a character-based RNN. Sequences of one-hot encoded characters $\mathbf{X}$ are passed through a time-distributed dense layer with parametric rectified linear unit (PReLU) activation (He et al., 2015), which form a preliminary embedding. This is shared with the subsequent layers. The intuition behind using a PReLU activation after the embedding stems from the fact that it can only improve the results or, at worst, be automatically bypassed: if a linear transformation (no activation) is really the best option, the model can still learn it (He et al., 2015).

For each class i, one gated recurrent unit (GRU;

Cho et al., 2014) is used, followed by a time-distributed dense layer with softmax output, yielding the next-character prediction sequence $\hat{\mathbf{X}}^{(i)}$. With that and the delayed version of $\mathbf{X}$, we calculate a class-conditioned error sequence $\mathbf{e}^{(i)}$ for each character (and zero-mask it according to the sequence length, if needed). In our experiments with one-hot encoded character inputs, $\mathbf{e}^{(i)}$ corresponds to categorical cross-entropy. The final loss is taken to be

$$\mathcal{L}\left(y, \mathbf{e}^{(1)}, \dots \mathbf{e}^{(c)}\right) = \sum_{i=1}^{c} \left(\frac{\mathbb{1}_{\{i\}}(y)}{n-1} \sum_{j=1}^{n-1} e_j^{(i)} \right),$$

where y is the class label of the instance, c is the total number of classes, n is the sequence length of the instance, and $\mathbb{1}()$ is an indicator function.

2.2 Normalization

To perform classification, we take the class-conditioned error sequences $\mathbf{e}^{(i)}$ provided by the language model, and concatenate them into a matrix $\mathbf{E} = [\mathbf{e}^{(1)}, \dots \mathbf{e}^{(c)}]$ for each instance. We then use an instance normalization layer

$$\bar{\mathbf{E}} = \sigma\left(g\mathbf{E}/\mu\right),$$

where $\sigma()$ is an activation function, g is a gain constant, and μ is the average over all the elements of $\mathbf{E}$ (taking sequence masking into account). In principle, we could learn g (or extended vector/matrix versions of it) and use any activation. However, we empirically found $g = 1/3$ and a sigmoid activation to work well enough with character-based cross-entropy sequences.

2.3 Classification

After computing $\bar{\mathbf{E}}$, we input it to a two-layer neural network with PReLU activations, dropout (Srivastava et al., 2014), and a softmax output. This architecture decision is motivated by the fact that we need at least one layer of an another neural network to form the binary classification, since after the language model we have as many errors as characters. A second layer is added to allow the model to perform nonlinear classification based on the error sequences. Regarding normalization, our initial experiments involved no normalization and the performance was much poorer, to the level of the considered alternatives or slightly below.

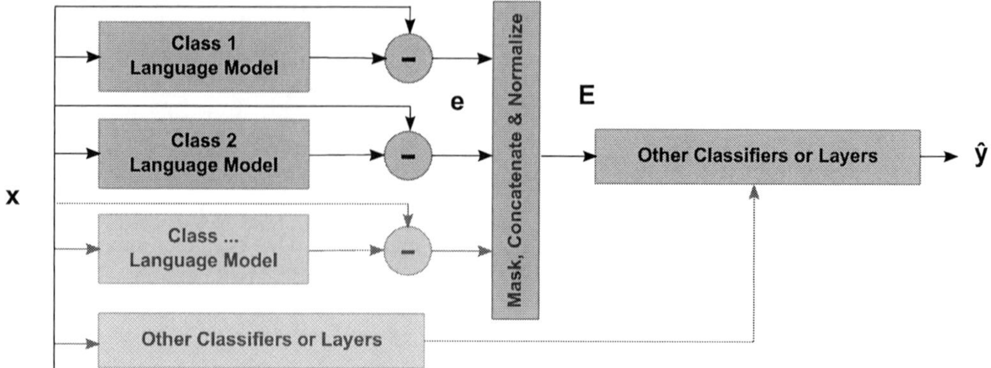

Figure 1: General schema of the proposed model. First, a language model for next-character prediction is trained with the data corresponding to each single class. Second, a normalized, sequential measurement of the performance of those language models is fed as input to a neural network classifier.

2.4 Model setup

We train our models using Adam gradient descent (Kingma and Ba, 2015) until we do not see an improvement on the validation set for 4 epochs. For the language model, we use layer dimensionalities 250 (embedding) and 500 (GRU). For the classification model, we use a dropout of 0.5 and dimensionality 100. At classification time, the language model's weights remain frozen. To implement our models we used Keras (Chollet, 2015) with Theano (Theano Development Team, 2016).

3 Evaluation data

To evaluate the suitability of the proposed concepts, we choose the task of detecting abusive tweets with out-of-vocabulary (OOV) words, using a sample of 2 million tweets from the Twitter 1% feed. Half of the sample is selected based on their use of 'hate words' from a crowdsourced dictionary[1], while the other half is selected randomly. We manually filter the dictionary to remove overly common and ambiguous words like "india", a localized slur for dark skinned people.

Due to lack of baselines and datasets that take into account OOV words, we create semi-synthetic splits with OOV words, in order to simulate data with new or heavily misspelled tokens. We randomly perform 10 train/validation/test splits, compute the area under the receiver operating characteristic curve (AUC), and report the mean and standard deviation over the 10 test splits. Two setups are considered:

- Easy – For the positive class, we take the hate-word list and split it into 70% for training and 15% for validation and testing. In performing such split, we force words with the same stem to end up in the same split. We then select tweets from the entire corpus that contain at least one stemmed word from each split. For the negative class, we just select randomly from the remaining tweets until we have balanced train/validation/test sets.

- Hard – Besides the list of hate words, we also consider a list of common words (top 1,000 to 3,000 most frequent English words[2]). We proceed as with the positive class of the Easy setup, and generate balanced train/validation/test splits for both abusive and non-abusive tweets. In addition, to increase difficulty, we remove tweets with list words appearing in more than one split (that is, we ensure that the intersection of listed words is null between train/validation/test).

To the best of our knowledge, there are no established benchmark datasets for the problem of OOV word detection. Recent work on characterizing OOV words in twitter attempted to build a dataset of such words (Maity et al., 2016), but mostly focused on content analysis and categorization (e.g., *wassup* and *iknow*, belong to word mergings). We plan to develop big crowd-sourced datasets of OOV social media texts and provide them free to the research community.

---

[1] http://hatebase.org

[2] http://www.ef.com/english-resources/english-vocabulary/

Setup	Word NB	Char NB	Word NB-LR	Char NB-LR	Char RNN	Proposed
Easy	0.900 (0.091)	0.849 (0.052)	0.912 (0.113)	0.902 (0.102)	0.858 (0.141)	**0.951** (0.080)
Hard	0.634 (0.109)	0.663 (0.080)	0.580 (0.089)	0.679 (0.038)	0.619 (0.101)	**0.705** (0.059)

Table 1: AUC scores for the considered baselines (see text) and the proposed approach. A null randomized model yields 0.514 (0.082) and 0.503 (0.090) for the Easy and Hard setups, respectively.

4 Results

We compare the proposed approach with 5 of the most common and competitive baselines in abusive language detection (Djuric et al., 2015; Mehdad and Tetreault, 2016). The first two are based on a naïve Bayes classifier using the TF-IDF of both word and character n-grams (NB). The next two are based on the approach proposed by Wang and Manning (2012): similarly, word and character n-grams are constructed, but NB ratios are calculated, and logistic regression is used as a classifier (NB-LR). The rationale behind this choice over other classifiers (e.g SVMs) was that Wang and Manning (2012) found that for short text sentiment tasks, NB actually does performs better than SVMs. For the previous non-neural count-based baselines, we use all combinations of $\{1,2,3\}$-grams with cutoff frequencies of 20 (NB) and 100 (NB-LR). These cutoff frequencies were chosen in-sample in order to maximize the performance of these baselines. The fifth baseline is a character-based RNN using a time-distributed embedding layer, followed by a PReLU activation, a GRU, a dense layer with PReLU activation, and a dense layer with sigmoid output. We try different values for the dimensionality of the aforementioned layers and finally use 200 (embedding), 400 (GRU), and 200 (dense).

The result of the comparison is reported in Table 4. We see that, among the 5 baselines, there is no clear winner for the two setups. Word-based NB-LR performs best in the Easy setup and character-based NB-LR performs best in the Hard setup. Nonetheless, the proposed approach outperforms them by 4.2 and 3.8%, respectively. Compared to the average baseline performance, we observe a relative improvement of 7.5 and 11.0%. We also note that the standard deviation of the proposed approach (across runs) is comparatively low with respect to the baselines.

5 Future work

In this paper, we deal with hate speech detection and, in particular, with abusive OOV words. To this extent we propose to use the error signal of class-based language models as input to text classification algorithms. In particular, we train a next-character prediction model for any given class, and then exploit the error of such class-based models to inform a neural network classifier. This way, we intend to shift from the 'ability to describe seen documents to the 'ability to predict unseen content. Experiments using OOV splits from abusive tweet data show promising results, outperforming competitive text categorization strategies by 4–11%.

We envision a number of potential extensions for the proposed approach: adding an 'all-class' predictor to the language models, improve (or learn) the error sequence normalization, studying the effect of adding further classifiers in parallel to the proposed classification model, ways of fusing those, play with class-based sentence or paragraph embeddings, etc. Generalizing the architecture to longer sequences is a main task for further research, perhaps considering recurrent, quasi-recurrent (Bradbury et al., 2017), or convolutional networks for the classification stage. A qualitative analysis of the output of above classifiers is planned as future work. Due to the fact that our data are weakly-labeled and come from dictionaries, we also plan to shift our focus to real-world, curated data sets of abusive language, as well as evaluate our models on human-annotated crowd-sourced data.

Acknowledgments

This work has been fully funded by the European Commission as part of the ENCASE project (H2020-MSCA-RISE of the European Union under GA number 691025).

References

S. Arora, Y. Liang, and T. Ma. 2017. A simple but tough to beat baseline for sentence embeddings. In *Proc. of the Int. Conf. on Learning Representations (ICLR)*. https://openreview.net/pdf?id=SyK00v5xx.

J. Bradbury, S. Merity, C. Xiong, and R. Socher. 2017. Quasi-recurrent neural networks. In *Proc. of the Int. Conf. on Learning Representations (ICLR)*. http://arxiv.org/abs/1611.01576.

S. Brody and N. Diakopoulos. 2011. Cooooooooooooooooollllllllllllllll!!!!!!!!!!!!!! Using word lengthening to detect sentiment in microblogs. In *Proc. of the Conf. on Empirical Methods in Natural Language Processing (EMNLP)*. pages 562–570.

Ying Chen, Yilu Zhou, Sencun Zhu, and Heng Xu. 2012. Detecting offensive language in social media to protect adolescent online safety. In *Privacy, Security, Risk and Trust (PASSAT), 2012 International Conference on and 2012 International Confernece on Social Computing (SocialCom)*. IEEE, pages 71–80.

K. Cho, B. Van Merriënboer, D. Bahdanau, and Y. Bengio. 2014. On the properties of neural machine translation: encoder-decoder approaches. In *Proc. of the Workshop on Syntax, Semantics and Structure in Statistical Translation (SSST)*. pages 103–111.

Franois Chollet. 2015. keras. `https://github.com/fchollet/keras`.

N. Djuric, J. Zhou, R. Morris, M. Grbovic, V. Radosavljevic, and N. Bhamidipati. 2015. Hate speech detection with comment embeddings. In *Proc. of the Int. Conf. on World Wide Web (WWW)*. pages 29–30.

K. He, X. Zhang, S. Ren, and J. Sun. 2015. Delving deep into rectifiers: surpassing human-level performance on ImageNet classification. In *Proc. of the IEEE Int. Conf. on Computer Vision (ICCV)*. pages 1026–1034.

G Hine, J Onaolapo, E De Cristofaro, N Kourtellis, I Leontiadis, R Samaras, G Stringhini, and J Blackburn. 2017. Kek, cucks, and god emperor trump: A measurement study of 4chan's politically incorrect forum and its effects on the web. In *International Conference on Web and Social Media (ICWSM)*. Association for the Advancement of Artificial Intelligence (AAAI).

E. Keogh and M. Pazzani. 2001. Derivative dynamic time warping. In *Proc. of the SIAM Int. Conf. on Data Mining (SDM)*.

D. P. Kingma and J. L. Ba. 2015. Adam: a method for stochastic optimization. In *Proc. of the Int. Conf. on Learning Representations (ICLR)*. https://arxiv.org/abs/1412.6980.

Q. Le and T. Mikolov. 2014. Distributed representations of sentences and documents. In *Proc. of the Int. Conf. on Machine Learning (ICML)*. volume 32, pages 1188–1196.

Suman Maity, Anshit Chaudhary, Shraman Kumar, Animesh Mukherjee, Chaitanya Sarda, Abhijeet Patil, and Akash Mondal. 2016. Wassup? lol: Characterizing out-of-vocabulary words in twitter. In *Proceedings of the 19th ACM Conference on Computer Supported Cooperative Work and Social Computing Companion*. ACM, pages 341–344.

Y. Mehdad and J. Tetreault. 2016. Do characters abuse more than words? In *Proc. of the Annual Meeting of the Special Interest Group on Discourse and Dialogue (SIGDIAL)*. pages 299–303.

T. Mikolov. 2012. *Statistical language models based on neural networks*. Ph.D. thesis, Brno University of Technology.

C. Nobata, J. Tetreault, A. Thomas, Y. Mehdad, and Y. Chang. 2016. Abusive language detection in online user content. In *Proc. of the Int. Conf. on World Wide Web (WWW)*. pages 145–153.

D. A. Reynolds, T. F. Quatieri, and R. B. Dunn. 2000. Speaker verification using adapted Gaussian mixture models. *Digital Signal Processing* 10(1-3):19–41.

Anna Schmidt and Michael Wiegand. 2017. A survey on hate speech detection using natural language processing. *SocialNLP 2017* page 1.

J. Serrà, H. Kantz, X. Serra, and R. G. Andrzejak. 2012. Predictability of music descriptor time series and its application to cover song detection. *IEEE Trans. on Audio, Speech and Language Processing* 20(2):514–525.

N. Srivastava, G. Hinton, A. Krizhevsky, I. Sutskever, and R. Salakhutdinov. 2014. Dropout: a simple way to prevent neural networks from overfitting. *Journal of Machine Learning Research* 15:1929–1958.

Theano Development Team. 2016. Theano: A Python framework for fast computation of mathematical expressions. *arXiv e-prints* abs/1605.02688. http://arxiv.org/abs/1605.02688.

S. Wang and C. D. Manning. 2012. Baselines and bigrams: simple, good sentiment and topic classification. In *Proc. of the Annual Meeting of the Association for Computational Linguistics (ACL)*. volume 2, pages 90–94.

One-step and Two-step Classification for Abusive Language Detection on Twitter

Ji Ho Park and Pascale Fung
Human Language Technology Center
Department of Electronic and Computer Engineering
Hong Kong University of Science and Technology
jhpark@connect.ust.hk, pascale@ece.ust.hk

Abstract

Automatic abusive language detection is a difficult but important task for online social media. Our research explores a two-step approach of performing classification on abusive language and then classifying into specific types and compares it with one-step approach of doing one multi-class classification for detecting sexist and racist languages. With a public English Twitter corpus of 20 thousand tweets in the type of sexism and racism, our approach shows a promising performance of 0.827 F-measure by using HybridCNN in one-step and 0.824 F-measure by using logistic regression in two-steps.

1 Introduction

Fighting abusive language online is becoming more and more important in a world where online social media plays a significant role in shaping people's minds (Perse and Lambe, 2016). Nevertheless, major social media companies like Twitter find it difficult to tackle this problem (Meyer, 2016), as the huge number of posts cannot be mediated with only human resources.

Warner and Hirschberg (2012) and Burnap and Williams (2015) are one of the early researches to use machine learning based classifiers for detecting abusive language. Djuric et al., (2015) incorporated representation word embeddings (Mikolov et al., 2013). Nobata et al. (2016) combined pre-defined language elements and word embedding to train a regression model. Waseem (2016) used logistic regression with n-grams and user-specific features such as gender and location. Davidson et al. (2017) conducted a deeper investigation on different types of abusive language. Badjatiya et al. (2017) experimented with

deep learning-based models using ensemble gradient boost classifiers to perform multi-class classification on sexist and racist language. All approaches have been on one step.

Many have addressed the difficulty of the definition of abusive language while annotating the data, because they are often subjective to individuals (Ross et al. 2016) and lack of context (Waseem and Hovy, 2016; Schmidt & Wiegand, 2017). This makes it harder for non-experts to annotate without having a certain amount of domain knowledge (Waseem, 2016).

In this research, we aim to experiment a two-step approach of detecting abusive language first and then classifying into specific types and compare with a one-step approach of doing one multi-class classification on sexist and racist language.

Moreover, we explore applying a convolutional neural network (CNN) to tackle the task of abusive language detection. We use three kinds of CNN models that use both character-level and word-level inputs to perform classification on different dataset segmentations. We measure the performance and ability of each model to capture characteristics of abusive language.

2 Methodology

We propose to implement three CNN-based models to classify sexist and racist abusive language: CharCNN, WordCNN, and HybridCNN. The major difference among these models is whether the input features are characters, words, or both.

The key components are the convolutional layers that each computes a one-dimensional convolution over the previous input with multiple filter sizes and large feature map sizes. Having different filter sizes is the same as looking at a sentence with different windows simultaneously. Max-pooling is performed after the convolution to

41

Proceedings of the First Workshop on Abusive Language Online, pages 41–45,
Vancouver, Canada, July 30 - August 4, 2017. ©2017 Association for Computational Linguistics

capture the feature that is most significant to the output.

2.1 CharCNN

CharCNN is a modification of the character-level convolutional network in (Zhang et al. 2015). Each character in the input sentence is first transformed into a one-hot encoding of 70 characters, including 26 English letters, 10 digits, 33 other characters, and a newline character (punctuations and special characters). All other non-standard characters are removed.

Zhang et al. (2015) uses 7 layers of convolutions and max-pooling layers, 2 fully-connected layers, and 1 softmax layer, but we also designed a shallow version with 2 convolutions and max-pooling layers, 1 fully-connected layers, and 1 softmax layers with dropout, due to the relatively small size of our dataset to prevent overfitting.

2.2 WordCNN

WordCNN is a CNN-static version proposed by Kim (2014). The input sentence is first segmented into words and converted into a 300-dimensional embedding *word2vec* trained on 100 billion words from Google News (Mikolov et al., 2013). Incorporating pre-trained vectors is a widely-used method to improve performance, especially when using a relatively small dataset. We set the embedding to be non-trainable since our dataset is small.

We propose to segment some out-of-vocabulary phrases as well. Since the Twitter tweets often contain hashtags such as *#womenagainstfeminism* and *#feminismisawful* we use a wordsegment library (Segaran and Hammerbacher, 2009) to capture more words.

2.3 HybridCNN

We design HybridCNN, a variation of WordCNN, since WordCNN has the limitation of only taking word features as input. Abusive language often contains either purposely or mistakenly misspelled words and made-up vocabularies such as *#feminazi*.

Therefore, since CharCNN and WordCNN do not use character and word inputs at the same time, we design the HybridCNN to experiment whether the model can capture features from both levels of inputs.

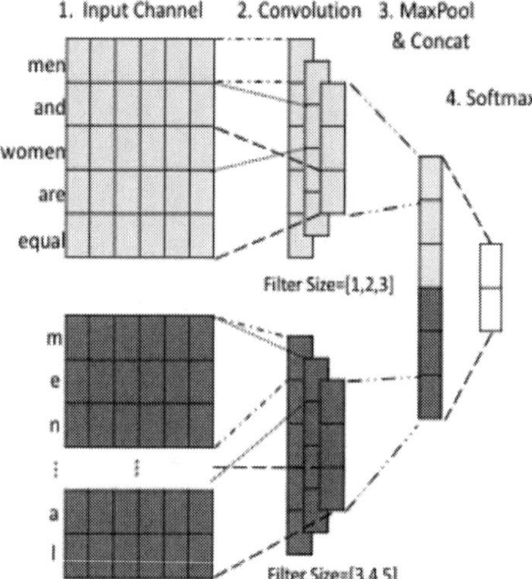

Figure 1 Architecture of HybridCNN

HybridCNN has two input channels. Each channel is fed into convolutional layers with three filter windows of different size. The output of the convolution are concatenated into one vector after 1-max-pooling. The vector is then fed into the final softmax layer to perform classification (See Figure 1).

3 Experiments

3.1 Datasets

We used the two English Twitter Datasets (Waseem and Hovy, 2016; Waseem, 2016) published as unshared tasks for the 1st Workshop on Abusive Language Online(ALW1). It contains tweets with sexist and racist comments. Waseem and Hovy (2016) created a list of criteria based on a critical race theory and let an expert annotate the corpus. First, we concatenated the two datasets into one and then divided that into three datasets for one-step and two-step classification (Table 1). One-step dataset is a segmentation for multi-class classification. For two-step classification, we merged the sexism and racism labels into one abusive label. Finally, we created another dataset with abusive languages to experiment a second classifier to distinguish "sexism" and "racism", given that the instance is classified as "abusive".

3.2 Training and Evaluation

We performed two classification experiments:
1. Detecting "none", "sexist", and "racist" language (one-step)

Dataset	One-step			Two-step-1		Two-step-2	
Label	None	Racism	Sexism	None	Abusive	Sexism	Racism
#	12,427	2,059	3,864	12,427	5,923	2,059	3,864

Table 1: Dataset Segmentation

2. Detecting "abusive language", then further classifying into "sexist" or "racist" (two-step)

The purpose of these experiments was to see whether dividing the problem space into two steps makes the detection more effective.

We trained the models using mini-batch stochastic gradient descent with AdamOptimizer (Kingma and Ba, 2014). For more efficient training in an unbalanced dataset, the mini-batch with a size of 32 had been sampled with equal distribution for all labels. The training continued until the evaluation set loss did not decrease any longer. All the results are average results of 10-fold cross validation.

As evaluation metric, we used F1 scores with precision and recall score and weighted averaged the scores to consider the imbalance of the labels. For this reason, total average F1 might not between average precision and recall.

As baseline, we used the character n-gram logistic regression classifier (indicated as LR on Table 2-4) from Waseem and Hovy (2016), Support Vector Machines (SVM) classifier, and FastText (Joulin et al., 2016) that uses average bag-of-words representations to classify sentences. It was the second best single model on the same dataset after CNN (Badjatiya et al., 2017).

3.3 Hyperparameters

For hyperparameter tuning, we evaluated on the validation set. These are the hyperparmeters used for evaluation.

- **CharCNN:** Shallow model with 1024 feature units for convolution layers with filter size 4, max-pooling size 3, and L2 regularization constant 1 and 2048 units for the fully-connected layer
- **WordCNN:** Convolution layers with 3 filters with the size of [1,2,3] and feature map size 50, max-pooling, and L2 regularization constant 1
- **HybridCNN:** For the character input channel, convolution layers with 3 filters with size of [3,4,5] and for word input

channel, 3 filters with size of [1,2,3]. Both channels had feature map size of 50, max-pooling, and L2 regularization constant 1.

4 Result and Discussions

4.1 One-step Classification

The results of the one-step multi-class classification are shown in the top part of Table 2.

Our newly proposed HybridCNN performs the best, giving an improvement over the result from WordCNN. We expected the additional character input channel improves the performance. We assumed that the reason CharCNN performing worse than WordCNN is that the dataset is too small for the character-based model to capture word-level features by itself.

Baseline methods tend to have high averaged F1 but low scores on racism and sexism labels due to low recall scores.

4.2 Two-step Classification

The two-step approach that combines two binary classifiers shows comparable results with one-step approach. The results of combining the two are shown in the bottom part of Table 3.

Combining two logistic regression classifiers in the two-step approach performs about as well as one-step HybridCNN and outperform one-step logistic regression classifier by more than 10 F1 points. This is surprising since logistic regression takes less features than the HybridCNN.

Furthermore, using HybridCNN on the first step to detect abusive language and logistic regression on the second step to classify racism and sexism worked better than just using HybridCNN.

Table 4 shows the results of abusive language classification. HybridCNN also performs best for abusive language detection, followed by WordCNN and logistic regression.

Table 5 shows the results of classifying into sexism and racism given that it is abusive. The second classifier has significant performance in predicting a specific type (in this case, sexism

Method	None			Racism			Sexism			Total		
	Prec.	Rec.	F1	Prec.	Rec.	F1	Prec.	Rec.	F1	Prec.	Rec.	F1
LR	.824	.945	.881	.810	.598	.687	.835	.556	.668	.825	.824	.814
SVM	.802	**.956**	.872	**.815**	.531	.643	**.851**	.483	.616	.814	.808	.793
FastText	.828	.922	**.882**	.759	.630	.685	.777	.557	.648	.810	.812	.804
CharCNN	.861	.867	.864	.693	.746	.718	.713	.666	.688	.801	.811	.811
WordCNN	.870	.868	.868	.704	.762	.731	.712	**.686**	.694	.818	.816	.816
HybridCNN	**.872**	.882	.877	.713	**.766**	**.736**	.743	.679	**.709**	**.827**	**.827**	**.827**
LR (two)	.841	.933	**.895**	.800	.664	.731	.809	.590	.683	**.828**	**.831**	**.824**
SVM (two)	.816	**.945**	.876	**.811**	.605	.689	**.823**	.511	.630	.816	.815	.803
HybridCNN (two)	.877	.864	.869	.690	**.759**	.721	.705	.701	**.699**	.807	.809	.807
HybridCNN + LR(two)	**.880**	.859	.869	.722	.751	**.735**	.683	**.717**	**.699**	.821	.817	.818

Table 2. Experiment Results: upper part is the one-step methods that perform multi-class classification and lower methods with (two) indicate two-step that combines two binary classifiers. HybridCNN is our newly created model.

and racism) of an abusive language. We can deduce that sexist and racist comments have obvious discriminating features that are easy for all classifiers to capture.

Since the precision and recall scores of the "abusive" label is higher than those of "racism" and "sexism" in the one-step approach, the two-step approach can perform as well as the one-step approach.

Model	Prec.	Rec.	F1
LR	.816	.640	.711
SVM	**.839**	.560	.668
FastText	.765	.616	.683
CharCNN	.743	.674	.707
WordCNN	.731	.722	.726
HybridCNN	.719	**.754**	**.734**

Table 3. Results on Abusive Language Detection

Model	Prec.	Rec.	F1
LR	**.954**	**.953**	**.952**
SVM	.954	.953	.952
FastText	.937	.937	.937
CharCNN	.941	.941	.941
WordCNN	.952	.952	.952
HybridCNN	.951	.950	.950

Table 4. Results on Sexist/Racist Classification

5   Conclusion and Future work

We explored a two-step approach of combining two classifiers - one to classify abusive language and another to classify a specific type of sexist and racist comments given that the language is abusive. With many different machine learning classifiers including our proposed HybridCNN, which takes both character and word features as input, we showed the potential in the two-step approach compared to the one-step approach which is simply a multi-class classification. In this way, we can boost the performance of simpler models like logistic regression, which is faster and easier to train, and combine different types of classifiers like convolutional neural network and logistic regression together depending on each of its performance on different datasets.

We believe that two-step approach has potential in that large abusive language datasets with specific label such as profanity, sexist, racist, homophobic, etc. is more difficult to acquire than those simply flagged as abusive.

For this reason, in the future we would like to explore training the two-step classifiers on separate datasets (for example, a large dataset with abusive language for the first-step classifier and smaller specific-labelled dataset for the second-step classifier) to build a more robust and detailed abusive language detector.

Acknowledgements

This work is partially funded by CERG16214415 of the Hong Kong Research Grants Council and ITS170 of the Innovation and Technology Commission.

References

Badjatiya, P., Gupta, S., Gupta, M., & Varma, V. (2017). Deep learning for hate speech detection in tweets. *Proceedings of the 26th International Conference on World Wide Web Companion,* 759-760.

Djuric, N., Zhou, J., Morris, R., Grbovic, M., Radosavljevic, V., & Bhamidipati, N. (2015). Hate speech detection with comment embeddings. *Proceedings of the 24th International Conference on World Wide Web,* 29-30.

Joulin, A., Grave, E., Bojanowski, P., & Mikolov, T. (2016). Bag of tricks for efficient text classification. *Proceedings of the 15th Conference of the European Chapter of the Association for Computational Linguistics: Volume 2, Short Papers,*

Kim, Y. (2014). Convolutional neural networks for sentence classification . *In Proceedings of EMNLP.,*

Kingma, D., & Ba, J. (2014). Adam: A method for stochastic optimization. *Proceedings of the 3rd International Conference on Learning Representations (ICLR)*

LeCun, Y., Kavukcuoglu, K., & Farabet, C. (2010). Convolutional networks and applications in vision. *Circuits and Systems (ISCAS), Proceedings of 2010 IEEE International Symposium on,* 253-256.

Meyer, R. (2016, 07/21). Twitter's famous racist problem. *The Atlantic,*

Mikolov, T., Sutskever, I., Chen, K., Corrado, G. S., & Dean, J. (2013). Distributed representations of words and phrases and their compositionality. *Advances in Neural Information Processing Systems,* 3111-3119.

Nobata, C., Tetreault, J., Thomas, A., Mehdad, Y., & Chang, Y. (2016). Abusive language detection in online user content. *Proceedings of the 25th International Conference on World Wide Web,* 145-153.

Perse, E. M., & Lambe, J. (2016). *Media effects and society* Routledge.

Ross, B., Rist, M., Carbonell, G., Cabrera, B., Kurowsky, N., & Wojatzki, M. (2017). Measuring the reliability of hate speech annotations: The case of the european refugee crisis In *Proceedings of the Workshop on Natural Language Processing for ComputerMediated Communication (NLP4CMC), pages 6–9*

Schmidt, A., & Wiegand, M. (2017). A survey on hate speech detection using natural language processing. *Socialnlp 2017, ,* 1.

Segaran, T., & Hammerbacher, J. (2009). *Beautiful data: The stories behind elegant data solutions* " O'Reilly Media, Inc.".

Wang, W., Chen, L., Thirunarayan, K., & Sheth, A. P. (2012). Harnessing twitter" big data" for automatic emotion identification. *Privacy, Security, Risk and Trust (PASSAT), 2012 International Conference on and 2012 International Confernece on Social Computing (SocialCom),* 587-592.

Warner, W., & Hirschberg, J. (2012). Detecting hate speech on the world wide web. *Proceedings of the Second Workshop on Language in Social Media,* 19-26.

Waseem, Z. (2016). Are you a racist or am I seeing things? annotator influence on hate speech detection on twitter. *Proceedings of the 1st Workshop on Natural Language Processing and Computational Social Science,* 138-142.

Waseem, Z., & Hovy, D. (2016). Hateful symbols or hateful people? predictive features for hate speech detection on twitter. *Proceedings of NAACL-HLT,* 88-93.

Zhang, X., Zhao, J., & LeCun, Y. (2015). Characterlevel convolutional networks for text classification. *Advances in Neural Information Processing Systems,* 649-657.

Legal Framework, Dataset and Annotation Schema for Socially Unacceptable Online Discourse Practices in Slovene

Darja Fišer
Faculty of Arts
University of Ljubljana
Aškerčeva cesta 2
1000 Ljubljana, Slovenia
`darja.fiser@ff.uni-lj.si`

Nikola Ljubešić	**Tomaž Erjavec**
Dept. of Knowledge Technologies	Dept. of Knowledge Technologies
Jožef Stefan Institute	Jožef Stefan Institute
Jamova cesta 39	Jamova cesta 39
1000 Ljubljana, Slovenia	1000 Ljubljana, Slovenia
`nikola.ljubesic@ijs.si`	`tomaz.erjavec@ijs.si`

Abstract

In this paper we present the legal framework, dataset and annotation schema of socially unacceptable discourse practices on social networking platforms in Slovenia. On this basis we aim to train an automatic identification and classification system with which we wish contribute towards an improved methodology, understanding and treatment of such practices in the contemporary, increasingly multicultural information society.

1 Introduction

In Slovenia, Socially Unacceptable Discourse (SUD) practices, such as prosecutable hate speech, threats, abuse and defamations, but also not prosecutable but still indecent and immoral insults and obscenities, are heavily researched by sociologists (Dragoš, 2007; Leskošek, 2004). They receive regular coverage in the media, public debates are held about it in the parliament, several national and international initiatives and activities address them (Motl and Bajt, 2016), all with the aim to raise awareness and propose efficient prevention strategies.

Despite all these efforts, their success has been limited as was clearly indicated in the second half of 2015 when extreme forms of SUD flooded social media as a response to the migrant crisis in the Balkans. This trend is confirmed by the records of the Spletno Oko (Web Eye) national hotline service for reporting online hate speech, which forwarded 75% more of the applications received to the police in 2015 than the year before (Vehovar and Motl, 2015). Even when criminal or civil cases are filed, very few of them make it as far as a court hearing, let alone a conviction. Here, the biggest bottleneck is not the definition of legally unacceptable forms of speech in the Penal Code (public promotion of hatred, violence or intolerance) but in the syllogism process, i.e. the application of the general legal norm to the facts of a particular case (Rovšek, 2011; Šalamon, 2015).

This shows that new interdisciplinary theoretical and analytical methods and approaches are needed to improve our understanding as well as to enable efficient and comprehensive identification and classification of SUD in the contemporary, increasingly multicultural information society. As of yet, there are no publications reporting on successful attempts to automate the identification of SUD for Slovene, which is hardly surprising as most work has so far been limited to English, with a few exceptions for Dutch (van Halteren and Oostdijk, 2013) and German (Ross et al., 2017). State-of-the-art approaches tackle this task through supervised machine learning (Sood et al., 2012; Dadvar et al., 2013). For this, of course, manually annotated datasets are needed.

A major limitation of most existing work in this area is that it is based on an ad-hoc treatment of SUD classification in natural language processing and a lack of detailed guidelines that are necessary for reliable annotation (Ross et al., 2017). Annotated datasets have started to emerge only recently (Nobata et al., 2016; Waseem and Hovy, 2016), but nevertheless they lack precise documentation on data annotation and make use of only very basic

Proceedings of the First Workshop on Abusive Language Online, pages 46–51,
Vancouver, Canada, July 30 - August 4, 2017. ©2017 Association for Computational Linguistics

annotation schemas. The community could benefit from input by experts from the area of SUD, which is the goal of this paper, in which we present the legal framework, the database, and the annotation schema of Slovene socially unacceptable online discourse practices that was developed in collaboration by sociologists and legal experts who specialize in SUD. Since Slovene legislation is in line with all the relevant EU directives, the proposed schema and annotation principles could be applied to other languages as well.

2 The FRENK Project

The work presented in this paper serves as the foundation for FRENK, a new 3-year interdisciplinary national basic research project funded by the Slovenian national research agency from May 2017 to May 2020. For the first time, the project combines researchers from the fields of NLP, sociolinguistics, sociology and law. Its goal is the development of resources, methods and tools for the understanding, identification and classification of various forms of SUD in the information society. The project aims to combine state-of-the-art quantitative and qualitative multidisciplinary approaches which will be employed to investigate the use of socially unacceptable discourse in its sociocultural context.

In the scope of the project we will use social media data to construct a large corpus of SUD that will be highly structured and their (often nonstandard) texts linguistically processed as well as enriched with various metadata with the help of our toolchain for the processing of noisy user-generated content (Fišer et al., 2017). Using the typology of socially unacceptable discourse and its targets and the manually annotated representative sample of texts presented in this paper we will apply machine learning techniques to flag and categorise SUD texts and their targets.

With the methodologies and instruments of corpus linguistics, critical discourse analysis and inferential statistics, interdisciplinary (socio)linguistic analyses will be performed on the collected and processed resources, focusing on migrants and Islamophobia, and homophobia and gay rights. These approaches will be supplemented with a corpus analysis of legal aspects of socially unacceptable discourse and sociological surveys on its the perception in the Slovene society.

3 Legal framework

The term *hate speech*, the strongest form of socially unacceptable discourse practices, is not explicitly used in the Slovene legislation. Instead, criminally prosecutable acts due to public promotion of hatred, violence or intolerance that can be understood as hate speech are included in Article 297 of the Penal Code. However, (Šalamon, 2015) warns that with the most recent amendment of the Code in 2012, the definition became much more precise and narrow, perhaps even too narrow, as it excludes acts of verbal outrage that do not include elements of a threat or abuse and cannot endanger law and order.

(Motl and Bajt, 2016) reach a similar conclusion in their overview of the legal framework and legal practice in Slovenia where they show that hate speech is becoming commonplace and still very rarely sanctioned. What is more, the issue of (non criminal) intolerant speech is more often than not underestimated and treated as occasional excess by the key stakeholders.

According to its treatment in the Slovene legal framework, (Vehovar et al., 2012) defined three levels of SUD found online. The largest share is represented by *Inappropriate Speech* with which they signify various forms of socially undesired, indecent and immoral discourse practices, such as swearwords, insults, vulgar or obscene language and profanities. While there are no legal grounds for the prosecution of such types of discourse practices as they are protected by the free speech provisions, they are typically regulated with codes of conduct by owners of online portals.

The second level are instances of *Inadmissible Speech*, which comprise discourse practices that contain false statements that harm the reputation of an individual, group of people or organization or those that threaten someone's life or security. Both are punishable by the Penal Code and, depending on whether they are directed towards a *social group* due to race, ethnicity, religion, sexual orientation of their members, or towards a *specific individual*, prosecuted ex officio or by the party concerned.

Finally, the highly restrictive account of *Hate Speech* is specifically reserved for discourse practices that are directed towards, promote intolerance and call to violence against a social subgroup based on their racial or ethnic profile, religion, sexual orientation or political affiliation.

4 Database of Slovene SUD

The biggest and most authoritative database of socially unacceptable online discourse practices in Slovene is being collected through the Spletno Oko[1] (Web Eye) hotline service that enables Internet users anonymous reporting of hate speech and child sexual abuse content they come across online. The hotline was established in 2006 within the international Safer Internet Program[2] and is financed by the European Commission (INEA agency) and the Slovenian Ministry of Public Administration. Its main mission is to reduce the amount of child sexual abuse content and hate speech online in cooperation with the police, internet service providers, and other governmental and non-governmental organizations. Apart from awareness raising campaigns and exchange of best practices with other hotlines in the network, the Safer Internet Centre performs a fast analysis of the submissions and reports the potentially criminal cases to the authorities.

The most recent version of the Spletno Oko database contains reported SUD instances from online networking and social media sites from 2010 onwards, comprising 13,000 text instances or about 900,000 tokens. All the reported text instances were examined and classified into one of the categories according to the legal framework by a professional analyst with a degree in sociology, criminology or law and specialised training for the job at the hotline service. In the first years of the hotline's operations, most of the reported text instances were news comments from online news portals. This is why the hotline drafted the "Code for the regulation of hate speech on online portals"[3] in 2013 which has since been signed by most major online news portals in the country. As a result, the amount of reported instances from online news portals has declined substantially. In the past few years, the prevailing, and increasing, source of reports to the hotline are Facebook groups and pages.

5 Annotation of Slovene SUD

A prerequisite of any automatic approaches to the detection and classification of SUD is the compilation of a manually annotated dataset. In the FRENK project we will build upon the invaluable Spletno Oko database but since the annotation at the hotline service was not set up in a way that would directly enable a successful transfer to the machine learning environment, a number of steps are needed to harmonise both initiatives, which we describe in this section.

First and foremost, the flat annotation schema needs to be redesigned in such a way that it allows for both coarse- and fine-grained SUD classification (see Section 5.1) and complemented by detailed annotation guidelines, which ensure consistent annotation as well as serve for documentation purposes and for potential future annotation campaigns to improve comparability of the results. To overcome low annotation agreement, instead of the existing single annotations multiple annotations need to be obtained for each data point in the early phases of the annotation campaign, followed by a post-hoc adjudication procedure.

This will help us arrive at gold-standard annotations as well as work out possible issues either in the annotation schema or the annotation guidelines. We will adopt the MATTER annotation framework (Pustejovsky and Stubbs, 2012), i.e. Modelling the phenomenon, Annotating it, Training and Testing the ML methods, Evaluating their fitness of purpose, and possibly Revising the procedure on the basis of the evaluation. The annotation process should not be linear but proceed in several cycles accompanied by the refinement of the annotation schema and the guidelines and resulting in a high-quality dataset that can at the same time be used also for linguistic, sociological as well as legal investigations of SUD. By following these principles we believe we can advance the state-of-the-art in computational linguistic SUD investigations, where such datasets have so far been annotated in a rather cursory fashion.

5.1 Annotation schema

For the annotation campaign within the FRENK project the typology developed by the "Spletno Oko" hotline experts (Vehovar et al., 2012) has been modified to better facilitate automatic identification and classification of SUD, our ultimate goal. The originally flat typology was reorganized into a two-level schema which allows for both coarse- (2-class: SUD, not SUD), medium- (4-class: category level 1 in Figure 1) and fine-

---

[1] http://www.spletno-oko.si/english/

[2] https://www.betterinternetforkids.eu/web/portal/policy/insafe-inhope

[3] http://www.spletno-oko.si/sovrazni-govor/za-urednike-spletnih-mest

Typology of SUD

1. No Elements of Problematic Speech
1.1 Reports are false, void
1.2 Texts contain no unacceptable speech
2. Inappropriate Speech
2.1 Texts contain insulting, offensive speech
2.2 Text contain obscenity, profanity, vulgarity
3. Inadmissible Speech
3.1 Texts contain defamatory speech
3.2 Texts contain abusive, threatening speech
4. Hate Speech
4.1 Socially unacceptable hate speech
4.2 Potentially legally punishable hate speech

Target of SUD

1. Ethnicity
2. Race
3. Sexual orientation
4. Political affiliation
5. Religion

Metadata

1. Date of submission
2. URL of the reported SUD
3. Text of the reported SUD

Figure 1: SUD Annotation schema used in the Spletno Oko database.

grained (8-class: category levels 1 and 2 in Figure 1) treatment of SUD. It will be interesting to explore which of those yield better results for each of the stakeholders (NLP researchers, sociologists, lawyers, moderators of online portals).

As can be seen in Figure 1, the underlying legal principles described in Section 2 serve as the basis of a hierarchical two-level SUD annotation schema that is applied to classify the reports submitted through the helpline, which yield the 4 top categories: *1. No Elements of Problematic Speech*, *2. Inappropriate Speech*, *3. Inadmissible Speech*, and *4. Hate Speech*.

Each of the top categories has two subcategories, all of which have a legal basis with one exception, namely the subcategory *4.1 Socially Unacceptable Hate Speech*. This additional subcategory was introduced in the final typology because real-life cases of highly volatile online discourse practices contain some but not all elements of hate speech as required by the Penal Code. While as opposed to potentially *Legally Punishable Hate Speech*, is not a legal category according to Slovene legislation, it is of high social and sociological relevance and therefore deserves special attention.

Reports that meet the criteria of *4.1 Socially Unacceptable* and *4.2 Potentially Legally Punishable Hate Speech* are further annotated with who is the *target* of SUD: ethnicity (e.g. Roma), race (e.g. African Americans), sexual orientation (e.g. gays), political affiliation (e.g. the United Left) and religion (e.g. Islam). The target information will be an interesting feature to examine in machine learning as as well as socio-linguistic and legal analyses.

In addition to SUD type and target, annotators also record when the report was submitted, where the disputed communication was observed, as well as the entire disputed text.

5.2 Analysis of annotations

Nearly half of all the reports in the Spletno Oko database contain no elements of problematic speech (no unacceptable content 23% or false report 20%). This shows that many users of the hotline often report content which they find generally upsetting or because they feel personally insulted or attacked.

Almost a quarter of the reports contain inappropriate speech (15% insulting or offensive content, 9% obscene or vulgar language, profanities, cursing, swearwords) and as such cannot be subject to prosecution but are restricted by most online content providers and removed by moderators. These results suggest that some online content providers either do not enforce their internal rules or cannot do it quickly enough to prevent exposure to SUD among their users.

Next, 16% of the reports contain inadmissible speech (15% defamatory content, 1% threats) which are prosecutable through public prosecution or by private lawsuit. As much as 13% of the reports meet some but not all of the criteria of Article 297 of the Penal Code (e.g. spread intolerance but do not promote violence). Even though it cannot be legally prosecuted as hate speech, such content is nevertheless perceived as socially unacceptable and therefore requires special attention and proper treatment by researchers, lawmakers and content providers alike.

Finally, 3% of the reports meet all the criteria for potentially legally punishable hate speech and were reported to the authorities.

6 Conclusions

This paper presented the legal framework, annotation schema and dataset of socially unacceptable online discourse practices for Slovene, which are the first important stepping stone towards the a comprehensive, interdisciplinary treatment of the linguistic, sociological, legal and technological dimensions of various forms of SUD in Slovenia. In our future work we will develop a tool for automatic identification and classification of SUD on social media. The research will result in a thorough examination of the characteristics of SUD as a linguistic phenomenon and the social context in which explicit or implicit forms of discriminatory language are manifested. These insights will facilitate an improved understanding of the differences between legally acceptable and unacceptable forms of communication.

For the first time in Slovenia, the FRENK project brings together computer science, linguistics, sociology and law, thereby contributing to the increasingly important new research directions of the Digital Humanities and Social Sciences (DHSS) and establishing infrastructure and knowledge transfer of approaches based on large amounts of textual, sociodemographic and behaviour data. The classifier we will develop within the project has a big potential to be integrated into the daily work of moderators of discussions on the most popular forums and administrators of readers' comments on the biggest online media sites who cannot cope with the volume of posts with manual methods and are finding simple, in-house-built lexicon methods insufficient.

Acknowledgments

The authors would like to thank the anonymous reviewers for their helpful comments. The work described in this paper was funded by the Slovenian Research Agency within the national basic research project Resources, methods and tools for the understanding, identification and classification of various forms of socially unacceptable discourse in the information society (J7-8280, 2017-2020).

References

Maral Dadvar, Dolf Trieschnigg, Roeland Ordelman, and Franciska de Jong. 2013. Improving Cyberbullying Detection with User Context. In *Proceedings of the 35th European Conference on Advances in Information Retrieval*. Springer-Verlag, Berlin, Heidelberg, ECIR'13, pages 693–696. https://doi.org/10.1007/978-3-642-36973-5_62.

Srečo Dragoš. 2007. Sovražni govor (Hate speech). *Socialno delo* 46(3):135–144.

Darja Fišer, Tomaž Erjavec, and Nikola Ljubešić. 2017. The compilation, processing and analysis of the Janes corpus of Slovene user-generated content. In Ciara R. Wigham and Gudron Ledegen, editors, *Corpus de communication médiée par les réseaux: construction, structuration, analyse*, LHarmattan, Collection Humanités Numériques.

Vesna Leskošek. 2004. Sovražni govor kot dejanje nasilja (Hate speech as an act of violence). In Vesna Leskošek, editor, *Mi in oni: Nestrpnost na Slovenskem*, Mirovni inštitut.

Andrej Motl and Veronika Bajt. 2016. Sovražni govor v Republiki Sloveniji: pregled stanja (Hate speech in the Republic of Slovenia: an overview of the situation). Technical report, Mirovni inštitut.

Chikashi Nobata, Joel Tetreault, Achint Thomas, Yashar Mehdad, and Yi Chang. 2016. Abusive Language Detection in Online User Content. In *Proceedings of the 25th International Conference on World Wide Web*. International World Wide Web Conferences Steering Committee, Republic and Canton of Geneva, Switzerland, WWW '16, pages 145–153. https://doi.org/10.1145/2872427.2883062.

James Pustejovsky and Amber Stubbs. 2012. *Natural Language Annotation for Machine Learning*. O'Reilly Media.

Björn Ross, Michael Rist, Guillermo Carbonell, Benjamin Cabrera, Nils Kurowsky, and Michael Wojatzki. 2017. Measuring the Reliability of Hate Speech Annotations: The Case of the European Refugee Crisis. *CoRR* abs/1701.08118. http://arxiv.org/abs/1701.08118.

Jernej Rovšek. 2011. Ali je sovražni govor sploh mogoče omejiti (Is it possible to limit hate speech at all?). http://mediawatch.mirovni-institut.si/bilten/seznam/39/sovrazni.

Sara Owsley Sood, Judd Antin, and Elizabeth F. Churchill. 2012. Using Crowdsourcing to Improve Profanity Detection. In *AAAI Spring Symposium: Wisdom of the Crowd*.

Hans van Halteren and Nelleke Oostdijk. 2013. Variability in Dutch Tweets. An estimate of the proportion of deviant word tokens. *Journal for Language Technology and Computational Linguistics* 29(2):97–123.

Vasja Vehovar and Andrej Motl. 2015. Letno poročilo, Spletno oko 2015. (Annual Report Web Eye 2015). Technical report, Center za varnejš internet, prijavna toča Spletno oko. Fakulteta za družbene vede. http://www.spletno-oko.si/sites/default/files/spletno_oko_-_letno_porocilo_2015.pdf.

Vasja Vehovar, Andrej Motl, Lija Mihelič, Boštjan Berčič, and Andraž Petrovčič. 2012. Zaznava sovražnega govora na slovenskem spletu (Detecting hate speech on the Web). *Teorija in praksa* 49(1):95–111. http://dk.fdv.uni-lj.si/db/pdfs/TiP2012_1_Vehovar_idr.pdf.

Neža Kogovšek Šalamon. 2015. Sovražni govor kot uradno pregonljivo kaznivo dejanje (Hate speech as officially sanctioned criminal offence). In *1. dnevi prava zasebnosti in svobode izražanja.* IUS Software, GV založba, pages 23–27.

Zeerak Waseem and Dirk Hovy. 2016. Hateful Symbols or Hateful People? Predictive Features for Hate Speech Detection on Twitter. In *Proceedings of the NAACL Student Research Workshop.* Association for Computational Linguistics, San Diego, California, pages 88–93. http://www.aclweb.org/anthology/N16-2013.

Abusive Language Detection on Arabic Social Media

Hamdy Mubarak, Kareem Darwish
Qatar Computing Research Institute,
HBKU, Doha, Qatar
{hmubarak,kdarwish}@qf.org.qa

Walid Magdy
School of Informatics,
The University of Edinburgh, UK.
wmagdy@inf.ed.ac.uk

Abstract

In this paper, we present our work on detecting abusive language on Arabic social media. We extract a list of obscene words and hashtags using common patterns used in offensive and rude communications. We also classify Twitter users according to whether they use any of these words or not in their tweets. We expand the list of obscene words using this classification, and we report results on a newly created dataset of classified Arabic tweets (obscene, offensive, and clean). We make this dataset freely available for research, in addition to the list of obscene words and hashtags. We are also publicly releasing a large corpus of classified user comments that were deleted from a popular Arabic news site due to violations the site's rules and guidelines.

1 Introduction

Social media is a popular medium for discussion, expression of views, sharing of content, and promotion of ideas and products. Like any other medium of communication, the content may be clean or obscene/profane or and cordial/polite or offensive/rude. Identification of profane and offensive exchanges on social media can be useful for a variety of applications. For example, users may be interested in filtering out obscenities or indecent content from their social media stream or in filtering out such content for their children. Further, detecting obscene or offensive language in a social media exchange may indicate the discussion of contentious/controversial subjects/content or the presence of hate speech that may be connected to or promoting hate crimes (Watch, 2014). Some sites such as Facebook

SafeSearch Filters

SafeSearch can help you block inappropriate or explicit images from your Google Search results.
The SafeSearch filter isn't 100% accurate.
but it helps you avoid most violent and adult content.

Turn on SafeSearch.   Lock SafeSearch

Figure 1: Google "safe search" setting

allows users to filter out content based on a word list that users provide. Similarly, as shown in Figure 1, popular web search engines, such as Google and Bing, and media sharing sites, such as YouTube, have settings for "safe search" that filters out obscenities and pornographic contents. On way to filter out such desirable content is to maintain a list of obscene words to filter content against. However, the manual construction and maintenance of such lists is arduous. This is due to the fact that list curators may not cover all words, particularly country/culture specific ones (written in local dialects or understood in certain cultures) and users may coin new words or alter the spelling of existing words (ex. by replacing letters with similarly looking characters, such as "0" instead of "O").

Jay and Janschewitz (2008) identified three categories of offensive speech, namely: **Vulgar**, which include explicit and rude sexual references, **Pornographic**, and **Hateful**, which includes offensive remarks concerning peoples race, religion, country, etc. The goal of this work is to detect vulgar and pornographic obscene speech in Arabic social media without the need for manually curating word lists. The detection of offensive language that includes personal attacks, demeaning comments, or hateful language is left for future work. Unlike previous work on obscenity and offensive language detection for different languages, such as

52

Proceedings of the First Workshop on Abusive Language Online, pages 52–56,
Vancouver, Canada, July 30 - August 4, 2017. ©2017 Association for Computational Linguistics

English (Mahmud et al., 2008; Spertus, 2007; Xiang et al., 2012) and German (Ross et al., 2016), very limited previous work for this task was done for Arabic (Abozinadah et al., 2016).

Arabic poses interesting challenges primarily due to the lexical variations of different Arabic dialects. Our approach is concerned with an automated approach to construct of an offensive word list. The approach mines tweets to nominate new obscene words, which can be provided to judges who would either add them to the word list (if obscene) or not. Our approach is based on the intuition that if we can identify users who often use obscene words from a seed word list of obscenities, then by contrasting these users against other users who never use words from the list, we can net additional obscenities. We also introduce two new datasets for this task. The first contains 1,100 manually labeled tweets, and the second contains 32K user comments that the moderators of a popular Arabic news site deemed inappropriate. We are publicly releasing the datasets along with the lexicons we created.

2 Approach

In our approach, we created a set of obscene words to work as our seeding list. We extracted the list from a large set of tweets containing 175 million tweets that we obtained from Twitter during March 2014 using the Twitter streaming API with language filter set to Arabic "lang:ar". We searched the tweets for some patterns that are usually used in offensive communications, such as: .. يا ابن ال..، يا ولاد ال (You, son(s) of, daughter(s) of, .. etc.) along with their variant spellings. The words appearing after these patterns were then collected and manually assessed for being obscene or not. The final list after manual assessment contained obscene 288 words and phrases. Additionally, we added the 127 hashtags that are used to screen pornographic pages in an online tweet aggregator TweetMogaz (Elsawy et al., 2014; Magdy, 2013)). The list can be downloaded from:
`http://alt.qcri.org/~hmubarak/offensive/ObsceneWords.txt`

Next, given our tweet set of 175 million tweets, we obtained a list of Twitter users, aka tweeps, who authored at least 100 tweets along with their tweets. The text of the tweets was cleaned and normalized in the manner described in (Darwish

et al., 2012). This included the normalization of different shapes of hamza, yaa, and taa marbuta, normalization of decorative characters, and proper segmentation of hashtags and URLs. Given the list of tweeps, we divided them into two groups, namely: those who authored tweets that did not include a single obscene word from our aforementioned list (clean group) and those who used at least one of the words from our list at least once (obscene group). Our hypothesis is that those who use at least one of the words in our list are likely to use other obscenities that may not be included in our list. The size of the clean and obscene groups were 166K tweeps, who authored 86M tweets, and 23K tweeps, who authored 16M tweets, respectively.

Given the tweets of the two groups, we computed unigram and bigram counts in both of them. Given these counts, we computed the Log Odds Ratio (LOR) (Forman, 2008) for each word unigram and bigram that appeared at least 10 times. The tweets authored by the clean tweeps are used as a background corpus, and the tweets authored by the obscene tweeps are used as a foreground corpus. The computation of the LOR is as follows:

$$LOR = \log\left[\frac{tp \cdot (pos - tp)}{fp \cdot (neg - fp)}\right]$$

where tp and fp are the counts in the foreground and background corpora respectively, and pos and neg are the tweet counts in the foreground and background corpora respectively. We retained unigrams and bigrams that yielded an LOR equals to infinity which means that they appeared in the foreground corpus only (obscene) but didnt appear in the background corpus (clean), and we added them to our original list of words and phrases. This enhanced the precision, and in future we will consider other ranges of LOR to enhance the recall without affecting the precision. This process can be done iteratively. We performed one iteration and we generated 3,430 word unigrams and bigrams. We refer to list of words generated using this method as the LOR list.

3 Experimental Setup

To measure the effectiveness of our approach, we used intrinsic as well as extrinsic evaluation. For intrinsic evaluation, we randomly selected 100 words (unigrams or bigrams) from the list of generated words with LOR equals to infinity. We marked the words as either obscene or not. Of the 100 words, 59 were found to be obscene.

For extrinsic evaluation, we built a test set for the obscene and offensive language detection that contains 100 highly discussed tweets that each had at least 10 replies. Specifically, we collected the 100 tweets by identifying 10 controversial tweeps from the top tweeps in Egypt, according to `SocialBakers.com`. For each of the tweeps, we randomly selected 10 tweets that have 10 or more comments/replies. In all, we had 100 original tweets plus 1,000 comment/reply tweets – 1,100 tweets all together. For the tweets, we submitted each tweet along with its context (thread of replies) to `CrowdFlower.com` to be judged by 3 different annotators from Egypt. The annotators could mark the tweets as: obscene, offensive (but not obscene), or clean. Figure 1 shows three tweets and the their output judgments. Of the judged tweets, the percentages of obscene, offensive (but not obscene), and clean tweets were 19.1%, 40.3%, and 40.6% respectively. The average inter-annotator agreement was 85%. In the context of this paper, we are only considering obscene tweets in our evaluation. Offensive tweets are left for future work. The 1,100 annotated tweets can be downloaded from `http://alt.qcri.org/~hmubarak/offensive/TweetClassification-Summary.xlsx`. Given the annotated test set and our list of obscene words, we automatically tagged each tweet in the test set as obscene if it contained a word in the list. We experimented with several lists namely: the SeedWords list, the LOR list (word unigrams only), the LOR list (word bigrams only), combined LOR (unigrams only) + SeedWords lists, and combined LOR (bigrams only) + SeedWords lists. Table 1 shows the results (Precision, Recall, and F1) using the different lists. As can be seen in the results, using word unigrams is superior to using word bigrams. The results suggests that the initial seed word list yields high precision with relatively low recall. Combining SeedWords and LOR (unigram) lists yielded slightly improved recall, while maintaining the precision.

Using list-based methods to detect abusive language is proved to be good and robust (Sood et al., 2012b; Chen et al., 2012a). However, this approach is limited by its reliance on lists. This is shown also in our results in the form of high precision and low recall. Chen et al. (Chen et al.,

2012a) suggest using lexical and syntactical features along with automatically generated black lists. We plan to explore such features to account for the complexities and richness of Arabic and its dialects. We also plan to look at morphological features to account for the rich morphology of Arabic. Breaking Arabic words into constituent clitics can be useful in generating appropriate morphological features.

List	P	R	F1
SeedWords (SW)	0.97	0.43	0.59
SW + LOR (unigrams)	0.97	0.44	**0.60**
SW + LOR (bigrams)	0.89	**0.45**	0.60
LOR (unigrams)	**0.98**	0.41	0.58
LOR (bigrams)	0.89	0.44	0.59

Table 1: Extrinsic evaluation results

4 Aljazeera Deleted Comments

In the interest of the research community, we are also releasing a dataset of 32K deleted comments from `Aljazeera.net`[1]. `Aljazeera.net`, a popular Arabic news channel, moderates all the comments that appear on their site. According to the site's "Community Rules and Guidelines" (`http://www.aljazeera.com/aboutus/2011/01/201111681520872288.html`), a user comment is not accepted if it is a personal attack, racist, sexist, or otherwise offensive, inciting violence, non-relevant, advertising, etc.

Initially we obtained a corpus of 400K comments on approximately 10K articles that cover many gneres such as politics, economy, society, and science. From these comments, we selected 32K comments whose lengths are between 3 and 200 characters to ease subsequent annotation. We annotated the selected comments using CrowdFlower, where three annotators were asked to classify comments as obscene, offensive, or clean. The annotators were also given article titles as we did not have the entire thread of comments. The breakdown of the annotation is as follows: 2% obscene, 79% offensive, and 19% clean. The inter-annotator agreement was 87%. Low percentage of obscene comments may be attributed to the fact that

---

[1] We would like to thank Aljazeera for courteously agreeing to release the data

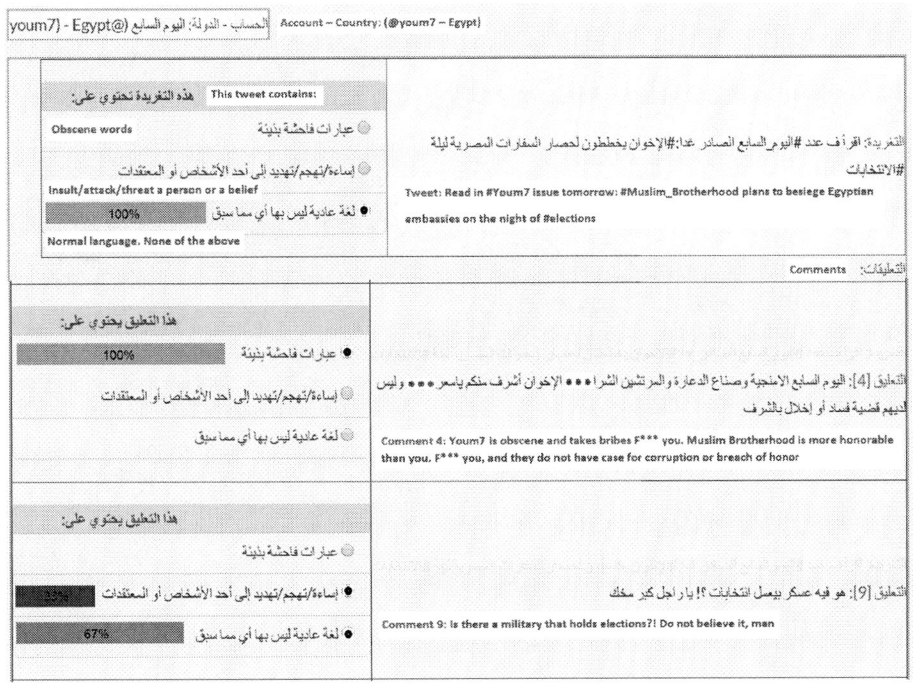

Figure 2: CrowdFlower judgment screen (translations are added for clarification)

users know in advance that their comments on news agencies are subject to moderation, which is not the case when they post freely on social media.

The comments are written in Modern Standard Arabic (MSA) and different dialects. Examples of different types of offensive comments are shown in Table 2. We plan to use this corpus to detect offensive language for attacking people and hate speech. The data can be downloaded from: `http://alt.qcri.org/~hmubarak/offensive/AJCommentsClassification-CF.xlsx`

5 Conclusion and Future Work

In this paper we present an automated method to create and expand a list of obscene words. We also introduce a new test set for the task, which we plan to make publicly available in addition to the list of obscene words and a large corpus of annotated user comments for obscene and offensive language detection.

For future work, we plan to enhance the recall by applying different algorithms, and to expand the test set to include tweets from multiple regions (Egypt, Gulf, Levant, Maghreb, and Iraq) to cover different dialects and cultures. Further, the work in this paper focused on identifying obscene tweets, and we plan to expand it to cover offensive language and hate speech. Additionally, we plan to study different levels of morphological and syntactic analysis, and using character n-grams as suggested by (Waseem, 2016) in addition to unigrams and bigrams to deal with the rich morphology of Arabic and its dialects. Hopefully, morphological processing can lead to improved recall.

Comment	Type
كذاب ابن ك** ابن ق*** Liar, son of the ***	Obscene
الارهابى انت و اجدادك You and grandparents are terrorists	Attack
كلب وجب قتله A dog who must be killed	Violence
لأن العرب عبيد وسيبقون كذلك Arabs are slaves and will remain	Racism
عيب تحكمنا واحدة ست Shameful to be ruled by a woman	Sexism

Table 2: Examples of offensive user comments

References

Ehab A Abozinadah, Jr Jones, and H James. 2016. Improved microblog classification for detecting abusive arabic twitter accounts. In *International Journal of Data Mining and Knowledge Management Process*. IJDKP.

Ying Chen, Yilu Zhou, Sencun Zhu, and Xu Heng. 2012a. Detecting offensive language in social media to protect adolescent online safety. In *In Privacy, Security, Risk and Trust (PASSAT), 2012 International Conference on and 2012 International Conference on Social Computing (SocialCom)*. IEEE, pages 71–80.

Kareem Darwish, Walid Magdy, and Ahmed Mourad. 2012. Language processing for arabic microblog retrieval. In *Proceedings of the 21st ACM international conference on Information and knowledge management*. ACM, pages 2427–2430.

Eslam Elsawy, Moamen Mokhtar, and Walid Magdy. 2014. Tweetmogaz v2: Identifying news stories in social media. In *Proceedings of the 23rd ACM International Conference on Conference on Information and Knowledge Management*. ACM.

George Forman. 2008. Bns feature scaling: an improved representation over tfidf for svm text classification. In *In Proceedings of the 17th ACM conference on Information and knowledge management*. ACM.

Timothy Jay and Kristin Janschewitz. 2008. The pragmatics of swearing. In *Journal of Politeness Research. Language, Behaviour, Culture 4, no. 2.*

Walid Magdy. 2013. Tweetmogaz: a news portal of tweets. In *In Proceedings of the 36th international ACM SIGIR conference on Research and development in information retrieval*. ACM.

Altaf Mahmud, Kazi Zubair Ahmed, and Mumit Khan. 2008. Detecting flames and insults in text. In *In Proceedings of the Sixth International Conference on Natural Language Processing.*

Björn Ross, Michael Rist, Guillermo Carbonell, Benjamin Cabrera, Nils Kurowsky, and Michael Wojatzki. 2016. Measuring the Reliability of Hate Speech Annotations: The Case of the European Refugee Crisis. In Michael Beißwenger, Michael Wojatzki, and Torsten Zesch, editors, *Proceedings of NLP4CMC III: 3rd Workshop on Natural Language Processing for Computer-Mediated Communication*. Bochum, volume 17 of *Bochumer Linguistische Arbeitsberichte*, pages 6–9.

Sara Sood, Judd Antin, and Elizabeth Churchill. 2012b. Using crowdsourcing to improve profanity detection. In *In AAAI Spring Symposium: Wisdom of the Crowd, volume SS-12-06 of AAAI Technical Report*. AAAI.

Ellen Spertus. 2007. Smokey: Automatic recognition of hostile messages. In *In Proceedings of the Ninth Conference on Innovative Applications of Artificial Intelligence.*

Zeerak Waseem. 2016. Are you a racist or am i seeing things? annotator influence on hate speech detection on twitter. In *Proceedings of the First Workshop on NLP and Computational Social Science*. Association for Computational Linguistics, Austin, Texas, pages 138–142. http://aclweb.org/anthology/W16-5618.

Hate Speech Watch. 2014. Hate crimes: Consequences of hate speech. In *http://www.nohatespeechmovement. org/hate-speech-watch/focus/ consequences-of-hate-speech.*

Guang Xiang, Bin Fan, Ling Wang, Jason Hong, and Carolyn Rose. 2012. Detecting offensive tweets via topical feature discovery over a large scale twitter corpus. In *In Proceedings of the 21st ACM international conference on Information and knowledge management*. ACM.

Vectors for Counterspeech on Twitter

Lucas Wright[4], Derek Ruths[2], Kelly P Dillon[3], Haji Mohammad Saleem[2], and Susan Benesch[1,4]

[1]Berkman Klein Center for Internet and Society, Harvard University, Massachusetts
sbenesch@cyber.law.harvard.edu
[2]School of Computer Science, McGill University, Montreal
[3]Department of Communication, Wittenberg University, Ohio
[4]Dangerous Speech Project, Washington DC

Abstract

A study of conversations on Twitter found that some arguments between strangers led to favorable change in discourse and even in attitudes. The authors propose that such exchanges can be usefully distinguished according to whether individuals or groups take part on each side, since the opportunity for a constructive exchange of views seems to vary accordingly.

1 Introduction

As abusive language proliferates online, researchers struggle to define it, to detect it reliably, and to find the best ways to diminish it. 'Counterspeech' is gaining currency as a grassroots alternative to takedown, for diminishing abuse and hatred online. Counterspeech - which we define as a direct response to hateful or harmful speech - can be practiced by almost anyone, requiring neither law nor institutions. In this paper, we report counterspeech that apparently had a favorable effect on people to whom it responded. We also offer distinctions that may be useful for more reliable detection of both counterspeech and of abusive language - and for designing more effective counterspeech.

Many authors observe, as we do, that counterspeech varies greatly, in tone and in communicative strategies, and several papers offer categories of counterspeech, providing useful frameworks for observation and further study (Bartlett & Krasodomski-Jones, 2015; Briggs & Feve, 2013; Saltman & Russell, 2014). Some authors use the term 'counterspeech' expansively, however, to refer to any content that counters or contradicts hateful or extremist content - not necessarily in response to any particular speech act. A much broader category than ours, this could include

forms of education, propaganda, and public information.

Our findings on counterspeech are preliminary, yet novel. The idea that 'more speech' is a remedy for harmful speech has become widely accepted since U.S. Supreme Court Justice Louis Brandeis propounded it in 1927[1] – without supporting data. We found counterspeech on Twitter[2] that, to our surprise, was followed by apologies or other signs of favorable impact on the account to which the counterspeech responded. Our findings are qualitative, since reliable quantitative detection of hateful speech or counterspeech is a puzzle yet to be fully solved due to the great variations in language employed, though we have made some progress on detection (Saleem, Dillon, Benesch, & Ruths, 2016). It is even more difficult to detect automatically 'successful counterspeech,' or counterspeech that has a favorable impact on an interlocutor. Therefore, although we used automated collection methods, most of the cases reported here were found in news reports and other literature.

Here we focus on a central idea: that just as "abusive language" is a very broad category, so is counterspeech, and in both cases, the nature and impact of the language varies with the number of people involved: whether it is produced by an

---

[1] Justice Brandeis asserted in his concurring opinion in Whitney v California that to expose "falsehood and fallacies" and to "avert the evil," "the remedy is more speech, not enforced silence" (Whitney v California, 1927, U.S. Supreme Court, p. 377)
[2] We first observed successful counterspeech on Twitter in Kenya in 2013, during a project to study hateful and dangerous speech online during the months leading to a presidential election. See iHub Research (2013). Subsequently, we worked with Twitter staff to find other examples of successful counterspeech, including in response to the selection of Nina Davuluri as Miss America 2014, and in response to homophobia on Twitter in France.

Proceedings of the First Workshop on Abusive Language Online, pages 57–62,
Vancouver, Canada, July 30 - August 4, 2017. ©2017 Association for Computational Linguistics

individual or a group, and whether it is directed at an individual or a group. Thus there are four "vectors" in each of which counterspeech functions quite differently, as abusive speech also does: one-to-one exchanges, many-to-one, one-to-many, and many-to-many. We also extrapolated a set of counterspeech communicative strategies from our data; those will be reported separately.

Hate speech and abusive speech online have been studied by multiple authors[3] yet they are still contested terms (Benesch, 2014; Mendel, 2012). Since it can be difficult to know a speaker's state of mind or intent, especially from a tweet, we use the term "hateful speech" to identify, and focus on, an expression of hate.

2 Challenges to detection of counterspeech

Computational approaches are required in order to study and engage counterspeech efforts at scale. The most fundamental computational capability we sought is automated detection of counterspeech (and the original posts to which the counterspeech responded).

To our knowledge, virtually no work has been published on the detection of counterspeech. Despite being entirely open, the typology outlined here offers several insights into the complexity of the detection problem and promising ways of understanding the relative hardness of different sub problems. Specifically, we have identified that counterspeech can involve a broad range of audience sizes - from single counterspeakers to whole communities. Further, we find that a single counterspeech act can exhibit a number of different communicative strategies including humor, emotional appeals, multi-stage dialog, and overt verbal attack itself. These two factors have implications for the difficulty of the detection task.

2.1 Forms of counterspeech acts

Counterspeech acts can assume many forms. Crucially, in our review of known counterspeech acts, we have observed no indication that these forms are templated - meaning that any two arbitrary counterspeech acts will not share language, syntax, or style. This contrasts, for example, with event references, conversations, mentions of politicians, and other tweet acts that carry more regu-

lar structure. The implication of this is that before automated methods can be developed, we require a better understanding of the (potentially quite subtle) structures that counterspeech acts have in common. Notably, a viable alternative to this would be using deep learning techniques, which would learn the relevant structures themselves. To use such approaches, we require very large datasets of known counterspeech acts in order to train a classifier.

2.2 Number of speakers

Given the sheer number of tweets generated each day, detection of specific tweet sets can become harder as the size of that set shrinks. This is particular true of tweet sets that lack easy-to-identify structural indicators (e.g., the use of a shared hashtag). As a result, counterspeech involving only one or a few counterspeakers is quite hard to identify: not only will there be few tweets in an entire 'conversation,' but the tweets may lack a strong signal that a classifier can use. On the other hand, counterspeech acts involving many users may adopt Twitter conventions such as mentions, retweets, and hashtags that could act as strong signals for a classifier.

Ultimately, it seems that some counterspeech acts and events will be easier to detect than others. While focusing on these easier sub problems presents a promising direction for future work, we - as a community - must remain aware that these classifiers will offer an incomplete picture of the broader counterspeech phenomenon on Twitter. Future studies should appropriately contextualize their findings and advances by also exploring the kinds of counterspeech their classifiers *cannot* detect.

3 Methods

As mentioned earlier, automatic detection of counterspeech is currently an unsolved problem. This made collecting data for our analysis a non-trivial task. Primarily, we closely followed developing news stories on controversial topics searched Twitter for discussion of such topics, and carried out informal surveys, searching for what we nicknamed "golden conversations" - three step exchanges between at least two accounts, in which hateful speech was met by counterspeech, followed by a sign of favorable impact on the first account or accounts. The last step could be an

---

[3] Cyberbullying also has an extensive literature, which is outside the scope of this project.

apology, a recanting, or a deleted tweet or account (the latter two were ambiguous signals, however).

We also collected our own sample of Twitter data with trending and relevant hashtags on the controversial topics, using Twitter streaming and search APIs to aggregate public tweets while the selected hashtags were still being used, sometimes for conversations. We then qualitatively analyzed the collected tweets and coded them as hateful speech or counter speech. In some cases, we used metadata from the collected tweets to find specific conversations on Twitter, to gain a better understanding of how a hashtag was used in context.

4 Vectors

We observed significant distinctions in counterspeech conversations, according to the number of participants in each stage or side. Harassment of an individual by a group of people, for example, is very different in nature and likely consequences, from hatred directed by one person against an entire racial or ethnic group.

Likewise, responses to an individual can be received very differently than responses to groups. Identifying numerous models for responses will help the chances of successful attempts, especially in media, including online (Pajares, Prestin, Chen, & Nabi, 2009, p. 293-297). These vectors can be helpful for individuals who witness abusive language, but are unsure how to respond. For example, the threshold to assume the responsibility to respond one-to-many may be too high, and thus a one-to-one response can be a more attractive or feasible counterspeech strategy.

4.1 One-to-one

Some of the most striking cases in which counterspeech seems to convince a person to change discourse are conversations between (only) two people. Where someone seems firmly committed not only to hateful ideology but to declaring it publicly, we would not expect counterspeech to sway that person. Yet in some cases, it apparently has – and has even helped to bring about lasting change in beliefs, not only speech. In these cases, we observe counterspeech strategies including: an empathic and/or kind tone, use of images, and use of humor. This counterspeech usually labels the content as hateful or racist, not its author.

A conversation in which nearly all of these strategies were used took place on January 19,

2015 – Martin Luther King (MLK) Jr. Day in the United States. It began with this tweet:

"In honor of MLK day today, I'm taking a vow to use the word "nigger" as many times as possible and in the most inappropriate times"

A writer and activist[4] discovered the tweet and responded with anti-hatred quotes from King, one after another. The first tweeter replied with a torrent of racist messages. The activist made an empathetic reference to the mother of the first tweeter. After several more exchanges, he abruptly wrote to the woman he had been attacking viciously, "you're so nice and I'm so sorry." (Payne, 2015).

Another striking example of one-to-one counterspeech is the case of Megan Phelps-Roper, who was fully convinced of the extreme homophobic tenets of the Westboro Baptist Church, in which she was raised - until she started a Twitter account to spread the views of the church. On Twitter she encountered people who challenged her views and engaged her in other ways, including humor and suggestions for music she might enjoy. Extended online conversations with two of them completely changed Phelps-Roper's views, by her own account. She ended up leaving the church. This case is described in detail by Adrian Chen (2015).

It is no surprise that deep and/or lasting change in discourse and beliefs - difficult to achieve by any means, online or offline - can take many tweets. Another distinguishing feature of one-to-one conversations is that, even on Twitter, they are not always public, since a message sent through Twitter's "direct message" feature is visible only to the sender and the receiver. In Megan Phelps-Roper's case, she and her new interlocutors also used one-to-one messaging apps other than Twitter.

In a less public online context, people may feel less guarded and therefore more open to dissenting views. On the other hand, if their conversations are invisible to the larger 'audience,' the audience can neither join in nor be favorably influenced by the conversation, except in rare cases when it is described elsewhere, as in Chen's article (2015).

---

[4] We've erred on the side of not revealing the identities of people in the cases we describe in order to protect them and to preserve their privacy. We've made exceptions, however, for public figures and/or those who have already chosen to discuss the case publicly.

4.2 One-to-Many

Some Twitter users have taken it upon themselves to try to change way in which others express themselves publicly on Twitter, by searching for the use of certain terms or phrases and rebuking those who use them. This sort of activist effort can be described as one-to-many counterspeech, though we note that it can also be understood as many one-to-one exchanges.

In one example, Dawud Walid, an African-American Muslim man, searched for variations of the word 'abeed' which means 'slave' and was used in tweets to refer to black people. He sent an op-ed he had written, entitled "Fellow humans are not abeed," to Twitter users who had tweeted the term. He received a variety of responses, from apologies and promises not to use the word again, to a tweet that repeated the word as many times as possible in 140 characters (Walid, 2013). Other similar efforts are the accounts @YesYoureRacist and @YesYoureSexist, which retweeted examples of racist and sexist content (often e.g. beginning with the phrase "I'm not racist, but…").

In each of these cases, counterspeech is met with a range of responses, from apologies to angry argument. In another example of one-to-many counterspeech, some users deliberately tweet on a hashtag with which they disagree, such as #stopislam, to reach people who agree with it.

4.3 Many-to-One

In some cases, news of an objectionable tweet (or hashtag) goes viral, and many Twitter users – sometimes thousands – join in counterspeech. This can be salutary where it catches enough of the attention of the original speaker to be successful but not harassing, as in the case of a user who tweeted his outrage that Nina Davuluri (whom he erroneously identified as an Arab) had been chosen as Miss America 2014. After receiving tweets that variously corrected his error and called him a racist, he first responded "I didn't realize it would explode like that #unreal" and then tweeted at Davuluri, apologizing. The furor died down quickly, and the user is still on Twitter, at this writing.

In other cases, however, huge numbers of angry Twitter users have overwhelmed others, rising to the level of harassment. Original speakers hastily delete tweets or even their accounts, but even that can be an insufficient refuge in the face of, for example, counterspeakers who contact their em-ployers, demanding that they be fired for tweets or posts. This has indeed led to firing in several cases (Ronson, 2015).

The blog "Racists Getting Fired" made a practice of punishing people who posted racist content by contacting their employers and, similarly, demanding that they be fired (McDonald, 2014). Such responses are no doubt successful at changing the online speech of their targets, but may only harden the hateful convictions of those targets, and constitute online mob justice.

4.4 Many-to-Many

Conversations among large numbers of people online are of interest, not least because of the impressive scale on which they often take place. We observed counterspeech surging when strangers met and argued online, often because they were interested in the same offline event. On Twitter, such conversations generally form around hashtags.

Hashtags can themselves constitute hateful and abusive language – or counterspeech – and they often gather or inspire 'many-to-many' conversations. The use of "a hashtag can be seen as an explicit attempt to address an imagined community of users… as each user participating in a hashtag conversation acts potentially as a bridge between the hashtag community and members of their own follower network" (Bruns & Burgess, 2012, p. 804). Often, one hashtag represents one general view or normative group, such as #BlackLivesMatter, with others represent opposing or dissenting views, such as #BlueLivesMatter (which refers to police for their blue uniforms), or #AllLivesMatter.

One of the most vitriolic hashtags we found, #KillAllMuslims, trended in the immediate aftermath of the Charlie Hebdo massacre of January 2015 - and then was quickly taken over by counterspeakers expressing their dismay that it existed. One counterspeech tweet that uses the hashtag was retweeted more 10,000 times: "Not muslim but never thought about this b4 #CharlieHebdo #KillAllMuslims #Muslims pic.twitter.com/ LL1pkPk6uk." The link was to an image of visual similarities among religious traditions, e.g. a Catholic nun in a habit and a Muslim woman in hijab.

Notably, trending hashtags can be more widely and quickly disseminated than any tweet. When #KillAllMuslims trended, for example, thousands of people on Twitter could not help but notice two things: the hashtag called for mass murder or genocide, and thousands of people had typed it and sent it.

The fact that a hashtag is trending can also have a major impact on how Twitter users perceive norms on the platform. It is dismaying when hateful hashtags trend, and reassuring when counterspeech does. The hashtag #YouAintNoMuslimBruv, for example, trended after a bystander yelled the same phrase at a would-be attacker in London in December 2015.

5   Further Research

A worthy topic for further study would be the norm-influencing capacity of hashtags around public events and controversies, for two reasons: they draw large numbers of people, and those people are often of strikingly different views.

Without such a catalyst, people of very different convictions are less likely to exchange them since they spend most of their time in like-minded silos, reading content with which they mainly agree (Anderson & Raine, 2010, p. 18; Conover et al., 2011; Lewandowsky et al., 2012, p. 111; Zuckerman, 2013). Certain 'places' online, including Twitter accounts that draw devoted fans and ardent critics, also draw strikingly different readers or audiences, who are thus exposed to one another's ideas. This famously leads to conflict; however in some cases there are constructive exchanges which are worth finding and studying.

Acknowledgments

We thank Public Safety Canada's Kanishka Project for funding the research described here, and the John D. and Catherine T. MacArthur Foundation for supporting the Dangerous Speech Project.

References

Janna Quitney Anderson and Lee Rainie. 2010, July 2. The future of social relations. *Pew Research Center's Internet & American Life Project*, Washington, DC. http://www.pewinternet.org/files/old-media/Files/Reports/2010/PIP_Future_of_Internet_%202010_social_relations.pdf.

Jamie Bartlett and Alex Krasodomski-Jones. 2015. Counter-speech: Examining content that challenges extremism online. *Demos*. https://www.demos.co.uk/wp-content/uploads/2015/10/Counter-speech.pdf

Susan Benesch. 2014. Defining and diminishing hate speech. In *Freedom from hate: State of the world's minorities and indigenous peoples 2014*. Minority Rights International, pages 18-25. http://minorityrights.org/wp-content/uploads/old-site-downloads/mrg-state-of-the-worlds-minorities-2014-chapter02.pdf.

Rachel Briggs and Sebastien Feve. 2013. Review of programs to counter narratives of violent extremism. *Institute of Strategic Dialogue*. https://www.counterextremism.org/download_file/117/134/444/

Axel Bruns and Jean E. Burgess. 2011. The use of Twitter hashtags in the formation of ad hoc publics. In *Proceedings of the 6th European Consortium for Political Research (ECPR) General Conference 2011*, University of Iceland, Reykjavik. http://eprints.qut.edu.au/46515/

Adrian Chen. 2015, November 23. Unfollow: How a prized daughter of the Westboro Baptist Church came to question its beliefs. *New Yorker*. http://www.newyorker.com/magazine/2015/11/23/conversion-via-twitter-westboro-baptist-church-megan-phelps-roper

Michael D. Conover, Jacob Ratkiewicz, Matthew Francisco, Bruno Goncalves, Filippo Menczer, and Alessandro Flammini. 2011. Political Polarization on Twitter. In *Proceedings of the Fifth International AAAI Conference on Weblogs and Social Media*, pages 89-96. https://www.aaai.org/ocs/index.php/ICWSM/ICWSM11/paper/view/2847

iHub Research. 2013. Umati Final Report, Sept. 2012 –May 2013. http://dangerousspeech.org/umati-final-report/

Stephan Lewandowsky, Ullrich K. H. Ecker, Colleen M. Seifert, Norbert Schwarz, and John Cook. 2012. Misinformation and its correction: Continued influence and successful debiasing. *Psychological Science in the Public Interest, 13(3)*, 106-131. https://doi.org/10.1177/1529100612451018

Soraya Nadia McDonald. 2014, December 2. 'Racists Getting Fired' exposes weaknesses of Internet vigilantism, no matter how well-intentioned. *The Washington Post*. https://www.washingtonpost.com/news/morning-mix/wp/2014/12/02/racists-getting-fired-exposes-weaknesses-of-internet-vigilantism-no-matter-how-well-intentioned/.

Toby Mendel. 2014. Does international law provide for consistent rules on hate speech? *International Journal of Constitutional Law*, 12(3):417-429. https://doi.org/10.1093/icon/mou053.

Steven Payne. 2015, January 20. An amazing woman fields a troll on MLK Day and it was nothing short of inspirational. http://www.dailykos.com/story/2015/1/20/1359055/-An-amazing-woman-feeds-a-troll-on-MLK-Day-and-it-was-nothing-short-of-inspirational.

Jon Ronson. 2015, February 12. How one stupid tweet blew up Justine Sacco's life. *The New York Times.* http://www.nytimes.com/2015/02/15/magazine/how-one-stupid-tweet-ruined-justine-saccos-life.html.

Haji Mohammed Saleem, Kelly P. Dillon, Susan Benesch, and Derek Ruths. 2016. A Web of Hate: Tackling hateful speech in online social spaces. In *Proceedings of the First Workshop on Text Analytics for Cybersecurity and Online Safety.* European Language Resource Association. http://www.tacos.org/node/17.

Erin Saltman and Jonathan Russell. 2014. The role of Prevent in countering online extremism. *The Quilliam Foundation.* http://preventviolentextremism.info/sites/default/files/White%20Paper%20–%20The%20Role%20of%20Prevent%20in%20Countering%20Online%20Extremism%20.pdf

Dawud Walid. 2013, November 24. Responses to my calling out the term 'abeed'. https:// dawud-walid.wordpress.com/2013/11/24/responses-to-my-calling-out-the-term-abeed/.

Ethan Zuckerman. 2013. Digital cosmopolitans: Why we think the Internet connects us, why it doesn't, and how to rewire it. WW Norton & Company.

Detecting Nastiness in Social Media

**Niloofar Safi Samghabadi[♠], Suraj Maharjan[♠], Alan Sprague[♣],
Raquel Diaz-Sprague[♣], Thamar Solorio[♠]**
[♠]Department of Computer Science, University of Houston
[♣]Department of Computer & Information Sciences, University of Alabama at Birmingham
nsafisamghabadi@uh.edu, smaharjan2@uh.edu,
sprague@cis.uab.edu, diazspra@uab.edu, tsolorio@uh.edu

Abstract

Although social media has made it easy for people to connect on a virtually unlimited basis, it has also opened doors to people who misuse it to undermine, harass, humiliate, threaten and bully others. There is a lack of adequate resources to detect and hinder its occurrence. In this paper, we present our initial NLP approach to detect invective posts as a first step to eventually detect and deter cyberbullying. We crawl data containing profanities and then determine whether or not it contains invective. Annotations on this data are improved iteratively by in-lab annotations and crowdsourcing. We pursue different NLP approaches containing various typical and some newer techniques to distinguish the use of swear words in a neutral way from those instances in which they are used in an insulting way. We also show that this model not only works for our data set, but also can be successfully applied to different data sets.

1 Introduction

As the internet has become the preferred means of communication worldwide[1], it has introduced new benefits as well as new dangers. One of the most unfortunate effects of online interconnectedness is Cyberbullying – defined as the deliberate use of information/communication technologies (ICT's) to cause harm to people by causing a loss of both self-esteem and the esteem of their friendship circles (Patchin and Hinduja, 2010). The groups most affected by this phenomenon are teens and pre-teens (Livingstone et al., 2010).

According to a High School Youth Risk Behavior Survey, 14.8% of students surveyed nationwide in the United States (US) reported being bullied electronically (nobullying.com, 2015). Another research done by the Cyberbullying Research Center (Patchin, 2015) from 2007 to 2015 shows that on average, 26.3% of middle and high school students from across the United States have been victims of cyberbullying at some point in their lives. Also, on average, about 16% of the students have admitted that they have cyberbullied others at some point in their lives. Studies have shown that cyberbullying victims face social, emotional, physiological and psychological disorders that lead them to harm themselves (Xu et al. (2012)).

In this research we perform the initial step towards detecting invective in online posts from social media sites used by teens, as we believe it can be the starting point of cyberbullying events. We first create a data set that includes highly negative posts from ask.fm. ask.fm is a semi-anonymous social network, where anyone can post a question to any other user, and may choose to do so anonymously. Given that people tend to engage in cyberbullying behavior under the cover of anonymity (Sticca and Perren, 2013), the anonymity option in ask.fm, as in other social media platforms, allows attackers the power to freely harass users by flooding their pages with profanity-laden questions and comments. Seeing a lot of vile messages in one's profile page often disturbs the user. Several teen suicides have been attributed to cyberbullying in ask.fm (Healy, 2014; Shute, 2013). This phenomenon motivated us to crawl a number of ask.fm accounts and to analyze them manually to ascertain how cyberbullying is carried out in this particular site. We learned that victims have their profile page flooded with abusive posts. Then from identifying victims of cyberbullying, we switched to looking for word patterns

---

[1]The New Era of Communication Among Americans
http://www.gallup.com/poll/179288/new-era-communication-americans.aspx

Proceedings of the First Workshop on Abusive Language Online, pages 63–72,
Vancouver, Canada, July 30 - August 4, 2017. ©2017 Association for Computational Linguistics

that make a post abusive. Since, abusive posts are rare compared to the rest of online posts, in order to ensure that we would obtain enough invective posts, we decided to focus exclusively on posts that contain profanity. This is analogous to the method used in data collection by Xu et al. (2012); they limited their Twitter data to tweets containing the words *bully, bullied, bullying.*

The main contributions of this paper are as follows: We create a new resource to investigate negative posts in a social media platform used predominantly by teens, and make our data set public. The most noticeable difference of our data set with previous similar corpora is that it provides a generalized view of invective posts, which is not biased towards a specific topic or target group. In our data, each post is judged by three different annotators. Then we perform experiments with both typical features (e.g. linguistic, sentiment and domain related) and newer features (e.g. embedding and topic modeling), and combinations of these features to automatically identify potential invective posts. We also show the robustness of our model by evaluating it on different data sets (Wikipedia Abusive Language Data Set, and Kaggle). Finally, we do an analysis of bad word distributions in our data that, among other things, reflects a sexualized teen culture.

2   Related Research

Since our research goal is to detect nastiness in social media as an initial step to detect cyberbullying, we analyze previous works focusing on cyberbullying detection. Researchers (Macbeth et al., 2013; Lieberman et al., 2011) have reported that cyberbullying posts are contextual, personalized and creative, which make them harder to detect than detecting spam. Even without using bad words, the post can be hostile to the receiver. On the other hand, the use of negative words does not necessarily have a cyberbullying effect (alKhateeb and Epiphaniou, 2016). Researchers have used different approaches to find cyberbullying traces.

Dinakar et al. (2012) concentrate on sexuality, race and culture, and intelligence as the primary categories related to cyberbullying. Then, they construct a common sense knowledge base - BullySpace - with knowledge about bullying situations and a wide range of everyday life topics. The overall success of this experiment is 66.7%

accuracy for detecting cyberbullying in YouTube comments. Xu et al. (2012) identify several key problems in using the social media data sources to study bullying and formulate them as NLP tasks. In one of their approaches, they use latent topic modeling to analyze the topics people commonly talk about in bullying comments, however they find most topics were hard to interpret. Van Hee et al. (2015) study ask.fm Dutch posts, and develop a new scheme for cyberbullying annotation based on the presence and severity of cyberbullying, the role of the post's author, and a number of fine-grained categories associated with cyberbullying. They use the same two class classification tasks as the previous studies to automatically detect cyberbullying posts and achieve an F-score of 55.39%. Kansara and Shekokar (2015) combine text and image analysis techniques and propose a framework for detecting potential cyberbullying threats that analyze texts and images using a bag of words and a bag of visual word models respectively.

There is also some research in the field of online harassment and hate speech detection. Yin et al. (2009) apply a supervised machine learning approach to the automatic detection of online harassment. They combine content, sentiment, and contextual features and achieve an F-score of 44%. Nobata et al. (2016) use data gathered from Yahoo! Finance and News, then present a hate speech detection framework using n-gram, linguistic, syntactic and distributional semantic features and get an F-score of 81% for a combination of all features.

In this study, we present a data set containing question-answer pairs from ask.fm, which are labeled as positive (neutral), or negative (invective). Our data is conversational data from teenagers. We also have metadata containing information about the users that eventually can help us to focus on users who are being bullied with frequent profanity and also in analyzing the patterns used by attackers. Moreover, compared to previous work, we apply a wider range of different types of typical and newer NLP features, and their combinations to improve the classification performance. Following this approach, we reach F-scores of 59% for identifying invective posts in our own data set. Applying our classification model on Kaggle and Wikipedia data (we will introduce them later) shows that our method is robust and applicable to other data. We also do an analysis of bad word distribution in our data set that shows that most of these bad words are often used in a casual way, so detecting cases in which there are potential invective requires careful feature engineering.

3 Data Collection and Annotation

Since most of the abusive posts we observed on our small scale study contained profanities, we decided to analyze the occurrence of bad words in a random collection of social media data. We crawled about 586K question-answer pairs from 1,954 random users in ask.fm from 28th January - 14th February, 2015. We limited crawling to posts in English by determining the percentage of English words ($\geq 70\%$) in the user's first page with an English dictionary (pyenchant [2]).

To create our bad words list, we compiled a list from Google's bad words list [3] and words listed in (Hosseinmardi et al., 2014). Based on frequency of use of each bad word in the list, we shortlisted some of them and their morphological variations and slang. We then looked at a small sample of data and filtered all posts containing any of these bad words. The resulting data set contains about 350 question-answer pairs. This small portion of data was divided among 5 different annotators for two-way annotation and disagreements were resolved by a third annotator. From these annotations, we computed the negative use rate (NUR) of each bad word (w_i). Equation 1 defines NUR. $Count(PI, w_i)$ and $Count(PN, w_i)$ are the counts of posts containing word w_i tagged as *invective* and *neutral* respectively.

$$NUR(w_i) = \frac{Count(PI, w_i)}{Count(PI, w_i) + Count(PN, w_i)} \tag{1}$$

According to NUR, we ranked the list of foul words, and removed words which were below the threshold (0.05). The final list includes the words *f*ck, a*s, sh*t, die, kill, h*e, as**ole, s*ck, n**ger, stfu, b*tch,* and *cut*. We called this small set of annotated data as "gold data" and use it for annotating a larger sample of data via Crowd-Flower [4].

---

[2]http://pythonhosted.org/pyenchant/
[3]https://code.google.com/p/badwordslist/downloads/detail?name=badwords.txt
[4]http://www.crowdflower.com/

3.1 Crowdsourcing Annotations

With our small gold annotated data, we started a crowdsourcing task of annotating around 600 question-answer pairs in CrowdFlower. We provided a simple annotation guideline for contributors with some positive and negative examples to ease their task. Each question-answer pair was annotated by three different contributors. Figure 1 shows the interface we designed for the task.

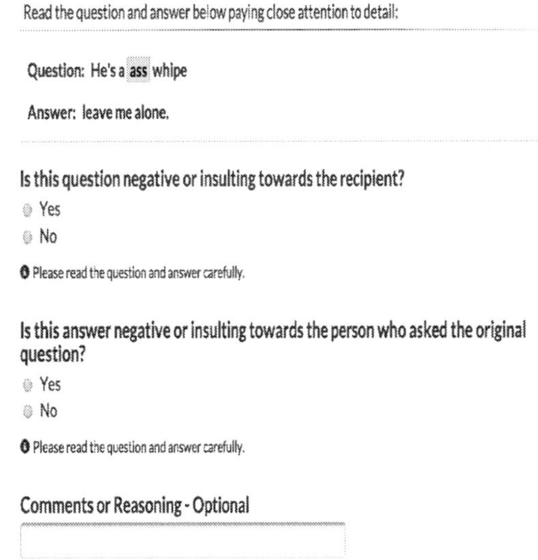

Figure 1: CrowdFlower interface to contributors

For ensuring high quality of the data, the same data was reviewed and annotated by 4 in-lab annotators using a two way annotation scheme. Initially, we found that the inter-annotator agreement was low. Hence, we changed the annotation guideline until the contributors and our internal annotators had reasonable agreement. We learned that although the task may seem simple, it may not so for the external contributors. Thus, it is necessary to iterate the process several times to ensure high quality data. Then, from the original set containing our gold data and extra 600 labeled pairs, we labeled more data with a combination of in-lab and crowdflower annotations into two classes: invective and neutral. Eventually, with this iterative process we annotated around 5,600 question and answer pairs. The average in-lab inter annotator agreement kappa score is 0.453. Table 1 shows the final data distribution. The data can be accessed via our website [5].

---

[5]http://ritual.uh.edu/resources/

Class	Question	Answer	Total
invective	1,114	909	2,023
neutral	4,483	4,688	9,171
Total	5,597	5,597	11,194

Table 1: Statistics for our ask.fm data

3.2 What is in the Data?

While annotating, we found instances of sexual harassment directed towards female users. Example 1 in Table 2 shows this type of abuse. In most of these cases, the attacking user is anonymous and he/she is constantly posting similar questions on the victim's profile.

We also found several instances where the purpose of the post is to defend/protect self or another person by standing up for a friend or posting hostile or threatening messages to the anonymous users (Example 2 in Table 2). This kind of post indirectly suggests that the user is being cyberbullied.

Also, the use of profane words does not necessarily convey hostility. In Example 3 in Table 2, looking at the question and answer pair, it is obvious that they are joking with each other.

In ask.fm, there are users that discourage cyberbullying by listening to the victims' feelings and motivating them to stay strong and not to hurt or kill themselves. Example 4 in Table 2 illustrates this case.

Ex.	Posts
1	*Question Send nudes to me babe? :) I'll send you some :)* **Answer:** *stfu* *Question: C'mon post something sexy. Like a yoga pants pic or your bra or thong*
2	*Question: She's not ugly you blind ass bat*
3	*Question: you + me + my bed = fuckkk (; **Answer:** Haha ooooooh shit (;*
4	*Question: well I just want you to know I'm suicidal and 13. and I'm probably gonna kill myself tonight ...**Answer:** No please don't seriously god put you on this earth for a reason and that reason was not for you to take yourself off of it ...*

Table 2: Examples of different topics in our data set

The above examples show that our data set covers a wide range of topics related to cyberbullying. We believe that the data set will be a resource for other researchers carrying out abusive language detection research.

3.3 Comparison with the Other Data sets

Kaggle data released in 2012 for a task hosted by Kaggle called Detecting Insults in Social Commentary [6]. This data contains posts on adult topics like politics, employment, military, etc. Compared with ours, the Kaggle data is more balanced (26.42% of data labeled as insult). Wikipedia abusive language data set (Wulczyn et al., 2016) includes approximately 115k labeled discussion comments from English Wikipedia. The data set was labeled via Crowdflower annotators on whether each comment contains a personal attack. Only 11.7% of the comments in this data set were labeled as personal attacks. Table 3 compares the average length of the posts and words between our data and two other data sets. As we can see in this table, posts in ask.fm are much shorter than Kaggle and Wikipedia data. It also seems that users in ask.fm tend to use shorter words or even more abbreviations.

Avg length of post	ask.fm	Kaggle	Wikipedia
Avg no. of words	13.92	38.35	81.29
Avg length of words	4.73	5.54	5.94

Table 3: Average length of the posts, and words in ask.fm, Kaggle, and Wikipedia data sets in terms of the average number of words and the average number of characters

4 Methodology

In this work, we apply a supervised classification algorithm, Linear SVM, to distinguish the use of bad words in a casual way from invective. We also define two sets of typical and newer NLP features to analyze different aspects of the posts.

4.1 Classic Features

We make use of the following different types of lexical, syntactic, and domain related features in this case:

Lexical: We use word n-grams, char n-grams, k-skip n-grams (to capture long distance context) as features. We weigh each term with its term frequency-inverse document frequency (TF-IDF).

POS colored n-grams: We use the n-gram of tokens with their POS tags to understand the importance of the role played by the syntactic class of the token in making a post invective. We use

Pattern	Example
L (You're) + R + D + A* + N (bad word)	You're just a pussy.
L (You're) + D + A* + N (bad word)	You're a one retarded b*tch.
V (bad word) + O	I want to kill(V) you(O).
O + N (bad word)	You shitheads.
N + N* (at least 2 bad words)	You stupid ass(N) dip(N) shit(N)
O (You) + A + N (bad word)	You stupid ass.
V (bad word) + D + N (bad word)	S**k my ass.

Table 4: Negative patterns for detecting nastiness. The capital letters are the abbreviations for the following POS tags: L = nominal + verbal (e.g. I'm)/verbal + nominal (e.g. let's), R = adverb, D = determiner, A = adjective, N = noun, O = pronoun (not possessive)

CMU's Part of Speech tagger[7] to get the POS tags for each document.

Emoticons (E): We use a normalized count of happy, sad and total emoticons as features to feed the classifier.

SentiWordNet (SWN): We use sentence neutrality, positive and negative scores using SentiWordNet (Baccianella et al., 2010), average count of nouns, verbs, adverbs and adjectives (Ark Tweet NLP (Owoputi et al., 2013)) as features.

LIWC (Linguistic Inquiry and Word Count): LIWC2007 (Pennebaker et al., 2007)) helps us to determine different language dimensions like the degree of positive or negative emotions, self-references, and casual words in each text. In this case, we use a normalized count of words separated by any of LIWC categories.

Style and Writing density (WR): This category focuses on the properties of the text by considering the number of words, characters, all uppercase words, exclamations, question marks, average word length, sentence length, and words per sentence as the features.

Question-Answer (QA): As we work with a data set from a semi-anonymous social network that contains question-answer pairs, certain features like type of post (question or answer), whether the post is a reply to an anonymous post, user mentions in the post, bad word ratio and bad words can be useful for detecting invective posts.

Patterns (P): Based on work by (Yin et al., 2009) and careful review of our training set, we extract the patterns (combination of lexical forms and POS tags) presented in Table 4, and define the binary feature vector to check the existence of any of them in the post.

---

[7] http://www.cs.cmu.edu/~ark/TweetNLP/#pos

4.2 Newer Features

In this set of features, we define the features listed below:

Embeddings: The idea behind this approach is to use a vector space model to improve lexical semantic modeling (Le and Mikolov, 2014). We use two different types of features in this case. The first one is defined by averaging the word embedding of all the words in each post, and the second one is based on a document embedding approach.

LDA: In order to find and analyze the topics involved in invective posts, we employ one of the best known topic modeling algorithms, Latent Dirichlet Allocation (LDA) (Blei et al., 2003). In this case, for each post we make a feature vector containing the probability of appearance of each topic in it.

5 Experiments and Results

In this section, we evaluate our methods on three different data sets we presented in Section 3. Our goal is to show our model works well not only for our data set, but also for the others.

5.1 Experimental Setup

For our data set, we randomly divide the data into training and test in a 70:30 training-to-test ratio, preserving the class distribution of both invective and neutral classes. We use 20% of the training data as a validation set to search for the best C parameters for the Linear SVM through grid search over different values. Since the data set is highly skewed, we perform oversampling of the invective instances during training to mitigate the imbalance data problem. Note that Kaggle corpus and Wikipedia corpus contain training, evaluation, and test sets separately.

Moreover, for the embedding features, we build the vector space by training 290,634 unique words coming from all 586K question-answer pairs we crawled from ask.fm. Also for the LDA feature, using all crawled data from ask.fm, we consider all pairs related to each user as a single document, and ignore the users with less than 10 pairs. For the other two data sets, we look at each comment as a single document. In the pre-processing step, we remove stopwords and words that occur less than 7 times, and set the number of topics to 20.

5.2 Evaluation

People use emoticons to help convey their emotions when they are posting online. In our baseline experiment, at first we simply check whether a post contains any emoticons in the list $\{<3, :-), :), (-:, (:, :o), :c)\}$ since by looking at the training data we found that these emoticons were used to show positive feelings. If the post contains at least one of these emoticons, we label it "neutral". Otherwise, we calculate the ratio of bad words to total words. If it is greater than a given threshold, our baseline system predicts the post as "invective".

$$invective(x) = \begin{cases} 0, & if\ badWordRatio(x) < T \\ 1, & if\ badWordRatio(x) \geq T \end{cases}$$
(2)

In this research, since we work with highly imbalanced data sets, we used "f1-score" and "area under the receiver operating characteristic curve (AUC)" as the evaluation metrics as they are less sensitive to imbalanced classes. Table 5 shows the results for our baseline experiment. We find the best threshold value among all threshold values $\{0.1, 0.2, 0.3, 0.4, 0.5, 0.6, 0.7, 0.8\}$ by performing grid search using the training set for training, and the validation set for testing.

With the feature collections we discussed in section 4, we train a Linear SVM classifier. Similar to the baseline experiment, for each set of features, we tuned SVM C parameter (inverse of regularization strength) with a grid search over values $\{0.00001, 0.0001, 0.001, 0.01, 0.1, 1.0, 10, 100, 1000, 10000\}$. Table 6 shows the classification results of invective class for all the features and some of their combinations for all three different data sets. Please note that Question-Answer feature can not be applied on Kaggle and Wikipedia data, because the comments format in these data sets are not of question-answer type.

5.3 Classification Results

The last row of Table 6 shows that combining all features does not always give the best F1-score. We obtained an F1-score of 0.59 for our data when we selectively combined different types of features. Although some features like SWN and P alone perform worse or not much better than the baseline (comparing AUC or F1-score), it seems that selectively combining them with other features improves the performance of the system. We can see in the results that when we combine a feature with others, in most cases but not all we get a higher AUC score compared to only using a single feature for training the classifier. This means each feature carries valuable information about different aspects of the posts. It is very interesting that combining emotion based features with the embedding ones (LIWC+E+SWN+W2V+D2V) gives us one of the best AUC scores. It shows that the emotions reflected from the text give us good information about whether it is hostile or not. However, the results we got from LDA features are not remarkable. Even combining this feature with the others does not seem to improve performance. One reason may be the sparsity of feature vectors in this case. LDA features ranks all trained topics over each document. It makes a vector for each post containing the probability of appearing each topic in it. Since generally, the length of online comments is very short, this vector would be very sparse.

Table 6 also shows the results for the Kaggle and Wikipedia data sets. Our results do not outperform the best AUC score reported by Kaggle's winner (0.842^8). However, we consider our method promising, since our features are not customized for Kaggle data set. Also, we compare our results with those reported for Wikipedia data (Wulczyn et al., 2016). They only presented the AUC of their different model architectures trained on the train split and evaluated on the development split. With the same configuration, we found that our results are similar to those they reported (e.g. using the same experimental set up, they got an AUC of 0.952 for word n-gram, and we got an AUC of 0.956 for word unigram). Overall, the results of applying our model on Kaggle and Wikipedia data show that it is applicable to

---

[8] https://www.kaggle.com/c/detecting-insults-in-social-commentary/leaderboard

	Our data set		Kaggle data set		Wikipedia data set	
Experiment	AUC	F-score	AUC	F-score	AUC	F-score
Random Baseline	0.492	0.26	0.513	0.35	0.509	0.17
Our Baseline	0.567	0.27	0.597	0.36	0.610	0.28

Table 5: Baseline experiment results for invective class

	Our data set		Kaggle data set		Wikipedia data set	
Feature	**AUC**	**F-score**	**AUC**	**F-score**	**AUC**	**F-score**
Unigram (U)	0.768	0.57	**0.813**	0.71	0.882	0.72
Bigram (B)	0.680	0.48	0.742	0.62	0.810	0.66
Trigram (T)	0.587	0.31	0.647	0.46	0.702	0.53
Word 1, 2, 3gram (UBT)	0.726	0.55	0.777	0.68	0.830	0.74
Char 3gram (CT)	0.753	0.55	0.805	0.70	0.883	0.69
Char 4gram (C4)	0.748	0.56	0.812	0.72	0.879	0.73
Char 5gram (C5)	0.717	0.52	0.793	0.71	0.869	0.74
Char 3, 4, 5gram (C345)	0.734	0.55	0.811	**0.73**	0.866	0.75
2 skip 2gram (2S2G)	0.654	0.44	0.756	0.65	0.764	0.65
2 skip 3gram (2S3G)	0.593	0.32	0.649	0.46	0.712	0.52
POS colored unigram (POSU)	0.762	0.56	0.803	0.70	0.874	0.71
POS colored bigram (POSB)	0.674	0.47	0.732	0.61	0.806	0.65
POS colored trigram (POST)	0.577	0.28	0.643	0.45	0.697	0.52
POSU+POSB+POST (POS123)	0.724	0.55	0.788	0.68	0.824	0.73
Question-Answer (QA)	0.744	0.52	N/A	N/A	N/A	N/A
Emoticon (E)	0.511	0.30	0.505	0.41	0.524	0.19
QA + E	0.743	0.52	N/A	N/A	N/A	N/A
SentiWordNet (SWN)	0.602	0.35	0.575	0.39	0.632	0.30
C345 + SWN	0.736	0.55	0.797	0.72	0.866	0.75
LIWC	0.662	0.42	0.715	0.57	0.787	0.53
QA + LIWC	0.764	0.55	N/A	N/A	N/A	N/A
Writing Density (WR)	0.564	0.30	0.566	0.42	0.682	0.31
U + WR	0.769	0.57	0.804	0.70	0.878	0.71
Patterns (P)	0.539	0.17	0.518	0.09	0.544	0.16
QA+LIWC+P	0.756	0.54	N/A	N/A	N/A	N/A
Word2vec (W2V)	0.745	0.51	0.759	0.63	0.854	0.61
Doc2vec (D2V)	0.750	0.52	0.792	0.66	0.886	0.60
LDA	0.626	0.37	0.559	0.40	0.577	0.26
LIWC+E+SWN+W2V+D2V	0.780	0.56	0.799	0.68	**0.889**	0.65
U+C4+QA+LIWC+E+SWN+W2V+D2V	**0.785**	0.57	N/A	N/A	N/A	N/A
U+C4+POSU+QA+D2V+LDA	0.781	0.58	N/A	N/A	N/A	N/A
C4+U+QA+E	0.766	**0.59**	N/A	N/A	N/A	N/A
All Features	0.756	0.56	0.798	0.71	0.882	**0.75**
Best Previous Reported score	–	–	0.842	–	–	–

Table 6: Classification results for invective class. N/A stands for the features that are not applicable to Kaggle and Wikipedia data sets

other data sets. According to the comparison of all three corpora in Section 3.3, we believe that the major reasons why we get higher scores in those two other data sets comparing with ours are:

1. In ask.fm, comments are question-answer pairs which are shorter than in other data sets. By looking at our data, we found that in many cases both question and answer include only one word – that makes the decision hard.

2. Online posts do not basically follow formal language conventions. Since ask.fm is mostly used by teenagers and youth, there are more misspellings and abbreviations inside the texts, which makes their processing much more difficult.

Among all the features, only P works poorly specifically in Kaggle data. But as mentioned in Section 4, for extracting those patterns, we only looked at our training data. So, it is understandable that they may not give us good results for the other data sets. So, it would be interesting to find a way for extracting the negative patterns from the text automatically.

Table 7 lists important features learned by the classifier. The "_" represents the whitespace char-

Feature	Our data set	Kaggle data set	Wikipedia data set
U	bitch, fuck, asshole, shut, stfu, off, you,stupid, fucking, ugly, pussy, u, ass, slut, face	you, idiot, stupid, dumb, loser, your, moron, ignorant, you're, faggot, bitch, shut, asshole, ass, retard	fuck, fucking, stupid, idiot, shit, asshole, ass, moron,bullshit, suck, idiots, bitch, sucks, dick, penis
C4	itch, bitc, _ass, _fuc, uck_, stfu, _hoe, _bit, tfu_, fuck, _stf, dumb, _off, _you, slut,	_you, you_, re a, diot, _idi, idio, dumb, moro, oron, _dum, your, bitc, tard, _fuc, oser	fuck, _fuc, shit, uck_, diot, _ass, suck, idio, moro, _shi, _gay, bitc, oron, dick

Table 7: Top negative features

acter. It is good to see that the classifier has learned to discriminate between neutral and invective words. The most interesting point obtained from this table is that the second-person pronoun is ranked as one of the top negative features. It supports our idea that invective posts have specific patterns in most of the cases. Also, in our data set, the word "face" ranked as a highly negative feature. It shows that attackers post negative comments about victims' faces, and in some cases as an answer to an uploaded picture. Moreover, the bad words captured from the other data sets (like *idiot*, *stupid*, *moron*) give us some idea to expand our bad word lists to enrich our data set.

	Posts
1	*Answer: stfu*
	Answer: Die
2	*Question: Fuck you brian lmao*
	Answer: xD ty
3	*Question: Can I kill you?*
	Question: Can we fuck please?
4	*Question: You are hot as fuck*

Table 8: Examples of misslabeled instances by the classifier

Analyzing mistakes, we found that the classifier gets confused with single profane word answers (Example 1 in Table 8), question and answer pairs in which users joke around using profanities (Example 2 in Table 8), posts with mixture of politeness and profanity (Example 3 in Table 8), and posts with bad words that are offered as compliments (Example 4 in Table 8).

5.4 Negativity of words

Table 9 shows the degree of negativity for the words in our bad-word list. We do this analysis in order to identify how negative each word in our bad word list is by itself. For computing this measure, we consider the posts that contain only one profane word. Then, for each bad word w_i in the list, we apply the same formula as Equation 1 to calculate the ratio of the negative posts containing w_i or any of its variations to the total posts in which w_i or any of its variations appears as their single bad word.

bad word	negativity	bad word	negativity
as**ole	51.16%	b*tch	41.65%
kill	12.47%	a*s	24.77%
f*ck	33.05%	die	7.41%
n**ger	13.30%	s*ck	26.88%
sh*t	15.23%	h*e	36.58%
cut	4.85%	stfu	51.55%

Table 9: Degree of negativity for bad words

From Table 9, it is clear that most of our bad words are used in a neutral or positive way more often than in a negative way. Although these numbers are related also to the overall incidence of nastiness, there are some noteworthy findings. For example, the word "f*ck", when used as a verb, referring to sexual activity, was used more often in a neutral or positive post, rather than a negative post. Thus its overall negative score is 33.05% compared to the word "as**ole" that had a negative score of 51.16%. This finding reflects a sexualized teen culture, part of a growing problem affecting young social media users. The low degree of negativity of the words "die", "kill", and "cut" are also interesting. By looking at the data, we find that the likelihood that these harm-related words reflect an online harassment is related to the appearance of the other bad words. Moreover, the data shows that these words are used sometimes to threaten people or encourage them to commit suicide. In contrast, the acronym "stfu" has the strongest degree of negativity. We believe that these observations are related to the versatility of the words. It is less likely to see the acronym "stfu" being used in a neutral and positive way than the other words. Also, some words like "suck" and "hoe" seem to carry a highly negative weight.

6 Conclusion and Future Work

In this paper, we present our evolving approaches for creating a linguistic resource to investigate nastiness in social media. We start out by selecting profanity-laden posts as a likely hostile starting point for invective potentially leading to cyberbullying events. We use various types of classic and new features, and try to combine them for distinguishing extremely negative text from the rest. Also, by applying our machine learning model on Kaggle and Wikipedia data, we show that this model can be applicable to other data sets. Interestingly, we find that profanities and vulgarities abound in teens posts and that the degree of negativity of profanities varies, from the strong negativity of the acronym "stfu" to the ambiguity of the term "f**k" which when used as a verb referring to sexual desire or propositioning is sometimes considered a compliment. We find interesting trends, degrees of negativity in profanity that possibly indicate heavy use of profanity among teens, and also reflect a sexualized teen culture.

We are continually enriching this linguistic resource by identifying more types of abusive posts. Future plans for our research are to capture more emotional aspects from the online comments, extract negative patterns from the text automatically, and consider a topic modeling algorithm specifically designed for short texts in order to extract only one topic per document. We also plan to work on a graph model of the users to better identify cyberbullying episodes.

Acknowledgments

We thank the anonymous reviewers for their valuable feedback on this research.

References

Haider M. al-Khateeb and Gregory Epiphaniou. 2016. How technology can mitigate and counteract cyberstalking and online grooming. *Computer Fraud & Security* 2016(1):14–18.

Stefano Baccianella, Andrea Esuli, and Fabrizio Sebastiani. 2010. Sentiwordnet 3.0: An enhanced lexical resource for sentiment analysis and opinion mining. In *LREC*. volume 10, pages 2200–2204.

David M. Blei, Andrew Y. Ng, and Michael I Jordan. 2003. Latent dirichlet allocation. *Journal of machine Learning research* 3(Jan):993–1022.

Karthik Dinakar, Birago Jones, Catherine Havasi, Henry Lieberman, and Rosalind Picard. 2012. Common sense reasoning for detection, prevention, and mitigation of cyberbullying. *ACM Transactions on Interactive Intelligent Systems (TiiS)* 2(3):18.

Healy. 2014. Ask.fm is relocating to ireland and no one is happy about it. `http://mashable.com/2014/11/05/ask-fm-relocation-ireland-cyberbullying-suicides-cold-shoulder/#SdafIlqyoGqg`.

Homa Hosseinmardi, Rick Han, Qin Lv, Shivakant Mishra, and Amir Ghasemianlangroodi. 2014. Towards understanding cyberbullying behavior in a semi-anonymous social network. In *Advances in Social Networks Analysis and Mining (ASONAM), 2014 IEEE/ACM International Conference on*. IEEE, pages 244–252.

Krishna B. Kansara and Narendra M. Shekokar. 2015. A framework for cyberbullying detection in social network. *International Journal of Current Engineering and Technology* 5(1).

Quoc V. Le and Tomas Mikolov. 2014. Distributed representations of sentences and documents. In *ICML*. volume 14, pages 1188–1196.

Henry Lieberman, Karthik Dinakar, and Birago Jones. 2011. Let's gang up on cyberbullying. *Computer* 44(9):93–96.

Sonia Livingstone, Leslie Haddon, Anke Görzig, and Kjartan Ólafsson. 2010. Risks and safety on the internet. *The Perspective of European Children. Final Findings from the EU Kids Online Survey of* pages 9–16.

Jamie Macbeth, Hanna Adeyema, Henry Lieberman, and Christopher Fry. 2013. Script-based story matching for cyberbullying prevention. In *CHI '13 Extended Abstracts on Human Factors in Computing Systems*. ACM, New York, NY, USA, CHI EA '13, pages 901–906. https://doi.org/10.1145/2468356.2468517.

Chikashi Nobata, Joel Tetreault, Achint Thomas, Yashar Mehdad, and Yi Chang. 2016. Abusive language detection in online user content. In *Proceedings of the 25th International Conference on World Wide Web*. International World Wide Web Conferences Steering Committee, Republic and Canton of Geneva, Switzerland, WWW '16, pages 145–153. https://doi.org/10.1145/2872427.2883062.

nobullying.com. 2015. The complicated web of teen lives - 2015 bullying report—nobullying—. `http://nobullying.com/the-complicated-web-of-teen-lives-2015-bullying-report/`.

Olutobi Owoputi, Brendan O'Connor, Chris Dyer, Kevin Gimpel, Nathan Schneider, and Noah A Smith. 2013. Improved part-of-speech tagging for online conversational text with word clusters. Association for Computational Linguistics.

Justin W. Patchin. 2015. Summary of our cyberbullying research (2004-2015). `http://cyberbullying.org/summary-of-our-cyberbullying-research`.

Justin W. Patchin and Sameer Hinduja. 2010. Cyberbullying and self-esteem. *Journal of School Health* 80(12):614–621.

James W. Pennebaker, Roger J. Booth, and Martha E. Francis. 2007. Liwc2007: Linguistic inquiry and word count. *Austin, Texas: liwc.net* .

Shute. 2013. Cyberbullying suicides: what will it take to have ask.fm shut down? - telegraph. `http://www.telegraph.co.uk/news/health/children/10225846/Cyberbullying-suicides-What-will-it-take-to-have-Ask.fm-shut-down.html`.

Fabio Sticca and Sonja Perren. 2013. Is cyberbullying worse than traditional bullying? Examining the differential roles of medium, publicity, and anonymity for the perceived severity of bullying. *Journal of youth and adolescence* 42(5):739–750.

Cynthia Van Hee, Els Lefever, Ben Verhoeven, Julie Mennes, Bart Desmet, Guy De Pauw, Walter Daelemans, and Veronique Hoste. 2015. Detection and fine-grained classification of cyberbullying events. In *Proceedings of the International Conference Recent Advances in Natural Language Processing*. INCOMA Ltd. Shoumen, Bulgaria, pages 672–680. http://aclweb.org/anthology/R15-1086.

Ellery Wulczyn, Nithum Thain, and Lucas Dixon. 2016. Ex machina: Personal attacks seen at scale. *CoRR* abs/1610.08914. http://arxiv.org/abs/1610.08914.

Jun-Ming Xu, Kwang-Sung Jun, Xiaojin Zhu, and Amy Bellmore. 2012. Learning from bullying traces in social media. In *Proceedings of the 2012 Conference of the North American Chapter of the Association for Computational Linguistics: Human Language Technologies*. Association for Computational Linguistics, Stroudsburg, PA, USA, NAACL HLT '12, pages 656–666. http://dl.acm.org/citation.cfm?id=2382029.2382139.

Dawei Yin, Brian D. Davison, Zhenzhen Xue, Liangjie Hong, April Kontostathis, and Lynne Edwards. 2009. Detection of harassment on web 2.0. *Proceedings of the Content Analysis in the Web 2.0 (CAW2.0)* 2:1–7.

Hack Harassment: Technology Solutions to Combat Online Harassment

George W. Kennedy III
Intel
Hillsboro, OR
`george.w.kennedy@intel.com`

Andrew W. McCollough
EdgeRock Technology Partners
Hillsboro, OR

Edward Dixon
Intel
Cork, Ireland
`edward.dixon@intel.com`

Alexie Bastidas
Intel
Santa Clara, CA

John Ryan
Intel
Cork, Ireland

Chris Loo
Intel
Santa Clara, CA

Saurav Sahay
Intel
Santa Clara, CA

Abstract

This work is part of a new initiative to use machine learning to identify online harassment in social media and comment streams. Online harassment goes under-reported due to the reliance on humans to identify and report harassment, reporting that is further slowed by requirements to fill out forms providing context. In addition, the time for moderators to respond and apply human judgment can take days, but response times in terms of minutes are needed in the online context. Though some of the major social media companies have been doing proprietary work in automating the detection of harassment, there are few tools available for use by the public. In addition, the amount of labeled online harassment data and availability of cross platform online harassment datasets is limited. We present the methodology used to create a harassment dataset and classifier and the dataset used to help the system learn what harassment looks like.

1 Introduction

Online harassment has been a problem to a greater or lesser extent since the early days of the internet. Previous work has applied anti-spam techniques like machine learning based text classifica-tion (Reynolds et al., 2011) to detecting harassing messages. However, existing public datasets are limited in size, with labels of varying quality.

The #HackHarassment (Harassment, 2017) initiative (an alliance of tech companies and NGOs devoted to fighting bullying on the internet) has begun to address this issue by creating a web tool to collect and label data, and using the tool to generate a large, high-quality, cross-platform dataset. The release of this tool is scheduled for Summer 2017. As we complete further rounds of labelling with a public audience, later iterations of this dataset will increase the available samples by at least an order of magnitude and enable corresponding improvements in the quality of machine learning models we have built for harassment detection. In this paper, we introduce an improved cross-platform harassment dataset and a machine learning model built on the dataset.

2 Related Work

Previous work in the area by (Bayzick et al., 2011) showed that natural language processing in combination with a rule-based system could detect bullying messages on an online forum, but with very poor accuracy. However, the same work also made clear that the limiting factor on such models was the availability of a suitable quantity of labeled examples, e.g. the Bayzick work relied on a dataset of 2,696 samples, only 196 of which were

73

Proceedings of the First Workshop on Abusive Language Online, pages 73–77,
Vancouver, Canada, July 30 - August 4, 2017. ©2017 Association for Computational Linguistics

found to be examples of bullying behavior. Additionally, this work relied on classical decision-tree models like J48 and JRIP, and k-nearest neighbors classifiers like IBk, as opposed to modern ensemble methods or deep neural-network-based approaches. In addition, Intel's #HackHarassment team published work (Bastidas et al., 2016) showing results for harassment detection using a variety of model types on a new dataset of comments and posts which their team had labelled.

More recently, major internet companies have focused efforts on combating various forms of harassment online. Yahoo researchers have developed machine learning models for detecting abusive language (Nobata et al., 2016) and a Google Jigsaw team partnered with the Wikimedia Foundation to develop solutions for reducing personal attacks or toxic comments, in Wikimedia editing (Wulczyn et al., 2017). Nobata outperformed state-of-the-art deep learning approaches with their supervised learning approach using a combination of linguistic, n-gram (including character n-grams), syntactic (POS), and semantic (using comment embeddings similar to word2vec) features. In addition, the Yahoo team has released the longitudinal New Feed data set used in the study on (Webscope, 2017). Wulczyn demonstrated that their machine models can perform as well as three human graders in identifying toxic comments in Wikipedia editing wars, and in addition released the Perspective API to enable developers to utilize their solution. However, see (Hosseini et al., 2017) for comments on adversarial attacks and the resultant fragility of the model - and other models that depend on token-level features. We extend these results and others by developing a system architecture for crowdsourcing sample labeling, a crosssocial-media-platform dataset, and providing an open source classifier for developers to build upon. The classifier is intended to be open sourced in Summer 2017.

3   Methods

In this work, we build upon our initial results using version 1.0 of our dataset (Bastidas et al., 2016). We followed a supervised classification method that uses a data with gold-standard labeled comments and a set discriminating linguistic properties, or features, of each comment to predict the class membership of new or untrained comments. Our features consisted primarily of n-gram and a small set of linguistic features on datasets drawn from The Guardian, Reddit, and Twitter. We performed no significant pre-processing on the data other than tokenization, though in the future we anticipate adding further feature-reduction steps, such as stemming, to improve model performance.

4   Data Source Selection

Three initial data sources were selected: The Guardian, Reddit, and Twitter. Text from each data source were extracted in several ways in Summer 2016. Comments on polarizing or hot-button news articles were extracted from the Guardian, an online news source. Comments from Reddit, a popular social media site, were selected from comment which had received at least 100 down votes. Short texts from Twitter, tweets were hand-curated from an initially machine-selected data set from Twitter, and then further tweets scraped by searching on polarizing or hot-button topics.

4.1   Reddit

Comments from Reddit were downloaded from a publicly available dataset on Google BigQuery, reddit_comments_all_2015. These comments were then filtered to those that had received at least 100 down votes. We used our initial version of the classifier to label these comments. The resulting 5700 harassing comments were then further manually labeled by an in-house team of analysts. Analysts were given instructions and examples for annotation of harassment or non-harassment. In addition, the raters were provided with an additional set of more fine-grained labels but instruction on annotation was not provided.). Each post was labeled independently by at least five Intel Security Web Analysts. A perfect consensus was relatively rare, and so we rated a post as harassing if 40%, 2 of our 5 raters, consider it to be harassing.

4.2   Twitter

Data were comprised of two sources: manual curation and annotation of a pre-existing machine-annotated dataset and a set of scraped tweets using proprietary sampling methods. The sampling should not be considered unbiased. The initial 5000 tweets were sourced from an online repository of tweets at. Additional tweets were scraped directly from Twitter during July 2016 using a custom twitterbot that queried on hot-button topics as keywords to the Twitter API. These additional

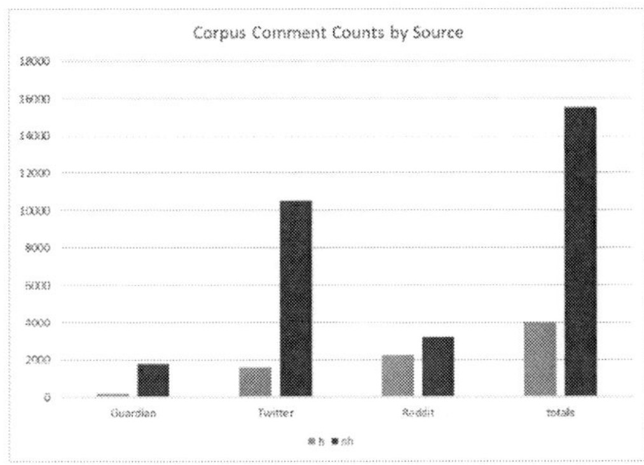

Figure 1: Corpus Comment Counts by Source

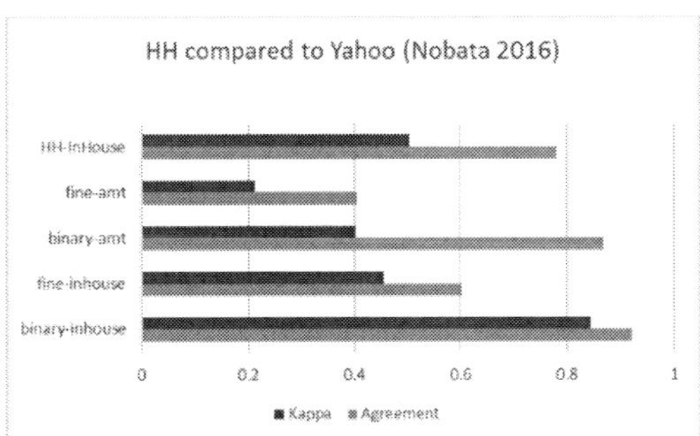

Figure 2: Inter-annotator agreement for Hack Harassment (HH) compared to Yahoo. HH uses Krippendorfs Alpha and Yahoo uses Kappa. Agreement is an average pairwise agreement.

tweets were first labeled by our early classifier and then manually labeled by our team (Hart, 2016).

4.3 The Guardian

Comments were scraped from 15 articles covering hot-button or polarizing topics. We believe that minimal harassing comments were found in the Guardian dataset as Guardian comments are curated by a team of moderators in accordance with their content policy. Therefore, minimal or no harassing comments should be expected, as we confirmed in the dataset.

Figure 1 shows that the current data set is reasonably unbalanced overall with a 1 : 4 ratio of non-harassing to harassing comments. In addition, the categories are unbalanced across source as well as category within source, such that Reddit, despite being only 28% of the total comments contributed 56% of the harassing comments.

As shown in Figure 2 and Figure 3, average agreement is below 90% for the Guardian

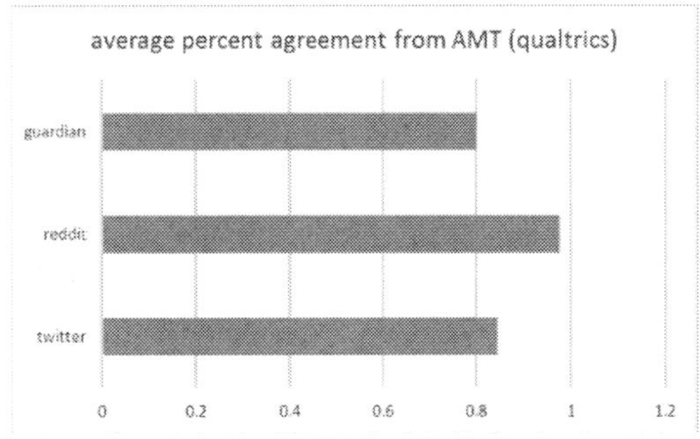

Figure 3: Average Percent of Agreement Among Amazon Mechanical Turk (AMT) Annotators

and Twitter surveys, with an average across all Qualtrics surveys only .875. This is well below what is typically suggested for raw agreement scores.

Guardian URLs
https://www.theguardian.com/discussion/p/4pcq2
https://www.theguardian.com/discussion/p/4pgek
https://www.theguardian.com/discussion/p/4an9q
https://www.theguardian.com/discussion/p/4p76x
https://www.theguardian.com/discussion/p/4pdqd
https://www.theguardian.com/discussion/p/4phck
https://www.theguardian.com/discussion/p/4pf70
https://www.theguardian.com/discussion/p/4pfe3
https://www.theguardian.com/discussion/p/4k4tx
https://www.theguardian.com/discussion/p/4pd76
https://www.theguardian.com/discussion/p/4jmg2
https://www.theguardian.com/discussion/p/4pg57
https://www.theguardian.com/discussion/p/4p6dt
https://www.theguardian.com/discussion/p/4p6gn
https://www.theguardian.com/discussion/p/4pgbx

Table 1: Guardian URLs used to scrape initial comments.

5 Data Ingest and Annotation Methods

Data ingest process and annotation were heterogeneous in nature. Manual curation was combined with machine annotation in several iterated steps to produce a final annotated dataset. The comment dataset was simply annotated with a Boolean indicating harassment. Harassment was determined on the gold data through a percent voting method: the reported metrics are for 40% and above simple agreement among raters that a given comment is harassment.

All preprocessing, training and evaluation was carried out in Python, using the popular SciKitLearn (for feature engineering and linear models) in combination with Numpy3 (for matrix operations) (Pedregosa et al., 2011; van der Walt et al.,

2011).

6 Feature Selection

Features were generated by tokenizing each comment, hashing the resulting n-grams, and computing a TF/IDF value for each token. The resultant feature vectors were used to train a Random Forest classifier. We used the following features:

- Unigram and Bigram TF-IDF: this is a standard feature used in text-categorization. We used unigrams and bigrams. Trigrams were not used because the size of the dataset meant almost all trigrams were too rare for their presence and absence to reach statistical significance.

- Character N-Gram TF-IDF from 3 to 6 characters: The goal with this was to target common alternative spellings of words, particularly frequent in online communication.

- Unigram Token Count: we utilized NLTKs Twitter Tokenizer to tokenize the tokens and count the number of tokens. The Twitter Tokenizer handles URLs and Hashtags much better than a standard punctuation based tokenizers found in NLTK or Sck-kit Learn. Our assumption behind using token count is that harassing texts tend to be brief assaults rather than long diatribes.

- Source: In combination with the token count, we selected a dummy coefficient (toggled as 1 or 0) to highlight if a comment is sourced from Twitter or not.

- Sentiment Polarities: we utilized NLTKs VADER Sentiment Analyzer to generate sentiment polarities for positive, neutral, and negative sentiment. Our assumption was that harassing comments tend to have more negative sentiment, whereas non-harassing comments tend to have more positive sentiment.

7 Training Dataset

The current training dataset contains: 20,432 unique comments. Of these comments, 4136 are labeled as harassment, 16296 are labeled as non-harassment. 12,049 comments are sourced from Twitter, with the remaining 8383 being from Reddit or the Guardian.

8 Machine Learning Model

Bastidas tested a variety of algorithms, including SVM, Decision Tree, Random Forest (ensemble Decision Trees), and Multinomial Nave Bayes (Bastidas et al., 2016). We increased the size of the Reddit dataset and included labeled comments that were sampled from Twitter and The Guardian. We collected performance results using this larger, cross-platform dataset, described in the Data Source Selection section, and a Scikit-Learn Random Forest classifier. For our hyperparameters we limited the number of trees to 200 and left the tree depth unbounded. Subsequently, the data were trained on the Random Forest by splitting the dataset into 80/20 training and evaluation sets, and then the training data were further split into Kfold (n=10) folds for cross-validation and the average results reported in Table 2. Of primary concern to us is to optimize for high recall. We want to minimize our false-negative rate for harassment.

Class	Precision	Recall	F1 Score
Not Harassing	0.93	0.95	0.94
Harassing	0.75	0.68	0.71
Average	0.89	0.90	0.90

Table 2: Random forest classifier results.

9 Future Work

New work from Facebook and OpenAI on text classification suggests obvious next steps. Bytelevel deep neural nets are capable of state-of-theart results on large datasets, can exploit unlabeled data, as described in recent work from OpenAI (Radford et al., 2017) and have the potential to resist the "adversarial" tokens described in (Hosseini et al., 2017). Using OpenAI's approach with a large, unlabeled dataset for pre-training is an obvious next step. A contrasting approach that requires further evaluation is the FastText model from Facebook's Advanced Research Lab, which, as described in (Joulin et al., 2016) and (Bojanowski et al., 2016), is competitive with deep convolutional neural networks and can exploit unlabeled data using pre-trained WordVectors, while requiring vastly less training time than competitive alternatives.

10 Conclusion

We have presented to our cross-platform harassment dataset, machine learning model. We intend to open our labeling platform to the public to expand the Hack Harassment cross platform dataset. As we complete further rounds of labelling with a public audience, later iterations of this dataset will increase the available samples by at least an order of magnitude, enabling corresponding improvements in the quality of machine learning models for harassment detection. We look forward to both the availability of a larger, cross-socialmediaplatform harassment dataset and seeing the development of classifiers that improve upon our work. We welcome partners able to contribute to expanding the dataset and improving the modeling.

References

A. Bastidas, E. Dixon, C. Loo, and J. Ryan. 2016. Harassment detection: a benchmark on the hackharassment dataset. In *Proceedings of the Collaborative European Research Conference (CERC 2016), Cork*. pages 76–79.

J. Bayzick, A. Kontostathis, and L. Edwards. 2011. Detecting the presence of cyberbullying using computer software.

P. Bojanowski, E. Grave, A. Joulin, and T. Mikolov. 2016. Enriching word vectors with subword information. `arXiv.org`.

Hack Harassment. 2017. Hack harassment. `https://www.hackharassment.com/`.

M. Hart. 2016. Twitterclassifier. `https://github.com/HackHarassment/TwitterClassifier`.

H. Hosseini, S. Kannan, B. Zhang, and R. Poovendran. 2017. Deceiving google's perspective api built for detecting toxic comments. `arXiv.org`.

A. Joulin, E. Grave, P. Bojanowski, and Mikolov. T. 2016. Bag of tricks for efficient text classification. `arXiv.org`.

Chikashi Nobata, Joel Tetreault, Achint Thomas, Yashar Mehdad, and Yi Chang. 2016. Abusive language detection in online user content. In *Proceedings of the 25th International Conference on World Wide Web*. International World Wide Web Conferences Steering Committee, Republic and Canton of Geneva, Switzerland, WWW '16, pages 145–153. https://doi.org/10.1145/2872427.2883062.

F. Pedregosa, G. Varoquaux, A. Gramfort, V. Michel, B. Thirion, O. Grisel, and et al. 2011. Scikit-learn: Machine learning in python. *Journal of Machine Learning Research* 12:145–153.

A. Radford, R. Jozefowicz, and I. Sutskever. 2017. Learning to generate reviews and discovering sentiment.

K. Reynolds, A. Kontostathis, and L. Edwards. 2011. Using machine learning to detect cyberbullying. In *Presented at the 2011 Tenth International Conference on Machine Learning and Applications(ICMLA 2011), IEEE.*. pages 241–244.

S. van der Walt, S. C. Colbert, and G. Varoquaux. 2011. The numpy array: A structure for efficient numerical computation. *Computing in Science & Engineering* 13(2):22–30.

Webscope. 2017. Webscope. `https://webscope.sandbox.yahoo.com/`.

E. Wulczyn, D. Taraborelli, N. Thain, and L Dixon. 2017. Algorithms and insults: Scaling up our understanding of harassment on wikipedia. https://medium.com/jigsaw/algorithms-and-insults-scaling-up-ourunderstanding-of-harassment-on-wikipedia-6cc417b9f7ff.

Understanding Abuse:
A Typology of Abusive Language Detection Subtasks

Zeerak Waseem
Department of Computer Science
University of Sheffield
United Kingdom
z.w.butt@sheffield.ac.uk

Thomas Davidson
Department of Sociology
Cornell University
Ithica, NY
trd54@cornell.edu

Dana Warmsley
Department for Applied Mathematics
Cornell University
Ithica, NY
dw457@cornell.edu

Ingmar Weber
Qatar Computing Research Institute
HBKU
Doha, Qatar
iweber@hbku.edu.qa

Abstract

As the body of research on abusive language detection and analysis grows, there is a need for critical consideration of the relationships between different subtasks that have been grouped under this label. Based on work on hate speech, cyberbullying, and online abuse we propose a typology that captures central similarities and differences between subtasks and we discuss its implications for data annotation and feature construction. We emphasize the practical actions that can be taken by researchers to best approach their abusive language detection subtask of interest.

1 Introduction

There has been a surge in interest in the detection of abusive language, hate speech, cyberbullying, and trolling in the past several years (Schmidt and Wiegand, 2017). Social media sites have also come under increasing pressure to tackle these issues. Similarities between these subtasks have led scholars to group them together under the umbrella terms of "abusive language", "harmful speech", and "hate speech" (Nobata et al., 2016; Faris et al., 2016; Schmidt and Wiegand, 2017) but little work has been done to examine the relationship between them. As each of these subtasks seeks to address a specific yet partially overlapping phenomenon, we believe that there is much to gain by studying how they are related.

The overlap between subtasks is illustrated by the variety of labels used in prior work. For example, in annotating for cyberbullying events, Van Hee et al. (2015b) identifies discriminative remarks (racist, sexist) as a subset of "insults", whereas Nobata et al. (2016) classifies similar remarks as "hate speech" or "derogatory language". Waseem and Hovy (2016) only consider "hate speech" without regard to any potential overlap with bullying or otherwise offensive language, while Davidson et al. (2017) distinguish hate speech from generally offensive language. Wulczyn et al. (2017) annotates for personal attacks, which likely encompasses identifying cyberbullying, hate speech, and offensive language. The lack of consensus has resulted in contradictory annotation guidelines - some messages considered as hate speech by Waseem and Hovy (2016) are only considered derogatory and offensive by Nobata et al. (2016) and Davidson et al. (2017).

To help to bring together these literatures and to avoid these contradictions, we propose a typology that synthesizes these different subtasks. We argue that the differences between subtasks within abusive language can be reduced to two primary factors:

1. *Is the language directed towards a specific individual or entity or is it directed towards a generalized group?*

2. *Is the abusive content explicit or implicit?*

Each of the different subtasks related to abu-

Proceedings of the First Workshop on Abusive Language Online, pages 78–84,
Vancouver, Canada, July 30 - August 4, 2017. ©2017 Association for Computational Linguistics

sive language occupies one or more segments of this typology. Our aim is to clarify the similarities and differences between subtasks in abusive language detection to help researchers select appropriate strategies for data annotation and modeling.

2 A typology of abusive language

Much of the work on abusive language subtasks can be synthesized in a two-fold typology that considers whether (i) the abuse is directed at a specific target, and (ii) the degree to which it is explicit.

Starting with the targets, abuse can either be directed towards a specific individual or entity, or it can be used towards a generalized *Other*, for example people with a certain ethnicity or sexual orientation. This is an important sociological distinction as the latter references a whole category of people rather than a specific individual, group, or organization (see Brubaker 2004, Wimmer 2013) and, as we discuss below, entails a linguistic distinction that can be productively used by researchers. To better illustrate this, the first row of Table 1 shows examples from the literature of directed abuse, where someone is either mentioned by name, tagged by a username, or referenced by a pronoun.[1] Cyberbullying and trolling are instances of directed abuse, aimed at individuals and online communities respectively. The second row shows cases with abusive expressions towards generalized groups such as racial categories and sexual orientations. Previous work has identified instances of hate speech that are both directed and generalized (Burnap and Williams, 2015; Waseem and Hovy, 2016; Davidson et al., 2017), although Nobata et al. (2016) come closest to making a distinction between directed and generalized hate.

The other dimension is the extent to which abusive language is explicit or implicit. This is roughly analogous to the distinction in linguistics and semiotics between *denotation*, the literal meaning of a term or symbol, and *connotation*, its sociocultural associations, famously articulated by Barthes (1957). Explicit abusive language is that which is unambiguous in its *potential* to be abusive, for example language that contains racial or homophobic slurs. Previous research has indicated a great deal of variation within such language (Warner and Hirschberg, 2012; David-

son et al., 2017), with abusive terms being used in a colloquial manner or by people who are victims of abuse. Implicit abusive language is that which does not immediately imply or denote abuse. Here, the true nature is often obscured by the use of ambiguous terms, sarcasm, lack of profanity or hateful terms, and other means, generally making it more difficult to detect by both annotators and machine learning approaches (Dinakar et al., 2011; Dadvar et al., 2013; Justo et al., 2014). Social scientists and activists have recently been paying more attention to implicit, and even unconscious, instances of abuse that have been termed "micro-aggressions" (Sue et al., 2007). As the examples show, such language may nonetheless have extremely abusive connotations. The first column of Table 1 shows instances of explicit abuse, where it should be apparent to the reader that the content is abusive. The messages in the second column are implicit and it is harder to determine whether they are abusive without knowing the context. For example, the word "them" in the first two examples in the generalized and implicit cell refers to an ethnic group, and the words "skypes" and "Google" are used as euphemisms for slurs about Jews and African-Americans respectively. Abuse using sarcasm can be even more elusive for detection systems, for instance the seemingly harmless comment praising someone's intelligence was a sarcastic response to a beauty pageant contestants unsatisfactory answer to a question (Dinakar et al., 2011).

3 Implications for future research

In the following section we outline the implications of this typology, highlighting where the existing literatures indicate how we can understand, measure, and model each subtype of abuse.

3.1 Implications for annotation

In the task of annotating documents that contain bullying, it appears that there is a common understanding of what cyberbullying entails: an intentionally harmful electronic attack by an individual or group against a victim, usually repetitive in nature (Dadvar et al., 2013). This consensus allows for a relatively consistent set of annotation guidelines across studies, most of which simply ask annotators to determine if a post contains bullying or harassment (Dadvar et al., 2014; Kontostathis et al., 2013; Bretschneider et al., 2014).

---

[1] All punctuation is as reported in original papers. We have added all the * symbols.

	Explicit	*Implicit*
Directed	"Go kill yourself", "You're a sad little f*ck" (Van Hee et al., 2015a), "@User shut yo beaner ass up sp*c and hop your f*ggot ass back across the border little n*gga" (Davidson et al., 2017), "Youre one of the ugliest b*tches Ive ever fucking seen" (Kontostathis et al., 2013).	"Hey Brendan, you look gorgeous today. What beauty salon did you visit?" (Dinakar et al., 2012), "((((@User))) and what is your job? Writing cuck articles and slurping Google balls? #Dumbgoogles" (Hine et al., 2017), "you're intelligence is so breathtaking!!!!!!" (Dinakar et al., 2011)
Generalized	"I am surprised they reported on this crap who cares about another dead n*gger?", "300 missiles are cool! Love to see um launched into Tel Aviv! Kill all the g*ys there!" (Nobata et al., 2016), "So an 11 year old n*gger girl killed herself over my tweets? ˆ_ˆ thats another n*gger off the streets!!" (Kwok and Wang, 2013).	"Totally fed up with the way this country has turned into a haven for terrorists. Send them all back home." (Burnap and Williams, 2015), "most of them come north and are good at just mowing lawns" (Dinakar et al., 2011), "Gas the skypes" (Magu et al., 2017)

Table 1: **Typology of abusive language.**

High inter-annotator agreement on cyberbullying tasks (93%) (Dadvar et al., 2013) further indicates a general consensus around the features of cyberbullying (Van Hee et al., 2015b). After bullying has been identified annotators are typically asked more detailed questions about the extremity of the bullying, the identification of phrases that indicate bullying, and the roles of users as bully/victim (Dadvar et al., 2014; Van Hee et al., 2015b; Kontostathis et al., 2013).

We expect that consensus may be due to the directed nature of the phenomenon. Cyberbullying involves a victim whom annotators can identify and relatively easily discern whether statements directed towards the victim should be considered abusive. In contrast, in work on annotating harassment, offensive language, and hate speech there appears to be little consensus on definitions and lower inter-annotator agreement ($\kappa \approx 0.60 - 0.80$) (Ross et al., 2016; Waseem, 2016a; Tulkens et al., 2016; Bretschneider and Peters, 2017) are obtained. Given that these tasks are often broadly defined and the target is often generalized, all else being equal, it is more difficult for annotators to determine whether statements should be considered abusive. Future work in these subtasks should aim to have annotators distinguish between targeted and generalized abuse so that each subtype can be modeled more effectively.

Annotation (via crowd-sourcing and other methods) tends to be more straightforward when explicit instances of abusive language can be identified and agreed upon (Waseem, 2016b), but is considerably more difficult when implicit abuse is considered (Dadvar et al., 2013; Justo et al., 2014; Dinakar et al., 2011). The connotations of language can be difficult to classify without domain-

specific knowledge. Furthermore, while some argue that detailed guidelines can help annotators to make more subtle distinctions (Davidson et al., 2017), others find that they do not improve the reliability of non-expert classifications (Ross et al., 2016). In such cases, expert annotators with domain specific knowledge are preferred as they tend to produce more accurate classifications (Waseem, 2016a).

Ultimately, the nature of abusive language can be extremely subjective, and researchers must endeavor to take this into account when using human annotators. Davidson et al. (2017), for instance, show that annotators tend to code racism as hate speech at a higher rate than sexism. As such, it is important that researchers consider the social biases that may lead people to disregard certain types of abuse.

The type of abuse that researchers are seeking to identify should guide the annotation strategy. Where subtasks occupy multiple cells in our typology, annotators should be allowed to make nuanced distinctions that differentiate between different types of abuse. In highlighting the major differences between different abusive language detection subtasks, our typology indicates that different annotation strategies are appropriate depending on the type of abuse.

3.2 Implications for modeling

Existing research on abusive language online has used a diverse set of features. Moving forward, it is important that researchers clarify which features are most useful for which subtasks and which subtasks present the greatest challenges. We do not attempt to review all the features used (see Schmidt and Wiegand 2017 for a detailed review) but make suggestions for which features could be most helpful for the different subtasks. For each aspect of the typology, we suggest features that have been shown to be successful predictors in prior work. Many features occur in more than one form of abuse. As such, we do not propose that particular features are necessarily unique to each phenomenon, rather that they provide different insights and should be employed depending on what the researcher is attempting to measure.

Directed abuse. Features that help to identify the target of abuse are crucial to directed abuse detection. Mentions, proper nouns, named entities, and co-reference resolution can all be used in different contexts to identify targets. Bretschneider and Peters (2017) use a multi-tiered system, first identifying offensive statements, then their severity, and finally the target. Syntactical features have also proven to be successful in identifying abusive language. A number of studies on hate speech use part-of-speech sequences to model the expression of hatred (Warner and Hirschberg, 2012; Gitari et al., 2015; Davidson et al., 2017). Typed dependencies offer a more sophisticated way to capture the relationship between terms (Burnap and Williams, 2015). Overall, there are many tools that researchers can use to model the relationship between abusive language and targets, although many of these require high-quality annotations to use as training data.

Generalized abuse. Generalized abuse online tends to target people belonging to a small set of categories, primarily racial, religious, and sexual minorities (Silva et al., 2016). Researchers should consider identifying forms of abuse unique to each target group addressed, as vocabularies may depend on the groups targeted. For example, the language used to abuse trans-people and that used against Latin American people are likely to differ, both in the nouns used to denote the target group and the other terms associated with them. In some cases a lexical method may therefore be an appropriate strategy. Further research is necessary to determine if there are underlying syntactic structures associated with generalized abusive language.

Explicit abuse Explicit abuse, whether directed or generalized, is often indicated by specific keywords. Hence, dictionary-based approaches may be well suited to identify this type of abuse (Warner and Hirschberg, 2012; Nobata et al., 2016), although the presence of particular words should not be the only criteria, even terms that denote abuse may be used in a variety of different ways (Kwok and Wang, 2013; Davidson et al., 2017). Negative polarity and sentiment of the text are also likely indicators of explicit abuse that can be leveraged by researchers (Gitari et al., 2015).

Implicit abuse. Building a specific lexicon may prove impractical, as in the case of the appropriation of the term "skype" in some forums (Magu et al., 2017). Still, even partial lexicons may be used as seeds to inductively discover other keywords by use of a semi-supervised method proposed by King et al. (2017). Additionally, character n-grams have been shown to be apt for abusive language tasks due to their ability to capture variation of words associated with abuse (Nobata et al., 2016; Waseem, 2016a). Word embeddings are also promising ways to capture terms associated with abuse (Djuric et al., 2015; Badjatiya et al., 2017), although they may still be insufficient for cases like 4Chan's connotation of "skype" where a word has a dominant meaning and a more subversive one. Furthermore, as some of the above examples show, implicit abuse often takes on complex linguistic forms like sarcasm, metonymy, and humor. Without high quality labeled data to learn these representations, it may be difficult for researchers to come up with models of syntactic structure that can help to identify implicit abuse. To overcome these limitations researchers may find it prudent to incorporate features beyond just textual analysis, including the characteristics of the individuals involved (Dadvar et al., 2013) and other extra-textual features.

4 Discussion

This typology has a number of implications for future work in the area.

First, we want to encourage researchers working on these subtasks to learn from advances in other areas. Researchers working on purportedly distinct subtasks are often working on the same problems in parallel. For example, the field of hate speech detection can be strengthened by interactions with work on cyberbullying, and vice versa, since a large part of both subtasks consists of identifying targeted abuse.

Second, we aim to highlight the important distinctions within subtasks that have hitherto been ignored. For example, in much hate speech research, diverse types of abuse have been lumped together under a single label, forcing models to account for a large amount of within-class variation. We suggest that fine-grained distinctions along the axes allows for more focused systems that may be more effective at identifying particular types of abuse.

Third, we call for closer consideration of how annotation guidelines are related to the phenomenon of interest. The type of annotation and even the choice of annotators should be motivated by the nature of the abuse. Further, we welcome discussion of annotation guidelines and the annotation process in published work. Many existing studies only tangentially mention these, sometimes never explaining how the data were annotated.

Fourth, we encourage researchers to consider which features are most appropriate for each subtask. Prior work has found a diverse array of features to be useful in understanding and identifying abuse, but we argue that different feature sets will be relevant to different subtasks. Future work should aim to build a more robust understanding of when to use which types of features.

Fifth, it is important to emphasize that not all abuse is equal, both in terms of its effects and its detection. We expect that social media and website operators will be more interested in identifying and dealing with explicit abuse, while activists, campaigners, and journalists may have more incentive to also identify implicit abuse. Targeted abuse such as cyberbullying may be more likely to be reported by victims and thus acted upon than generalized abuse. We also expect that implicit abuse will be more difficult to detect and model, although methodological advances may make such tasks more feasible.

5   Conclusion

We have presented a typology that synthesizes the different subtasks in abusive language detection. Our aim is to bring together findings in these different areas and to clarify the key aspects of abusive language detection. There are important analytical distinctions that have been largely overlooked in prior work and through acknowledging these and their implications we hope to improve abuse detection systems and our understanding of abusive language.

Rather than attempting to resolve the "definitional quagmire" (Faris et al., 2016) involved in

neatly bounding and defining each subtask we encourage researchers to think carefully about the phenomena they want to measure and the appropriate research design. We intend for our typology to be used both at the stage of data collection and annotation and the stage of feature creation and modeling. We hope that future work will be more transparent in discussing the annotation and modeling strategies used, and will closely examine the similarities and differences between these subtasks through empirical analyses.

References

Pinkesh Badjatiya, Shashank Gupta, Manish Gupta, and Vasudeva Varma. 2017. Deep learning for hate speech detection in tweets. In *Proceedings of the 26th International Conference on World Wide Web Companion.* pages 759–760.

Roland Barthes. 1957. *Mythologies.* Seuil.

Uwe Bretschneider and Ralf Peters. 2017. Detecting offensive statements towards foreigners in social media. In *Proceedings of the 50th Hawaii International Conference on System Sciences.*

Uwe Bretschneider, Thomas Whner, and Ralf Peters. 2014. Detecting online harassment in social networks. In *ICIS 2014 Proceedings: Conference Theme Track: Building a Better World through IS.*

Rogers Brubaker. 2004. *Ethnicity without groups.* Harvard University Press.

Pete Burnap and Matthew L Williams. 2015. Cyber hate speech on twitter: An application of machine classification and statistical modeling for policy and decision making. *Policy & Internet* 7(2):223–242.

Maral Dadvar, Dolf Trieschnigg, and Franciska de Jong. 2014. Experts and machines against bullies: a hybrid approach to detect cyberbullies. In *Conference on Artificial Intelligence.* Springer International Publishing.

Maral Dadvar, Dolf Trieschnigg, Roeland Ordelman, and Franciska de Jong. 2013. Improving cyberbullying detection with user context. In *European Conference on Information Retrieval.* Springer, pages 693–696.

Thomas Davidson, Dana Warmsley, Micheel Macy, and Ingmar Weber. 2017. Automated hate speech detection and the problem of offensive language. In *Proceedings of the Eleventh International Conference on Web and Social Media.* Montreal, Canada, pages 512–515.

Karthik Dinakar, Birago Jones, Catherine Havasi, Henry Lieberman, and Rosalind Picard. 2012. Common sense reasoning for detection, prevention, and mitigation of cyberbullying. *ACM Transactions on Interactive Intelligent Systems (TiiS)* 2(3):18.

Karthik Dinakar, Roi Reichart, and Henry Lieberman. 2011. Modeling the detection of textual cyberbullying. *The Social Mobile Web* 11(02).

Nemanja Djuric, Jing Zhou, Robin Morris, Mihajlo Grbovic, Vladan Radosavljevic, and Narayan Bhamidipati. 2015. Hate speech detection with comment embeddings. In *Proceedings of the 24th International Conference on World Wide Web*. ACM, pages 29–30.

Robert Faris, Amar Ashar, Urs Gasser, and Daisy Joo. 2016. Understanding harmful speech online. *Berkman Klein Center Research Publication* 21.

Njagi Dennis Gitari, Zhang Zuping, Hanyurwimfura Damien, and Jun Long. 2015. A lexicon-based approach for hate speech detection. *International Journal of Multimedia and Ubiquitous Engineering* 10(4):215–230.

Gabriel Emile Hine, Jeremiah Onaolapo, Emiliano De Cristofaro, Nicolas Kourtellis, Ilias Leontiadis, Riginos Samaras, Gianluca Stringhini, and Jeremy Blackburn. 2017. A longitudinal measurement study of 4chan's politically incorrect forum and its effect on the web. In *Proceedings of the Eleventh International Conference on Web and Social Media*. Montreal, Canada, pages 92–101.

Raquel Justo, Thomas Corcoran, Stephanie M. Lukin, Marilyn Walker, and M. Ins Torres. 2014. Extracting relevant knowledge for the detection of sarcasm and nastiness in the social web. *Knowledge-Based Systems* 69:124 – 133.

Gary King, Patrick Lam, and Margaret E Roberts. 2017. Computer-assisted keyword and document set discovery from unstructured text. *American Journal of Political Science* .

April Kontostathis, Kelly Reynolds, Andy Garron, and Lynne Edwards. 2013. Detecting cyberbullying: Query terms and techniques. In *Proceedings of the 5th Annual ACM Web Science Conference*. ACM, New York, NY, USA, WebSci '13, pages 195–204.

Irene Kwok and Yuzhou Wang. 2013. Locate the hate: Detecting tweets against blacks. In *Proceedings of the Twenty-Seventh AAAI Conference on Artificial Intelligence*. AAAI Press, AAAI'13, pages 1621–1622.

Rijul Magu, Kshitij Joshi, and Jiebo Luo. 2017. Detecting the hate code on social media. In *Proceedings of the Eleventh International Conference on Web and Social Media*. Montreal, Canada, pages 608–612.

Chikashi Nobata, Joel Tetreault, Achint Thomas, Yashar Mehdad, and Yi Chang. 2016. Abusive language detection in online user content. In *Proceedings of the 25th International Conference on World Wide Web*. pages 145–153.

Björn Ross, Michael Rist, Guillermo Carbonell, Benjamin Cabrera, Nils Kurowsky, and Michael Wojatzki. 2016. Measuring the Reliability of Hate Speech Annotations: The Case of the European Refugee Crisis. In *Proceedings of NLP4CMC III: 3rd Workshop on Natural Language Processing for Computer-Mediated Communication*. pages 6–9.

Anna Schmidt and Michael Wiegand. 2017. A survey on hate speech detection using natural language processing. In *Proceedings of the Fifth International Workshop on Natural Language Processing for Social Media*. Association for Computational Linguistics, Valencia, Spain, pages 1–10.

Leandro Araújo Silva, Mainack Mondal, Denzil Correa, Fabrício Benevenuto, and Ingmar Weber. 2016. Analyzing the targets of hate in online social media. In *Proceedings of the Tenth International Conference on Web and Social Media*. Cologne, Germany, pages 687–690.

Derald Wing Sue, Christina M Capodilupo, Gina C Torino, Jennifer M Bucceri, Aisha Holder, Kevin L Nadal, and Marta Esquilin. 2007. Racial microaggressions in everyday life: implications for clinical practice. *American Psychologist* 62(4):271–286.

Stéphan Tulkens, Lisa Hilte, Elise Lodewyckx, Ben Verhoeven, and Walter Daelemans. 2016. The automated detection of racist discourse in dutch social media. *CLIN Journal* 6:3–20.

Cynthia Van Hee, Els Lefever, Ben Verhoeven, Julie Mennes, Bart Desmet, Guy De Pauw, Walter Daelemans, and Veronique Hoste. 2015a. Detection and fine-grained classification of cyberbullying events. In *Proceedings of the International Conference Recent Advances in Natural Language Processing*. Hissar, Bulgaria, pages 672–680.

Cynthia Van Hee, Ben Verhoeven, Els Lefever, Guy De Pauw, Véronique Hoste, and Walter Daelemans. 2015b. Guidelines for the fine-grained analysis of cyberbullying. Technical report, LT3, Ghent University, Belgium.

William Warner and Julia Hirschberg. 2012. Detecting hate speech on the world wide web. In *Proceedings of the Second Workshop on Language in Social Media*. Association for Computational Linguistics, LSM '12, pages 19–26.

Zeerak Waseem. 2016a. Are you a racist or am i seeing things? annotator influence on hate speech detection on twitter. In *Proceedings of the First Workshop on NLP and Computational Social Science*. Association for Computational Linguistics, Austin, Texas, pages 138–142.

Zeerak Waseem. 2016b. *Automatic Hate Speech Detection*. Master's thesis, University of Copenhagen.

Zeerak Waseem and Dirk Hovy. 2016. Hateful symbols or hateful people? predictive features for hate speech detection on twitter. In *Proceedings of the*

NAACL Student Research Workshop. Association for Computational Linguistics, San Diego, California, pages 88–93.

Andreas Wimmer. 2013. *Ethnic boundary making: Institutions, power, networks*. Oxford University Press.

Ellery Wulczyn, Nithum Thain, and Lucas Dixon. 2017. Ex machina: Personal attacks seen at scale. In *Proceedings of the 26th International Conference on World Wide Web*.

Using Convolutional Neural Networks to Classify Hate-Speech

Björn Gambäck and **Utpal Kumar Sikdar**
Department of Computer Science
Norwegian University of Science and Technology
NO–7491 Trondheim, Norway
gamback@ntnu.no   utpal.sikdar@gmail.com

Abstract

The paper introduces a deep learning-based Twitter hate-speech text classification system. The classifier assigns each tweet to one of four predefined categories: racism, sexism, both (racism and sexism) and non-hate-speech. Four Convolutional Neural Network models were trained on resp. character 4-grams, word vectors based on semantic information built using word2vec, randomly generated word vectors, and word vectors combined with character n-grams. The feature set was down-sized in the networks by max-pooling, and a softmax function used to classify tweets. Tested by 10-fold cross-validation, the model based on word2vec embeddings performed best, with higher precision than recall, and a 78.3% F-score.

1 Introduction

During the Spring of 2017, parliamentary committees in Germany and the UK strongly criticised leading social media sites such as Facebook, Twitter and Youtube (Google) for failing to take sufficient and quick enough action against hate-speech, with the German government threatening to fine the social networks up to 50 million euros per year if they continue to fail to act on hateful postings (and posters) within a week (Thomasson, 2017).

When called to witness in front of the UK Home Affairs Committee, all the social media companies refused to reveal both the number of people they employ to battle hate-speech and the amount they spend on this. However, Google claimed to have invested "hundreds of millions" while Facebook stated that they had thousands of people working on the problem. The German government estimated that the companies combined already spend some 50 million euros per year and that the suggested new German law would increase that amount by 50% (CDU/CSU & SPD, 2017, p.14).

Regardless of the resources actually devoted by the social media networks, it is clear that their current efforts are not enough: "we are disappointed at the pace of development of technological solutions" (Home Affairs Committee, 2017, p.24). The UK and German governments also indicate that they are moving in the direction of treating online content providers in analogy with publishers of printed material, with the same obligations to abide to publishing laws.

With legislation in other countries set to follow (Nielsen, 2017), properly identifying hate-speech is a pressing issue, not only for the major players, but also for smaller companies, clubs, and organisations that allow for user-generated content on their sites (albeit the current German law proposal makes an exception for sites with less than 2 million users). Many such sites currently use slow, manual moderation, which mean that abusive posts will be left online for too long without appropriate action being taken or that content will be published with delay (which might be unacceptable to the users, e.g., in online chat rooms).

Following the work by Collobert et al. (2011), deep neural networks have been shown to effectively solve several language processing tasks such as part-of-speech tagging, sentiment analysis, and named entity recognition. Here a Convolutional Neural Network (CNN) model with various features is utilised for hate-speech categorisation. Word vectors based on semantic information are built for all tokens using an unsupervised learning algorithm, word2vec. The word vectors are merged with a set of extracted features, down-sized using max-pooling, and together with character n-grams (4-grams) fed to the neural network model to predict the categories of each tweet.

Proceedings of the First Workshop on Abusive Language Online, pages 85–90,
Vancouver, Canada, July 30 - August 4, 2017. ©2017 Association for Computational Linguistics

The paper is organised as follows: Previous work on hate-speech identification is discussed in Section 2. Section 3 describes the deep learning-based hate-speech categorisation strategy, while experiments and results are reported in Section 4. Finally, Section 5 summarises the discussion.

2 Related Work

Although the above-noted law-maker interest in the issue is fairly recent, the task of identifying hate speech and abusive language in online content has already been topical in the research community for 20 years. Spertus (1997) built the decision tree-based classifier 'Smokey' which utilised 47 syntactic and semantic sentential features. When trained on a small set of 720 web page posts manually annotated (as "flame", "okay" or "maybe") and evaluated on 502 other messages, 'Smokey' performed well on classifying the non-inflamatory messages, but fell completely short on flame texts (thus obtaining an accuracy of only 88.2% on a task with a majority-class baseline of 86.1%).

Addressing the dataset size problem, Sood et al. (2012) collected 1.6 million comments from a Yahoo! social news site, of which 6,500 were randomly selected for annotation by 221 persons on Amazon Mechanical Turk (AMT). Several Support Vector Machine classifiers were trained on varying-size parts of this dataset using mainly word n-gram features, indicating that classification performance kept improving with increased datasets, but not as rapidly after the data size had passed 1,500 items. Looking at another set of AMT-annotated Yahoo! news posts, Nobata et al. (2016) experimented with several different word-internal, n-gram-based, syntactic, and distributional semantic features, concluding that character n-grams alone contribute sufficiently strongly for an online gradient descent learner to perform well on this type of data.

Moving away from features based solely on the language used in online messages, Chen et al. (2012) proposed a model also taking into account the posting patterns of the users in order to single out persons exhibiting abusive behaviour. Similarly, Buckels et al. (2014) aimed to extract traits from online user behaviour that would indicate antisocial personality. This is of particular importance for swift moderation of online chat rooms, as addressed by, e.g., Yin et al. (2009) and Papegnies et al. (2017), with the latter suggesting several types of features (at the morphological, syntactic and user behaviour levels) that can be used for identifying when gamers on a French MMO (massively multiplayer online) game site move from discussing game-related issues to posting personal inflammatory remarks.

Of particular relevance to the present work are previous efforts on identifying abusive language on Twitter. Xiang et al. (2012) created offensive-language topic clusters using Logistic Regression over a set of 860,071 tweets automatically annotated using a boot-strapping technique and supplemented with a dictionary of 339 offensive words. When tested on 4,029 randomly selected tweets collected just after the training set, the lexicon-enhanced clustering outperformed a keyword matching baseline. Logistic Regression and a dictionary was also utilised by Davidson et al. (2017); however, they used crowd-sourcing to create their hate-speech dictionary and aimed to separate the tweets into three classes: hate-speech, offensive language, and neither. Working on a set of 24,802 manually labelled tweets, they achieved good recall and precision overall, but noted that almost 40% of the actual hate-speech tweets were misclassified, although with 3/4 of those being mistaken for offensive language only.

A recurring problem with several of these experiments has been that the annotated datasets have not always been made publically available. However, Ross et al. (2016) had a set of 541 German tweets annotated, in particular addressing the issues of annotator and annotation reliability, and what information should be provided to the annotators. Waseem (2016) discusses similar issues while providing a set of 6,909 English tweets hate-speech annotated by CrowdFlower users,[1] and extending a previous such dataset (Waseem and Hovy, 2016). This dataset will be used in the experiments reported below.

Wulczyn et al. (2016) also used CrowdFlower to obtain human annotations of 115,737 comments on Wikipedia as to whether they contained personal attacks and harassment. They furthermore experimented with strategies to automatically expand the dataset, comparing Multi-Layer Perceptrons (a single-hidden-layer neural network) to Logistic Regression, and word n-grams to character n-grams; concluding the Logistic Regression with character n-grams performed best.

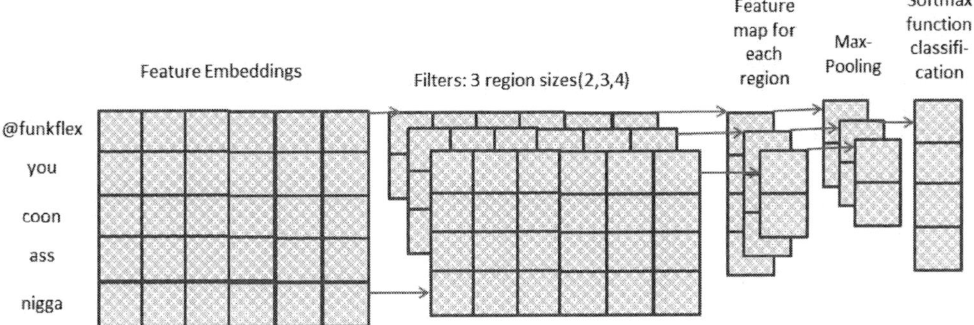

Figure 1: Hate-speech classifier

3 CNN-based Hate-Speech Classification

This section describes the hate-speech identification system architecture based on Convolutional Neural Networks (CNN). An overview of the system is shown in Figure 1. The first step of the system is to generate feature embeddings. Feature embeddings for all words were constructed by using word embeddings and character n-grams.

The word embeddings were generated in two ways, through word2vec (Mikolov et al., 2013a,b) and through random vectors. In the random vector setting, all the words in the corpora are initialised with random values. In the word2vec version, word vectors are generated based on the context. There are two types of such embeddings: continuous-bags-of-words (CBOW) and skip-gram models. In the CBOW architecture, the model predicts the current word from a window of surrounding context words. In the skip-gram model, the context words are predicted using the current word.

In addition to the word embeddings, length 28 one-hot character n-gram vectors were generated, with 26 elements for the English alphabet, one for digits, and one for all other characters/symbols. The feature embeddings were produced by concatenating the word embeddings with these character n-gram vectors.

A pooling layer in the network converts each tweet into a fixed length vector, capturing the information from the entire tweet. A max-pooling layer then captures the most important latent semantic factors from the tweets.

On the output side, a softmax layer calculates the class probability distributions for each tweet and assigns the hate-speech classes / labels based on the probability values.

4 Experiments

Four approaches to hate-speech classification were tested, based on different feature embeddings. All models were applied to the English Twitter hate-speech dataset created by Waseem (2016).[2] Each tweet in the dataset has been annotated by one Expert annotator and three Amateur annotators, with four labels: non-hate-speech (84% of the data), racism, sexism, and both (i.e., racism *and* sexism).

Waseem (2016) defined the "Expert" annotators as those having both a theoretical and applied knowledge of hate speech (those were recruited among feminist and antiracism activists), while the "Amateur" annotations were obtained by crowd-sourcing (on the CrowdFlower platform). We combined the annotated tags for each tweet based on majority voting, where the Expert was given double unit votes and each of the Amateurs was given a single unit vote.

The class distributions of the dataset are shown in Table 1. The total size of the dataset (6,655 tweets) is slightly lower than the original set (Waseem reported it as containing 6,909 tweets), since some of the annotated tweets were unavailable or had been deleted.

Data	Number of tweets
Racism	91
Sexism	946
Both (racism & sexism)	18
Non-hate-speech	5600
Total	6655

Table 1: Twitter hate-speech dataset statistics

---

[2]http://github.com/zeerakw/hatespeech

System setup		Precision	Recall	F_1-score
	Random vectors	**0.8668**	0.6726	0.7563
CNN	word2vec	0.8566	0.7214	**0.7829**
	Character n-grams	0.8557	0.7011	0.7695
	word2vec + character n-grams	0.8661	0.7042	0.7738
Logistic Regression with character n-grams (Waseem and Hovy, 2016)		0.7287	**0.7775**	0.7389

Table 2: System performance (10-fold cross-validated)

4.1 Results

The average 10-fold cross-validated results for all four Convolutional Neural Network (CNN) models are shown in Table 2, and compared to the Logistic Regression (LogReg) model used by Waseem and Hovy (2016).

In the first CNN model, random word vectors were considered as feature embeddings when training the network. This baseline model achieved precision, recall and F-score values of 86.68%, 67.26% and 75.63%, respectively, marking a drastic improvement in precision compared to the LogReg model, but at the expense of lower recall. In the second approach, word2vec word vectors were taken as feature embeddings to learn the CNN model, resulting in clearly (7.3%) improved recall, for an F-score of 78.29%, even though the precision actually was slightly reduced compared to using the random vectors.

The third and fourth models both added character n-grams to the input of the CNN model. In line with the experiments reported on the same dataset by Waseem and Hovy (2016), length 4 character n-grams were used. In the third model, only the character n-gram were considered as feature embeddings when training the CNN model, while in the fourth model, the feature embeddings were generated by concatenating word2vec word embeddings and character n-grams. Tested by 10-fold cross-validation, the latter system showed better precision (86.61%) than recall (70.42%), for an F-score of 77.38%.

However, although the character n-grams thus helped a little in improving precision, the word2vec model without character n-grams still achieved the best results of all the compared models, with the precision, recall and F-score values of 85.66%, 72.14% and 78.29%, respectively. Note that all CNN models convincingly outperformed Logistic Regression in terms of both precision and F_1-score, while the LogReg model achieved better recall than all the neural network models.

4.2 Error Analysis

An error analysis was carried out for each of the 10 folds. The confusion matrices are shown in Table 3. It can be observed that the model overall did not identify many tweets as hate-speech tweets. This may be due to insufficient training instances. Furthermore, the system wrongly identified some non-hate-speech tweets as hate-speech.

In particular, the system was not able to identify properly the category 'both', since the examples of this category are very few (1 or 2 per fold) with respect to the whole set of training instances. The system performed better in the 'sexism' category than in the other hate-speech categories ('both' and 'racism') because the number of tweets of this category are larger.

5 Conclusion and Future Work

Here we have experimented with a system for Twitter hate-speech text classification based on a deep-learning, Convolutional Neural Network model. The classifier assigns each tweet to one of four predefined categories: racism, sexism, both (racism and sexism) and neither.

Two CNN models were created based on different input vectors sets that were fed to the neural networks for training and classification. Word vectors based on semantic information were built using an unsupervised strategy, word2vec, and compared to a randomly generated vector baseline. In additional, two CNN models were trained on character 4-grams, as well as on a combination of word vectors and character n-grams. The feature set is down-sized in the networks by a max-pooling layer, while a softmax layer is utilised to assign the tweets their most probable label category.

CNN True	Fold-1				Fold-2				Fold-3				Fold-4				Fold-5			
	b	s	r	n	b	s	r	n	b	s	r	n	b	s	r	n	b	s	r	n
both	0	0	0	1	0	2	0	0	0	0	0	1	1	1	0	0	0	1	0	0
sexism	1	70	0	25	0	71	0	20	0	78	0	19	0	82	0	18	0	69	0	23
racism	0	0	5	6	0	0	0	6	0	0	2	8	0	0	5	7	0	0	1	8
neither	0	13	1	543	0	15	4	547	0	11	2	544	0	11	3	537	0	13	0	550

	Fold-6				Fold-7				Fold-8				Fold-9				Fold-10			
both	1	1	0	0	0	1	0	0	0	1	0	0	0	2	0	1	1	3	0	0
sexism	0	66	0	17	0	72	0	18	0	80	0	33	0	70	0	26	0	70	0	18
racism	0	0	3	1	0	0	1	3	0	0	6	9	0	0	1	9	0	0	6	4
neither	0	9	4	563	0	10	0	560	0	7	2	527	0	16	0	540	0	6	0	562

Table 3: Confusion matrices for each fold, with rows showing the true labels and columns system outputs. Legend: 'b' = both, 's' = sexism, 'r' = racism and 'n' = neither.

Trained and tested by 10-fold cross-validation, the system based on word2vec word vectors performed best overall, with an F_1-score of 78.3%. Adding character n-grams slightly increased the precision, but resulted in lower recall and F-score.

The tested models and neural network architectures could be extended in several ways: The word2vec embeddings used here were built on skip-grams that predict the context words using the current word. An alternative would be to use continuous-bags-of-words that basically do the opposite and predict the current word from a window of surrounding context words. Also, following Waseem and Hovy (2016) only length 4 character n-grams were used. Clearly it would be interesting to explore whether these are uniformly ineffective when changing the n-gram size.

The experiments reported here were carried out on a convolutional network architecture, but other types of deep neural networks could obviously be tried. In particular, the bi-directional Long Short-Term Memory (LSTM) recurrent neural network architecture has shown itself to be useful to language processing problems where utilising the sequential nature of the input is more essential, such as named entity recognition and sentiment analysis, although most of the best performing systems in SemEval 2016 (the International Workshop on Semantic Evaluation; Task 4: Sentiment Analysis in Twitter) actually utilised convolutional neural networks or combinations of CNNs and other approaches (Nakov et al., 2016).

A long those lines, Sikdar and Gambäck (2017) report experiments with a set-up for named entity recognition combining an LSTM with a more traditional machine learning classifier based on Conditional Random Fields (CRF). Such an approach could be tested also for the abusive language classification task, either using the LSTM/CRF combination or including CNN.

Acknowledgments

The work reported here was carried out within the CZ09 Czech-Norwegian Research Programme under Project Contract 7F14047, HaBiT ("Harvesting big text data for under-resourced languages"; `http://www.habit-project.eu`) funded by the Research Council of Norway (NFR) and the Czech Republic's Ministry of Education, Youth and Sports (MŠMT) through the EEA/Norway Financial Mechanism.

Thanks to the four anonymous reviewers for comments that helped improve the paper.

References

Erin E. Buckels, Paul D. Trapnell, and Delroy L. Paulhus. 2014. Trolls just want to have fun. *Personality and Individual Differences* 67:97–102.

CDU/CSU & SPD. 2017. Gesetzentwurf der Fraktionen der CDU/CSU und SPD: Entwurf eines Gesetzes zur Verbesserung der Rechtsdurchsetzung in sozialen Netzwerken (Netzwerkdurchsetzungsgesetz — NetzDG). Drs. 18/12356, Deutscher Bundestag, Berlin, Germany.

Ying Chen, Yilu Zhou, Sencun Zhu, and Heng Xu. 2012. Detecting offensive language in social media to protect adolescent online safety. In *Proceedings of the 2012 ASE/IEEE International Conference on Social Computing and 2012 ASE/IEEE International Conference on Privacy, Security, Risk and Trust*. IEEE Computer Society, Amsterdam, The Netherlands, pages 71–80.

Ronan Collobert, Jason Weston, Léon Bottou, Michael Karlen, Koray Kavukcuoglu, and Pavel Kuksa. 2011. Natural language processing (almost) from scratch. *Journal of Machine Learning Research* 12:2493–2537.

Thomas Davidson, Dana Warmsley, Michael Macy, and Ingmar Weber. 2017. Automated hate speech detection and the problem of offensive language. In *Proceedings of the International AAAI Conference on Web and Social Media (ICWSM)*. American Association for Artificial Intelligence, Toronto, Canada. To appear.

Home Affairs Committee. 2017. Hate crime: abuse, hate and extremism online. Fourteenth Report of Session 2016–17 HC 609, House of Commons, London, UK.

Tomas Mikolov, Kai Chen, Greg Corrado, and Jeffrey Dean. 2013a. Efficient estimation of word representations in vector space. *CoRR* abs/1301.3781.

Tomas Mikolov, Ilya Sutskever, Kai Chen, Greg Corrado, and Jeffrey Dean. 2013b. Distributed representations of words and phrases and their compositionality. In *Advances in Neural Information Processing Systems 26 (NIPS 2013)*. Curran Associates, Red Hook, NY, USA, pages 3111–3119.

Preslav Nakov, Alan Ritter, Sara Rosenthal, Fabrizio Sebastiani, and Veselin Stoyanov. 2016. SemEval-2016 Task 4: Sentiment analysis in Twitter. In *Proceedings of the 10th International Workshop on Semantic Evaluation*. ACL, San Diego, California.

Nikolaj Nielsen. 2017. EU states back bill against online hate speech. EUobserver, May 24. https://euobserver.com/justice/138009.

Chikashi Nobata, Joel Tetreault, Achint Thomas, Yashar Mehdad, and Yi Chang. 2016. Abusive language detection in online user content. In *Proceedings of the 25th International Conference on World Wide Web*. International World Wide Web Conferences Steering Committee, Montreal, Canada, pages 145–153.

Etienne Papegnies, Vincent Labatut, Richard Dufour, and Georges Linarès. 2017. Impact of content features for automatic online abuse detection. In Alexander Gelbukh, editor, *Computational Linguistics and Intelligent Text Processing: Proceedings of the 18th International Conference*. Springer, Budapest, Hungary.

Björn Ross, Michael Rist, Guillermo Carbonell, Benjamin Cabrera, Nils Kurowsky, and Michael Wojatzki. 2016. Measuring the reliability of hate speech annotations: The case of the European refugee crisis. In *3rd Workshop on Natural Language Processing for Computer-Mediated Communication*. Bochum, Germany, pages 6–9.

Utpal Kumar Sikdar and Björn Gambäck. 2017. Named entity recognition for Amharic using stack-based deep learning. In Alexander Gelbukh, editor, *Computational Linguistics and Intelligent Text Processing: Proceedings of the 18th International Conference*. Springer, Budapest, Hungary.

Sara Owsley Sood, Elizabeth F. Churchill, and Judd Antin. 2012. Automatic identification of personal insults on social news sites. *Journal of the American Society for Information Science and Technology* 63(2):270–285.

Ellen Spertus. 1997. Smokey: Automatic recognition of hostile messages. In *Proceedings of the 14th National Conference on Artificial Intelligence and 9th Conference on Innovative Applications of Artificial Intelligence*. American Association for Artificial Intelligence, Providence, Rhode Island, pages 1058–1065.

Emma Thomasson. 2017. German cabinet agrees to fine social media over hate speech. Reuters, Apr 5. http://uk.reuters.com/article/idUKKBN1771FK.

Zeerak Waseem. 2016. Are you a racist or am i seeing things? Annotator influence on hate speech detection on Twitter. In *Proceedings of 2016 EMNLP Workshop on Natural Language Processing and Computational Social Science*. ACL, Austin, Texas, pages 138–142.

Zeerak Waseem and Dirk Hovy. 2016. Hateful symbols or hateful people? Predictive features for hate speech detection on Twitter. In *Proceedings of the 15th Annual Conference of the North American Chapter of the Association for Computational Linguistics: Human Language Technologies*. ACL, San Diego, California, pages 88–93.

Ellery Wulczyn, Nithum Thain, and Lucas Dixon. 2016. Ex Machina: Personal attacks seen at scale. *CoRR* abs/1610.08914.

Guang Xiang, Bin Fan, Ling Wang, Jason I. Hong, and Carolyn P. Rose. 2012. Detecting offensive tweets via topical feature discovery over a large scale Twitter corpus. In *Proceedings of the 21st ACM International Conference on Information and Knowledge Management*. ACM, Maui, Hawaii, pages 1980–1984.

Dawei Yin, Zhenzhen Xue, Liangjie Hong, Brian D. Davison, April Kontostathis, and Lynne Edwards. 2009. Detection of harassment on Web 2.0. In *Proceedings of the Content Analysis in the WEB 2.0 Workshop at WWW2009*. Madrid, Spain.

Illegal is not a Noun:
Linguistic Form for Detection of Pejorative Nominalizations

Alexis Palmer, Melissa Robinson, Kristy Phillips
Department of Linguistics
University of North Texas
Denton, Texas, 76203, USA
{alexis.palmer,kristy.phillips}@unt.edu, melissa.robinson@my.unt.edu

Abstract

This paper focuses on a particular type of abusive language, targeting expressions in which typically neutral adjectives take on pejorative meaning when used as nouns - compare *gay people* to *the gays*. We first collect and analyze a corpus of hand-curated, expert-annotated pejorative nominalizations for four target adjectives: *female*, *gay*, *illegal*, and *poor*. We then collect a second corpus of automatically-extracted and POS-tagged, crowd-annotated tweets. For both corpora, we find support for the hypothesis that some adjectives, when nominalized, take on negative meaning. The targeted constructions are non-standard yet widely-used, and part-of-speech taggers mistag some nominal forms as adjectives. We implement a tool called NomCatcher to correct these mistaggings, and find that the same tool is effective for identifying new adjectives subject to transformation via nominalization into abusive language.

1 Introduction

Detection of abusive language tends to focus on identification of key words and character sequences that indicate expression of strongly negative attitudes toward individuals or groups of people (for example, Warner and Hirschberg, 2012; Waseem and Hovy, 2016; Nobata et al., 2016). Some key words, such as racial or ethnic slurs, are highly effective predictors, while other key words may signal contentious topics rather than actual abusive language. This second type of key word is semantically flexible. Depending on the context of individual occurrences, these words may be used abusively, neutrally, or even to express positive sentiment.

In this paper we focus on pejorative uses (i.e., uses expressing contempt, disapproval, or other negative sentiment) of words that are alternately neutral or pejorative, depending on their syntactic context. Specifically, we are interested in negatively-characterizing phrases such as *the blacks* or *the gays*. Formally, these expressions involve nominalization of adjectives, where one particular characteristic (e.g. homosexuality) becomes associated with a wide range of stereotypical notions (Wierzbiecka, 1986). Though these constructions are nothing new - the online Corpus of Historical American English,[1] for example, has one occurrence of *the blacks* as early as 1810 - they came to new public prominence during the 2016 U.S. Presidential election (Rebels, 2016; Liberman, 2016b,a).

A phrase like *the Mexicans* may not immediately register as pejorative, but the associated negative sentiment (1) becomes clear through contrast with a different type of noun phrase (2):

1. *I think **the Mexicans** are going to end up loving Donald Trump.* [cited in Liberman (2016b)]

2. *I think **the Mexican people** are going to end up loving Donald Trump.* [constructed]

In (2), *Mexican* is an adjective modifying the noun *people*; in (1), *Mexican* has been nominalized.[2]

This paper presents work in progress exploring the utility of linguistic form (i.e. particular syntactic constructions, discussed in Section 2) for automatically identifying this more subtle form of abusive language. We start by investigating a

---

[1] http://corpus.byu.edu/coha/
[2] The analysis of the form in (1) as nominal is supported by its compatibility with the nominal plural inflection *-s*.

Proceedings of the First Workshop on Abusive Language Online, pages 91–100,
Vancouver, Canada, July 30 - August 4, 2017. ©2017 Association for Computational Linguistics

hand-collected, expert-annotated corpus of nominal uses of *female, gay, illegal,* and *poor* (Section 3). For this data set and the four adjectives it targets, analysis shows a strong correspondence between nominal status and pejorative meaning.

Because our ultimate interest is in automatic detection of abusive language in unrestricted online data, we assemble a second corpus via automatic data extraction, use automatic part-of-speech (POS) labels as a proxy for linguistic form, and turn to the crowd for annotation (Section 4). This study again shows correspondence between negative sentiment and linguistic form, although the results are complicated by annotation issues.

Finally, we present two short investigations into the feasibility of the current approach for automatic detection of abusive language (Section 5). One interesting result shows that output from an automatic POS tagger can be used to identify new pejorative nominalizations in unrestricted data.

NOTE: This paper contains a number of examples of abusive and/or offensive language. These do not represent the views of the authors! Please proceed with caution and awareness.

2 Pejorative meaning and linguistic form

Locating pejorative meaning. Disentangling the pejorative load of an individual lexical item from the sentiment of the utterance in which it occurs is difficult, sometimes even impossible. The ultimate aim of the research agenda this paper contributes to is to mark *individual occurrences* of certain lexical items as pejorative or not. Sometimes the nominalizations of interest occur embedded in a clearly abusive context, as in example (6) below. In other instances, though, the context itself is relatively neutral, and use of the nominalization is precisely what shifts the utterance from neutral to pejorative (as in example (1) above).

The two corpora discussed in this paper differ in the care with which they distinguish between: a) pejorative meaning of a lexical item, and b) negative sentiment of an utterance. The PEJNOM corpus (Section 3) was annotated by one expert linguist. This annotator paid close attention to the location issue, developing guidelines for when to attribute pejorative meaning to a lexical item and when not to. Making this distinction requires closely examining the semantic contributions both of the targeted lexical item and of its context. The

two must be separately interpreted.

The TWTARGETS corpus (Section 4), on the other hand, was annotated using crowd-sourcing, with simple instructions given to anonymous, amateur annotators. The annotations suggest that crowd annotators do not always make the distinction as carefully as we would like.

Relationship with sentiment analysis. There is a clear connection between this work and sentiment analysis, given that pejorative meaning is *by definition* the expression of negative sentiment. However, most methods for sentiment analysis target the level of the utterance or the entire document. Our analysis focuses in on the level of the individual lexical item, as we aim to automatically classify occurrences of particular target words as pejorative or non-pejorative.

Pejoration as a process. From a theoretical perspective, pejoration is a process by which lexical items acquire negative meaning. In the case of adjectival nominalization (i.e. for our target forms), pejoration occurs as certain adjectival forms begin to be used as nouns.

In our proposed process of ADJ→N pejoration, the first step is from adjective (e.g. *My **rich** aunt paid for my schooling*) to the zero plural form (e.g. ***The rich** should pay more taxes than the poor*).[3] The zero plural may be seen as an intermediate step between adjectival and nominal forms (Günther, to appear). So far these are standard forms, with no inherent pejorative meaning.

Pejoration happens when the word crosses the boundary from zero plural to true nominal forms. As Wierzbicka states, nouns (typically) refer to individuals or groups of individuals, and adjectives (generally) ascribe characteristics to individuals. In this nominalization, a kind or category of entity is formed around the (former) adjective. In addition to the single attribute denoted by the adjective, stereotypical properties become associated with the kind, such as *dumb* and *sexy* for the nominalized *blonde*.

Using Wierzbicka's theory, we take a step further in our analysis, arguing that a certain dehumanization or deindividualization can come with nominalization, as individuals are referred to not as complex human beings but by making reference to *a single characteristic* of the individual. Addi-

---

[3]This form is known as *zero plural* because it denotes plural reference without plural inflection on the noun.

tionally, the properties associated with the nominal forms often lack the human properties associated with more standard variants. Consider the semantic properties of *woman* and *female*.

- Woman: FEMALE, HUMAN, ADULT
- Female: BIOLOGICAL SEX

HUMAN is one of the properties of the word *woman*, but this is not the case for *female*.

Once the adjective has been nominalized, it can occur in different forms. In English, nominal forms vary with respect to definiteness and number (see Section 3.2 for examples). Some forms are more marked than others, and non-standard, bare plural uses like those in (3) are widely found in online environments.

3. *Our system is free and accessible to every citizen, **richs** and **poors**. #debate #presidentialdebate* [Twitter, 2016]

3 Corpus Study 1: Hand-curated data, annotated by an expert

Four data sets are used across the two studies; the number of instances in each appears in Table 1. For the PEJNOM corpus, one **instance** is one occurrence of a target adjective, within an utterance of 1-3 sentences. One utterance can contain more than one instance. For TWTARGETS and TWOPEN, one **instance** is one tweet.

Our first corpus study addresses a manually-collected data set. The data set was curated over a number of months by a graduate student in Linguistics with a theoretical interest in understanding why there is such a striking contrast between adjectival and (some) nominal uses of four adjectives: *female*, *gay*, *illegal*, and *poor*. The initial focus of this data set was to assemble a large collection of pejorative nominalizations, as an empirical foundation for linguistic analysis.

The original version of the corpus (PEJNOM-ORIG) focuses on identifying pejorative nominalizations, resulting in a thoroughly unbalanced data set. To expand the data set without collecting additional data, we annotate *all* occurrences of the four target forms in the corpus, not only those which triggered inclusion of instances in the corpus in the first place. This second annotation round added 444 instances to the corpus; the expanded version is named PEJNOM-EXP.

3.1 The corpus and the target forms

The PEJNOM-ORIG corpus was assembled from Twitter, Reddit, news articles and interviews, political debates, and video and written blogs. The majority of the data is written, though some spoken data was transcribed and included.

Each of the four target adjectives is most likely to occur in its negative/abusive form in particular environments related to the term. In order to find pejorative uses, selected topics revolving around immigration, anti-feminism, homophobia, and poverty were searched.

Illegal. Data for *illegal* was primarily collected during the 2016 U.S. Presidential elections, with examples harvested from politicians during debates and interviews as well as online commentary from voters on political issues. Common topics were deportation, illegal immigration, and Donald Trump's border wall (e.g. 4).

4. *And those liberal SJWs don't want the wall.... And want to keep **illegals** in the US... Lmfao* [Reddit, June, 2016]

Female. Relevant forms of *female* are commonly found in Mens Rights blogs, specifically items tagged with MGTOW (Men Going Their Own Way). The Mens Rights movement is a collection of online groups that claim to exist to promote rights needed by men. However, within the MGTOW community, it is common for the discussion to focus on anti-feminist topics (e.g. 5). Other blogs with anti-feminist topics were also inspected for pejorative uses of *female*.

5. *As a gay shaman who has been victimized by a succession of narcissist **females**, MGTOW is giving me hope that the human race can survive the female psychopath.* [Youtube, 2015]

Gay. While most of the data for *gay* was collected from Twitter, anti-gay blogs and forums were inspected to find pejorative uses of *gay* (e.g. 6). The topics often center around gay marriage, gay rights, or hate crimes.

6. ***Gays** cannot reproduce, **gays** are not beneficial for humans in anyway and your love for them is without merit or reason.* [Reddit, 2014]

Poor. Pejorative examples of nominalized *poor* were found largely in satirical news articles focused on social topics, such as limits on welfare.

Data set	# *female*	# *gay*	# *illegal*	# *poor*	**All**
PEJNOM-ORIG	715	149	564	241	1669
PEJNOM-EXP	1108	160	592	253	2113
TWTARGETS	200	200	200	200	800
TWOPEN					56237

Table 1: Per data set, instances per target form.

Additional examples were found on Twitter. The pejorative use of *poor* varies from the other target forms, as it is mostly used to voice a perceived attitude of another person or group, as in (7).

7. *"Hoover was in charge of the Great Depression, I only used words to say **poors** were dumb for paying taxes and staying poor." - Trump logic* [Twitter, Oct. 16, 2016]

Each instance in PEJNOM-EXP was annotated for two categories: **linguistic form** (3.2) and **pejorative meaning** (3.3).

3.2 A closer look at linguistic form

Each instance in the corpus is coded for its grammatical structure. The four main nominal forms are indefinite singular (*a gay*), definite singular (*the female*), bare plural (*poors*), and definite plural (*the illegals*). In order to make more fine-grained distinctions, additional categories were added, including demonstratives, quantifiers, and pronouns. Figure 1 shows the distribution of target forms across linguistic form categories, for PEJNOM-ORIG.

	Examples	Female	Illegal	Poor	Gay
Indefinite singular	*A poor*	125	110	29	12
Definite singular	*The gay*	27	7		4
Bare plural	*Females*	409	245	62	78
Definite plural	*The illegals*	62	167	133	43
Quantified plural	*Many poors*	39	28	3	6
Quantified singular	*Any gay*	15		1	2
Demonstrative singular	*This female*	5			
Demonstrative plural	*Those illegals*	22	5	6	2
Pronoun Singular	*My poor*	2			
Pronoun plural	*You gays*	9	2	7	2
Total		715	564	241	149

Figure 1: Linguistic forms in PEJNOM-ORIG.

The definite plural form is of particular interest. Acton (2014) argues that the definite plural structure can indicate the speaker's nonmembership in the group mentioned, as well as distancing the speaker from the group mentioned. In this case, the definite plural is a marked variant of the bare plural form. With this in mind, definite plurals are also coded when modified by a relative clause, as the relative clause may provide syntactic reasons for using the definite plural (e.g. 8).

8. *Do **the #illegals who were given greencards supposedly by accident** factor into #HRC vetting #debates #Trumptrain* [Twitter, Oct. 2016]

The manual collection process used search terms on raw text. In order to locate definite and indefinite singular forms, while ruling out adjectival forms, we added selected verb forms (e.g. forms of copular *be*) to the search terms, targeting token sequences like *a poor is* (e.g. 9).

9. *yeah dude being poor happens from time to time, but being **A poor is** a way of life. LOL. :)* [Twitter, Jul. 13, 2016]

Utterances in which the target form is used in reference to itself (e.g. 10) are coded separately.

10. *sorry, but calling someone **an illegal** isn't racist! Illegal isn't a race* [Twitter, Jun 26, 2016]

Likewise, if the referent of the target form is non-human, such as *illegal* used to refer to illegal fireworks (11), or different from the expected referent, such as *illegal* for underaged drinkers (12), the instance is coded separately.

11. ***An illegal** went off on the ground and the sparks flew EVERYWHERE and one of them hit my forehead LOOOOOL* [Twitter, Jul. 4, 2015]

12. *Dunno if this is still true, but used to be an **ILLEGAL** wasn't considered a man unless he could finish 18 pack and drive home.* [Twitter, May 17, 2014]

Finally, instances with questionable spelling or other irregularities leading to ambiguity (e.g. 13) are excluded from the corpus.

13. *They are if **a poorz** has one or both.* [Wonkette.com, Sept. 2016]

3.3 Annotating pejorative meaning

Each instance is annotated for the presence of pejorative meaning, using four different labels: pejorative (PEJ), non-pejorative (NONP), uncertain (UNC), and satirical (SAT). The goal of this annotation is to capture **whether pejorative meaning is intended on the part of the speaker**.

What counts as pejorative? Through the course of annotation, the expert annotator refined her annotation guidelines, aiming to clarify precisely which factors trigger an annotation of PEJ. Some factors are consistent over all four target forms, while others are specific to one target form. The following factors signify pejorative uses of target forms; most are illustrated by examples:

- (14) negative adjective(s) modifying the target nominal form;
- (15) co-occurrence with phrases referring to particular stereotypes or behaviors associated with the relevant referent group (e.g. *freeloading* with an occurrence of *poor*);
- (16) appearance near negative verbs such as *hate* or *despise*, or negative phrases such as *get rid of* or *hardly any good*;
- coreference with other negative terms, such as *slut* for *female* or *wetback* for *illegal* was an indication for pejorative meaning as well;
- (17) other negative implications not tied to a specific lexical item or phrase.

14. *"You have the distinct odor of poverty. Trust me, I can smell you from here! **Sad filthy poors.**" - Trump in PA* [Twitter, Oct. 10, 2016]

15. *Why don't **gays** like being girly? Cause **a gay** is normally called girly.* [Twitter, Aug. 13, 2016]

16. *Whites **hate illegals**. Blacks **hate illegals**. Native Americans **hate illegals**. Asians **hate illegals**. legals **hate illegals**.* [Reddit, May 2016]

17. *this feminist nonsense is to give every man the daily message that **A Man Needs a Female Like a Fish Needs a Lobotomy**.* [Youtube, 2016]

Some target forms have specific indicators of pejorative/non-pejorative meanings. For example, if *female* occurs while discussing gender-focused topics (e.g. 18) or in pro-feminist contexts, it tends to be non-pejorative.

18. *Estrogen makes **females** more emotionally driven on average compared to males.* [Youtube, 2016]

Characteristically, the pejorative form of *female* is often paired with somehow mis-matched gendered nouns: such as *man* rather than *male*. The "matched" counterpart of *female* is *male*; *man*'s counterpart should be *woman*. When *female* is used in direct contrast to *man*, the semantic mismatch signals pejorative meaning (19).

19. *The president of the United States, to me, should be **a man** not **a female**.* [CNN interview, 2015]

Non-pejorative instances. We extend the corpus by annotating *all* occurrences of the four target words. Most adjectival occurrences (e.g. 20) and zero plural forms are annotated as NONP.

20. *Most of the arguments that I see against **gay marriage** invoke religious texts or figures.* [Reddit, 2015]

Satire/sarcasm. The satirical category (SAT) codes a different type of pejorative use. This category includes sarcastic uses and uses that voice the perceived attitude of a person, group, or society other than the speaker (see 21, for example). This tag is still considered to be pejorative, but is coded separately as it functions differently from blatant, explicitly negative uses. The SAT label occurs most frequently for *poor*, but does occur with other forms as well. Warner and Hirschberg (2012) also recognize sarcastic/satirical uses as a distinct category of abusive language.

21. *How dare **the poors** eat a steak! It offends my upper middle class sensibilities! Or something.* [Twitter, Oct. 20, 2016]

Uncertain. Lastly, the uncertain category (UNC) exists to capture instances for which the expert annotator did not feel confident choosing either PEJ or NONP. Often this is due to a limited amount of context, an unclear implication or sentence, or negative elements within questions, making it unclear whether pejorative meaning was intended on the part of the speaker.

Expert	#	Adj	ZP	Nom	Other
ALL	2106	410	6	1649	41
%PEJ	1113	0.5	16.65	**66.8**	4.9
%NONP	564	**99.0**	16.65	9.3	9.8
%SAT	217	0.25	-	13.0	2.4
%UNC	181	0.25	-	10.9	-
%UNK	9	-	-	-	21.9
%NOAN	22	-	66.7	-	61.0

Table 2: Correspondence between pejorative meaning and linguistic form, expert annotator, PEJNOM-EXP. 7 additional instances marked both **NoLF** and NOAN.

22. *At work trying to explain how this man I know have **a gay** is so hard to explain especially without a good picture* [Twitter, Sept. 26, 2016]

3.4 Analysis: correspondence between pejorative meaning and linguistic form

Table 2 shows the correspondence between linguistic form (LF) and pejorative status for PEJNOM-EXP, taking only the annotations from the expert. For each LF category, the table shows the percentage of instances assigned to each of the four pejoration labels.

For this analysis, the fine-grained LF categories are collapsed into four categories. Adjectives and zero plurals, as expected, are overwhelmingly annotated as NONP, with all but 4 of the 410 adjectival occurrences of the four target forms. This is unsurprising, given the collection methodology used for the corpus, yet it confirms the expectation that these words are absent pejorative meaning when used as adjectives.

Of 1649 nominal occurrences across the four target forms, nearly 67% are annotated as PEJ, with the remaining instances spread across NONP (n=153), SAT (n=214), and UNC (n=180). An example of a non-pejorative nominal use is (23).

23. *It should not be understood as gay marriage (ie marriage for **gays**) but marriage that includes **gays** (ie the marriage is the same for all and is extended to **gays**), which is different.* [Reddit, 2015]

The category **Other** consists of those cases excluded from the main corpus (meta-references, non-human referents, etc.). Finally, a small number of cases in the corpus have no label either for LF or for pejorative meaning. These appear in the table as **NoLF**, UNK, and NOAN.

3.5 Analysis: multiple expert annotators

The PEJNOM-EXP corpus was annotated in its entirety by a single expert (**Annotator A**). To determine how replicable these annotations are, we recruited two additional expert annotators (**Annotators B1** and **B2**). All three are graduate students of linguistics. Neither B1 nor B2 had participated in this project before annotating.

Annotators B1 and B2 were given written annotation guidelines and asked to label (as PEJ or NONP) a subset of 121 instances, almost equally balanced across the four target forms. We call this data set PEJNOM-SUBSET.

Anno2 \\ Anno1	A		B1	
	%	K	%	K
B1	86.0%	0.717	–	
B2	71.9%	0.461	74.4%	0.499

Table 3: Agreement (% and Cohen's K) between expert annotators, PEJNOM-SUBSET.

Table 3 shows agreement figures for each pair of annotators, measured in both simple percent agreement and Cohen's Kappa.[4] We see that agreement between Annotator A and Annotator B1 is quite good, with K=0.717. Annotator B2 shows lower agreement with both of the other annotators, with Kappa scores of 0.461 and 0.499. Agreement across the three annotators (measured as Fleiss's Kappa) is a similarly modest 0.546.

Annotator	# PEJ	# NONP
A	54	67
B1	57	64
B2	84	37

Table 4: Ratings from multiple expert annotators (A=primary expert, B1&B2=additional experts), PEJNOM-SUBSET.

To better understand the differences between annotators, we look at the distributions of the two labels for each annotator (Table 4). It is clear that Annotator B2 is much more likely than the other two annotators to label instances as PEJ. This annotator seems to label based on the entire instance and not just the target form. We will see this behavior again in the crowd-sourced annotations described in Section 4.3.

---

[4]Agreement computed in R using the `irr` package.

4 Corpus Study 2: Data harvested online and annotated by the crowd

The first corpus study confirms the hypothesis that these four adjectives, when nominalized, take on pejorative meaning. This result, though, comes with a giant caveat: the corpus was collected precisely to investigate pejorative nominalizations. To test this hypothesis in a less-biased setting, we build a second corpus of instances extracted automatically from Twitter using twarc.[5] To move closer to automatic detection of abusive language, LF is assigned by an automatic part-of-speech tagger, and annotation is done via crowd-sourcing.

4.1 The corpus

This corpus has two subsets: TwTARGETS and TwOPEN. Both subcorpora were de-duplicated using twarc's built-in utilities.

TwTargets. The first subcorpus consists of tweets which contain at least one of the four target forms discussed in Section 3. Using twarc, we searched for tweets containing either the singular or plural form of the target forms.[6] The full TwTARGETS data set consists of the most recent 6000 tweets for each of the four target forms.

TwOpen. The second subcorpus consists of 100,000 English-language tweets with geocodes located within a 2000 mile radius of the geographic center of the United States.[7]

The larger data set is next pruned by length, keeping only tweets with more than six words. The six-word limit does not include usernames, URLs, hashtags, emoticons, cardinal numbers, or punctuation. The remaining roughly 56K tweets make up the TwOPEN data set.

4.2 Approximating LF with POS tagging

The previous analysis suggests that, given good annotations, LF could serve as a reasonable baseline for identifying pejorative uses of certain adjectives. In an application setting, though, it is unreasonable to expect human-quality labeling of LF, so we turn to automatic POS taggers.

The particular set of constructions poses a challenge for automatic POS taggers, because these are lexical items occurring with a syntactic category (N) that is *not* the most likely category.

Tagger selection. Before selecting a tagger, we investigated several different options, running all taggers with default settings: the standard English POS tagging model from Stanford CoreNLP (Toutanova et al., 2003); the GATE Twitter POS tagger (Derczynski et al., 2013);[8] and TweetNLP (Owoputi et al., 2013).[9] For a small test suite (57 instances), TweetNLP with its native tag set gave the best results for the four target words, looking at both adjectival and nominal uses. The TweetNLP tag set is a coarse-grained tag set extended with Twitter-specific tags for elements like hashtags and URLs. Of interest for our task are the tags N for nouns and A for adjectives.

NomCatcher: tag correction for nominalizations. A number of the target nominalizations are wrongly labeled as A, in particular definite and indefinite singular instances. Plural instances are largely labeled correctly as N.

In order to perform analysis of whether nominalized adjectives are likely to be pejorative, it's essential that the nominalizations are tagged correctly. To this end we implement **NomCatcher**, a filter based on POS sequences, designed to identify and correct mistagged nominalizations.

In essence, NomCatcher searches for sequences that look like noun phrases lacking their head noun. NomCatcher targets any sequence with one or more article-like elements (tags D, S, O, \$, Z) followed by some combination of the same tags, adjectives, and punctuation, and ending in an adjective. When this sequence is followed by end-of-sentence punctuation or a verb, NomCatcher changes the final A tag to N.

```
you_O can_V tell_V a_D gay_A is_V
from_P florida_^ just_R by_P
looking_V at_P them_O
```

In the example above, the tag for *gay* is changed from A to N. TweetNLP and NomCatcher are applied to both TwTARGETS and TwOPEN.

4.3 Annotation by the crowd

For each of the four target forms, 200 instances were selected at random, evenly split between N and A. The instances were shuffled and split into

---

[5]https://github.com/DocNow/twarc

[6]Additional parameters: restricted to English-language tweets occurring in the prior 7 days, data downloaded on April 25th and 26th, 2017.

[7]Harvested on April 28th, 2017.

[8]https://gate.ac.uk/wiki/twitter-postagger.html

[9]http://www.cs.cmu.edu/ ark/TweetNLP/

n=800	5agree		4agree		3agree		NoMaj	
Sent.Label	14.5%		26.3%		46.9%		12.3%	
	N	A	N	A	N	A	N	A
NEG	72	16	61	51	71	67		
NEUT	11	8	34	49	83	120		
POS	3	6	4	12	14	20		
							47	51

Table 5: Degree of overlap between crowd annotators, per LF and per label, TWTARGETS.

Majority vote	Adj 400	Noun 400
%NEGATIVE	33.5	**51.0**
%NEUTRAL	**44.2**	32.0
%POSITIVE	**9.5**	5.2
%NOMAJ	12.8	11.8

Table 6: Correspondence between pejorative meaning and linguistic form, majority vote from crowd annotations, TWTARGETS.

5 batches. Each batch was combined with 10 instances from PEJNOM-EXP, without considering the LF of the additional 10 instances. Each batch of 50 instances was labeled by 5 different annotators via the crowd-sourcing platform Amazon Mechanical Turk.[10] Participation was restricted to Amazon MT Masters only, and annotators were paid US$0.50/batch.

Annotators were instructed to indicate whether certain highlighted words (one word highlighted per instance) were used with POSITIVE, NEGATIVE, or NEUTRAL meaning. The following three examples were given as part of the instructions:

a POSITIVE: If you want the job done right, ask a **female** to do it.

b NEGATIVE: I don't understand why **females** think they know how to drive.

c NEUTRAL: My first pet ever was a **female** lizard.

Annotators were warned about potentially offensive data, told that the data would help develop systems for automatically detecting negative uses of words, and reminded to mark "sentiment for the word itself, not for the entire tweet."

Agreement between annotators. Table 5 presents detailed counts of the overlap between the 5 crowd annotators per instance. A clear majority vote (**3agree**) can be established for

[10] https://www.mturk.com/mturk/

more than 85% of the 800 instances annotated by Turkers, and complete agreement (**5agree**) was reached for almost 15% of the cases. The full-agreement instances are mostly nouns, and mostly labeled NEG. Overall, the POS label is used infrequently, and crowd annotators tend to agree more on labels for nouns than for adjectives.

4.4 Analysis: correspondence between pejoration and linguistic form

Finally, we look at whether the hypothesis that nominalized occurrences of these adjectives tend to be used with negative meaning holds up in the non-expert setting.

Table 6 shows the correspondence between automatically-tagged LF and whether the majority vote of the annotators was Negative, Neutral, or Positive. For completeness, we include cases where no majority was reached.

Of the instances tagged with A, almost 54% are labeled as non-pejorative (majority vote: at least 3/5 annotators), counting both NEUT and POS as non-pejorative labels. 51% of the instances tagged with N are labeled as pejorative (NEG), with 37% receiving non-pejorative labels.

The numbers are small but encouraging, especially given that these are crowd-sourced annotations, annotators received no training, and no annotations were rejected. Despite clear instructions, in a number of cases it appears that annotators considered the sentiment of the entire tweet instead of just the word in question. For example, a majority vote of NEG was made for the following tweet:

24. *lol that's the best reason you could come up with in response to a group of **gays** supporting muslims?*

Nothing in the tweet itself suggests that this nominal use of **gays** is pejorative, and annotators were not given any additional context for the tweets.

5 Investigations

Expert annotations vs. crowd annotations. As a sanity check, 50 instances for each of the four target forms in PEJNOM-EXP were submitted for crowd-sourced annotation. Table 8 shows the mappings from expert annotations to the majority vote from the crowd.

This analysis is only suggestive, given that so few of the 200 PEJNOM-EXP instances in this batch have labels other than PEJ. We can note a

(1) Characteristics of individual humans	muslims, blacks, immigrants, riches, whites, sexists, homosexuals, feminists, fascists, blondes, illiterates, liberals, stupids
(2) Human, lexically pejorative	criminals, terrorists, rogues, racists
(3) Human-related, unlikely to be pejorative	others, individuals, (10-year-)olds, browns (sports team)
(4) Non-human	news, rights, lives, extremes, likes, standards, tops, seconds, presents, riches, shorts, graphics, finals, nonprofits, offensives, positives, evils, ideals
(5) Verbs	owns, lives, opens, likes, lasts, tops, seconds, presents, grosses,

Table 7: Lexical items identified as potential pejorative nominalizations. Shown in plural form.

Expert	CS: Neg	CS: Neut	CS: Pos	NoMaj
PEJ	86	26	1	12
NONP	11	16	2	4
SAT	13	4	1	4
UNC	2	11	0	5
NOAN	2	0	0	0

Table 8: Correspondence between crowd-sourced labels (majority vote) and expert annotations, 200 instances from PEJNOM-EXP. Numbers are counts, not percentages.

few tendencies: PEJ instances are largely marked as NEG, NON-PEJ instances are divided between NEG and NEUT, sarcastic utterances tend to be labeled as NEG, and UNC cases either are marked as NEUT or fail to reach a majority.

Identification of new pejorative nominalizations. Our analysis so far is restricted, treating just four adjectives. With NomCatcher (Section 4.2), we can quickly and automatically identify new adjectives that undergo the same kind of meaning shift. We apply NomCatcher to TWOPEN and to the hate speech corpus of (Waseem and Hovy, 2016), finding words whose POS tag is changed by NomCatcher from A to N.

From the 16K tweets in the hate speech corpus, NomCatcher's filter identifies 206 distinct lexical items. Some are good catches, but the majority are proper adjectives occurring between a determiner/article and a noun mistagged as V, as in [their_D hypocritical_A whining_V]. To narrow down the set of adjectives identified, a second filtering step is applied, checking the corpus for plural forms of the 206 words caught by NomCatcher. This step cuts the number of word types identified down to 43, which can be grouped as in Table 7.

Row 1 contains forms denoting human characteristics; these are the most likely to undergo semantic transformation to pejorative meaning. Row 2 contains human characteristics which are inherently pejorative. Row 3 is especially interesting; the two high-frequency forms (*others* and *individuals*) both avoid mentioning any particular characteristic. Rows 4 and 5 are not relevant for abusive language, as they are not referential to humans.

NomCatcher has similar results for our TWOPEN corpus; 314 lexical items are filtered down to 90. The categories remain the same, and the overlap with the words identified from the hate speech corpus is high.

6 Conclusions and future work

The aim of this work is to detect pejorative uses of lexical items that can be used either in completely harmless ways or in ways that are abusive and harmful. This is a challenging task, given that it relies on many layers of human interpretation.

Our approach focuses on the role of linguistic form, and our two corpus studies support the hypothesis that certain adjectives, when used as nouns, acquire pejorative meaning. The Nom-Catcher tool uses LF for quick identification of likely candidates for pejorative nominalization. Immediate next steps are to explore the effectiveness of sentiment analysis methods for this task.

As the work progresses, we will deepen the current analyses and expand the data sets, applying our methods to a large Reddit corpus, and eventually incorporate linguistic form into a full system for detecting abusive language online.

An exciting avenue for future inquiry is the role of sarcasm. Existing work identifying sarcasm on Twitter (Sulis et al., 2016; Ling and Klinger, 2016; Wang, 2013) finds that sarcastic tweets tend to express pejorative meaning with positive words. The sarcastic instances in our data show a different pattern, using pejorative nominalizations with other negative words to mock discriminatory mindsets, in the end conveying negative sentiment towards those who use this type of abusive language.

Acknowledgments

First and foremost, thanks to Patricia Cukor-Avila for many useful discussions, starting from the very beginning of this project. Thanks go to Mary Burke and Karla Villarreal for their short-notice expert annotations, and to the many unnamed crowd annotators involved in this project. We also thank our four anonymous reviewers for interesting comments and useful suggestions. This work was funded in part through research support to the first author from the UNT Department of Linguistics and the UNT College of Information.

References

Eric Acton. 2014. *Pragmatics and the social meaning of determiners (Doctoral dissertation)*. Ph.D. thesis, Stanford, CA.

Leon Derczynski, Alan Ritter, Sam Clark, and Kalina Bontcheva. 2013. Twitter part-of-speech tagging for all: Overcoming sparse and noisy data. In *Proceedings of the International Conference on Recent Advances in Natural Language Processing*. Association for Computational Linguistics.

Christine Günther. to appear. The rich, the poor, the obvious – Arguing for an ellipsis approach to "adjectives used as nouns". In *NPs in English: past and present*. John Benjamins.

Mark Liberman. 2016a. "Ask the gays". http://languagelog.ldc.upenn.edu/nll/?p=26223.

Mark Liberman. 2016b. The NOUNs. http://languagelog.ldc.upenn.edu/nll/?p=26254.

Jennifer Ling and Roman Klinger. 2016. An empirical, quantitative analysis of the differences between sarcasm and irony. In *International Semantic Web Conference*. Springer, pages 203–216.

Chikashi Nobata, Joel Tetreault, Achint Thomas, Yashar Mehdad, and Yi Chang. 2016. Abusive language detection in online user content. In *Proceedings of the 25th International Conference on World Wide Web*. International World Wide Web Conferences Steering Committee, Republic and Canton of Geneva, Switzerland, WWW '16, pages 145–153. https://doi.org/10.1145/2872427.2883062.

Olutobi Owoputi, Brendan O'Connor, Chris Dyer, Kevin Gimpel, Nathan Schneider, and Noah A Smith. 2013. Improved part-of-speech tagging for online conversational text with word clusters. Association for Computational Linguistics.

Latino Rebels. 2016. Maria Hinojosa Tells Latino Trump Surrogate on MSNBC's AM JOY That 'Illegals Is Not a Noun'. http://www.latinorebels.com/2016/10/29/maria-hinojosa-tells-latino-trump-surrogate-on-msnbcs-am-joy-that-illegals-is-not-a-noun-video/.

Emilio Sulis, Delia Irazú Hernández Farías, Paolo Rosso, Viviana Patti, and Giancarlo Ruffo. 2016. Figurative messages and affect in twitter: Differences between #irony, #sarcasm and #not. *Knowledge-Based Systems* 108:132–143.

Kristina Toutanova, Dan Klein, Christopher D Manning, and Yoram Singer. 2003. Feature-rich part-of-speech tagging with a cyclic dependency network. In *Proceedings of the 2003 Conference of the North American Chapter of the Association for Computational Linguistics on Human Language Technology-Volume 1*. Association for Computational Linguistics, pages 173–180.

Po-Ya Angela Wang. 2013. #Irony or #Sarcasm - A Quantitative and Qualitative Study Based on Twitter. In *Proceedings of the 27th Pacific Asia Conference on Language, Information, and Computation*.

William Warner and Julia Hirschberg. 2012. Detecting hate speech on the world wide web. In *Proceedings of the Second Workshop on Language in Social Media*. Association for Computational Linguistics, Stroudsburg, PA, USA, LSM '12, pages 19–26. http://dl.acm.org/citation.cfm?id=2390374.2390377.

Zeerak Waseem and Dirk Hovy. 2016. Hateful symbols or hateful people? predictive features for hate speech detection on twitter. In *Proceedings of the NAACL Student Research Workshop*. Association for Computational Linguistics, San Diego, California.

Anna Wierzbiecka. 1986. What's in a noun? (or: How do nouns differ in meaning from adjectives?). *Studies in Language* 10(2):353–389.

Author Index